Formations
OF NATION
AND PEOPLE

 ROUTLEDGE & KEGAN PAUL
London, Boston, Melbourne and Henley

First published in 1984
by Routledge & Kegan Paul plc
39 Store Street, London WC1E 7DD, England
9 Park Street, Boston, Mass. 02108, USA
464 St Kilda Road, Melbourne,
Victoria 3004 Australia and
Broadway House, Newtown Road,
Henley-on-Thames, Oxon RG9 1EN, England
Set in Palatino and Gill by
Rowland Phototypesetting Ltd
Bury St Edmunds, Suffolk
and printed in Great Britain by
St Edmundsbury Press Ltd
Bury St Edmunds, Suffolk

ISBN 0-7102-0044-7

CONTENTS

ACKNOWLEDGEMENTS

Illustrations are reproduced with the kind permission of *The Daily Telegraph* (p. 45), Express Newspapers (p. 213), Arthur Horner (p. 215), The Imperial War Museum (p. 143), IPC Magazines (pp. 191, 195, 200, 204, 207, 209), *Punch* (pp. 178, 179), Ralph Steadman (pp. 21, 27, 32, 36) and *The Sun* newspaper (p. 44). Although every effort has been made to trace copyright holders, we apologize in advance for any unintentional omission or neglect and will be pleased to insert the appropriate acknowledgment to companies or individuals in any subsequent edition of this publication. We would like to thank James Schoff of the Centre for the Study of Cartoons and Caricature, University of Kent, for his help.

NOTES ON CONTRIBUTORS

Bill Schwarz and **Alan O'Shea** teach cultural studies at North East London Polytechnic . . . **Patrick Wright** currently works with the National Council for Voluntary Organizations . . . **Andrjez Krauze** contributed to several magazines, published two collections of cartoons and illustrated many posters and books before leaving Poland in 1979. Since settling in England in 1982, he has published in *The Times, Guardian, Observer, Daily Express* and *New Society* . . . **David Forgacs** lectures in the School of European Studies at the University of Sussex . . . **Iain Chambers** teaches at the University of Naples, researches into popular culture and is author of *Pop Music and Popular Culture: A history of British pop music, 1956–81* (Macmillan, 1983) . . . **Lidia Curti** teaches at the Istituto Universitario Orientale, Naples, and has written extensively on the British theatre, British television and cultural studies . . . **Fernando Ferrara** is professor of English at the Istituto Universitario Orientale, Naples, and editor of *Anglistica*, a review of English literary and cultural studies; among his publications are studies of Orwell's novels, *Lady Chatterley's Lover* and political festivals (*Le Feste e il Potere*, 1983) . . . **Lucy Bland** teaches women's studies in adult education . . . **Frank Mort** is a research assistant in the Faculty of Arts at the Open University . . . **Caroline Rowan** is researching feminist history and teaches in adult education . . . **Neil Grant** is currently teaching in an observation and assessment unit in Birmingham . . . **Janice Winship** teaches women's studies and is doing research on sexuality and women's magazines . . . **Louise London** is a lawyer who works in the area of immigration and nationality . . . **Nira Yuval-Davis** is a sociologist who has been working on the interrelations between racism and sexism in general and national reproduction in particular.

Bill Schwarz

THE LANGUAGE OF CONSTITUTIONALISM:
Baldwinite Conservatism

In a debate in the House of Commons in August 1918 Stanley Baldwin, then a Conservative junior minister in Lloyd George's coalition government, declared: 'Propaganda is not a word that has a pleasant sound to English ears.' He deplored its use, finding such direct and explicit state management of public opinion distasteful. Yet the political and social crisis generated by the war was so grave that he was ready to accept its necessity, 'like anti-submarine work' – the image suggesting the existence of submerged and clandestine political forces ranged in opposition to the domestic social order. But more than this, he had also come to appreciate that: 'Public opinion today has a far greater weight in the moulding of governments than it ever had before.'[1] The implicit distinction made by Baldwin between propaganda and public opinion is significant not only for understanding the new Conservative formation, created in 1922 in a bid to free the party from the incubus of the alliance with those Liberals led by Lloyd George (who himself was something of a specialist in the dirty tricks of propaganda), but also for explaining the reconstruction of the very conception of politics in the post-First World War conjuncture. Notions of public opinion became the pivot of political strategies, and indeed it is from this period that the term itself first emerges as a common catchphrase. But also significant was Baldwin's ability to construct the distinction between propaganda and public opinion on the grounds of *Englishness*. His conception of constitutional politics went hand in hand with his nationalism. If Baldwin saw his task as winning a largely reluctant Conservative Party to the imperatives of democratic politics, he achieved this as much as anything by playing upon the idea of the English nation. Thus if propaganda was statist and un-English, then public opinion (and its appropriate politics) arose spontaneously from the depths of civil society and contributed another strand to the evolution of English liberalism and voluntarism. Or so the rhetoric went.

Today such assumptions may appear to be no more than the characteristic, mindless pulp of contemporary constitutionalist ideologies. But I want to argue that what we take for granted both in modern (or at least pre-Thatcher) Conservatism, and in the political field as a whole, was first produced in a specific conjuncture of events in the early 1920s – that it was in these years that the contemporary mould of British politics was first cast. One of the paradoxes which needs to be untangled is that what emerged in this period as the dominant political discourse, despite its striking novelty, was swiftly integrated into a constitutional tradition, which again was itself in the process of being re-invented as a peculiarly English, unbroken continuum.

In more abstract terms it can also be argued that from the late nineteenth century to the 1920s the field of 'the political' was transformed, and that the concepts of public opinion which predominated at the end of the period turned on quite new strategic considerations. The professionalization of electoral politics in the 1880s, the early attempts at systematic studies of voting behaviour (the forerunners of psephology) and the construction of the new collective subject of 'the electorate' combined to render passive the role of the subordinate classes in formal politics at the very moment when participation was first made possible. The new media were of critical importance in the re-formation of politics as spectacle, as a set of images packaged for mass consumption. In 1896 the first edition of the *Daily Mail* was published, Marconi arrived in Britain and filed his first radio patent, and the first commerical film was transferred to the Empire Music Hall, Leicester Square, where it ran for eighteen months. These represent not a quaint landmark in the history of leisure but a decisive moment in the development of the media which were to be crucial in the regulation and organization of public opinion in the first half of the twentieth century, and in the expansion of the domain of the public and the political.

This general process culminated in the creation of the 'universal' democratic subject legally institutionalized by the Representation of the People Act of 1918, and the formation of the representative state. The act provided the resources for the emergence of a new political language based on broader categories of citizenship and near universal suffrage. The precise *forms* of this language remained indeterminate and open until the period of the most intense industrial and class confrontations in 1925–6. It was in those years that the democratic advances embodied in the act were finally tied to Baldwinite Conservatism, and that hopes for a more assertive, radical and popular conception of democracy – both representative and direct – were decisively smashed.

This settlement presented an undoubted, if fragile, victory to the Conservative Party, sustaining it through the inter-war period. But although Baldwin either broke or contained alternative political forces, the formation he represented cannot usefully be described as hegemonic, in the broad Gramscian sense. Baldwinism was never successfully fashioned into a conception of civilization such that it reached every dimension of social life, articulating to its political and cultural programme a broad range of demands and beliefs emanating from subordinate groups. Far from it. It never came near to capturing the mass of the Labour Party or labour movement. But what was temporarily achieved by the Conservative Party under Baldwin's leadership was the construction of a consensus within the dominant fractions of the power bloc, which in addition could claim some measure of popular support. This consensus was founded on the belief that democracy, as such, equalled the right to vote in regular elections and the possibility that in the rotation of parties, the independent representatives of labour might take their turn in governing the nation.

Constitutional Conservatism

It is difficult from our present standpoint to grasp the novelty of this consensus. It so much frames the official rhetoric of the dominant parties, and is so firmly cemented in their practice, that it requires an effort of will to think back to a period when things were altogether different. It is part of the common sense of the modern political scene that the Conservative Party sets out to abide by the constitution, to establish a working concordat with Labour in order to get through the debates and committee business of parliamentary life, and to represent – if not the citizen – then at least the voter and public opinion. As a corollary, modern Conservatives make good their claim to be the inheritors of a national constitutional tradition, protecting the individual from state-regulated compulsion. In this politics, and in much of the dominant historiography of the twenties and thirties, we find a constitutionalism abstracted and dehistoricized, inserted into a multiplicity of notions about the English character, the English way of life or, indeed, the English landscape. One effect of this ideological work is to blur moments of rupture and breakdown, privileging continuity rather than transformation; and as a result such constitutionalist ideologies systematically conceal the historical conditions of their own emergence.

It was in just such a period of deep political crisis, from 1910 to 1926, that the tradition of constitutional Conservatism, in its modern, representative and universal form, was first produced. It was only through a complex process of ideological construction and reconstruction, neutralizing and dissolving alternative perspectives, that an essential continuity between this Conservatism and older constitutional forms could be established and legitimated. This evolutionist interpretation, however, does not make much sense. The crisis of the state between 1910 and 1926 encompassed the rise of Labour, an insurgent feminist movement, the devastation of mid-Victorian constitutionalism as a direct repercussion of the struggles over Ireland, the deepest shift in political allegiance of the working class yet seen this century, the collapse of the rotation of parties, the impact of the Great War, and the attempts to reorganize a political order behind the defensive armour of coalition. At critical moments it looked as if the Conservative Party itself was about to be swallowed up into a national, anti-socialist bloc of a Mussolini variety. Constitutional politics was fiercely challenged by both right and left.

Moreover, there existed no ready-made Conservative identity through which the party could come to terms with the new constitutional conditions. Conservatism had been pulled into the twentieth century on the back of the Unionist alliance and the authoritarian populism of the Tariff Reform League, and from the latter derived some coherence as a political party. The programme of the League was contentious but straightforward: it aimed to create, through a system of protection and tariffs, a single economic bloc based on the British Empire which would be sufficiently strong to rival the emergent industrial economies of Germany, the United States and Japan. Its political leaders hoped to unite both industrial capitalists and the working class under the banner of Empire, addressing all those who feared the collapse of British imperial hegemony. The organization of the League was eventually captured by the right and indiscernibly merged with the various proto-fascist sects. However, its legacy forced into the Conservative programme a virulent imperialism, racism and anti-feminism, which were most frequently premised on an explicit anti-constitutionalism – the desire to reverse Britain's liberal-constitutional social historical route. The process by which these political forces re-worked the language of the 'free-born Englishman' was already well under way by the onset of the imperial crisis in the 1890s. But in the increasing disarray and fragmentation of Unionism after 1910 the tariff programme, even in its broadest political and cultural version, could no longer hold together the discordant elements of the radical right. The most concerted and forceful attempt to rebuild Conservatism so that it could survive as a party disintegrated in both ideology and organization. Anti-constitutionalism took hold of the party as a whole. As Lord Milner perceived most clearly, the fundamental dilemma for Conservatives rested on the question of whether it was possible to hold back Labour *and* stick with the constitution.

In 1916 this dilemma was largely resolved for the Conservative leadership when Lloyd George assumed premiership of the war coalition, appearing as the saviour of all that Conservatism had stood for. The uncompromising reaction of the coalition promised to end the succession of abortive attempts to create a national, anti-socialist party of the 'centre'. Many of the distinctly Conservative elements of social imperialism and of the radical right, set adrift since the collapse of the Tariff Reform League and threatening to blow the party asunder, cohered in the political alliance of the various collectivisms under Lloyd George. The fracturing of the Liberal Party and the absorption of the Conservatives into a single party of the state, combined with an incipient corporatism, put constitutional, two-party politics at the bottom of the agenda.

Lloyd George's coalition survived until 1922. The most dazzling figures in the Conservative leadership (such as Lord Birkenhead and Austen Chamberlain) placed all their bets on a formal fusion of the coalition forces and thus, in effect, on the dismemberment of the Conservative Party. However, there was not a soul who could trust Lloyd George, least of all those Conservatives excluded from power and consigned to a political life of largely ineffective backbench speech-making. The solution which finally predominated first emerged in 1922 in the backbench rebellion led by Baldwin. The long-term success of this rebellion depended on a number of factors. First, it meant breaking the coalition and its managed electoralism of the 'coupon', and dislodging the most famous Conservative names of the day from the centre of the political stage. This strategy was staked not on the dismantling of constitutional politics, but on raising it to a position of absolute centrality. Second, it involved the disciplining of the Conservative right wing, particularly the forces organized by Northcliffe, Beaverbrook and Rothermere, the press barons – all of whom, by the end of the war, were prominent in the Ministry of Information, practising with the full backing of the state what must have appeared to Baldwin to have been the most shameless propaganda. Third, and above all, it depended upon educating Labour into an acceptance of constitutionalism. For this last objective to be achieved the line between constitutional and non-constitutional had to be defined, fought for and then held, come what may. To this end the Conservatives were prepared to call upon the full coercive powers of the state. Baldwin's Conservative Party could only guarantee formal constitutional rights by ensuring that the primary defensive organizations of labour were either smashed or drastically curtailed. By the end of May 1926 this is what had effectively taken place.

In the process Baldwin and his allies developed a new political language and a new cultural identity for Conservatism. His speech against Lloyd George at the Carlton Club in October 1922 was based on the belief that the time had arrived to return to normality after a period of exceptionalism. His attack was made in the name of an older Conservatism and moralism, a moralism pitched against the systematic double-dealing which had been the hallmark of the coalition. To Conservatives this appeal was potent, but in practice it could mean little, for the old Conservatism had largely been appropriated by Lloyd George. Baldwin's initial, instinctive reflex was to re-work the stock repertoire of pre-war Unionism and revive tariff reform as a political programme. In the autumn of 1923, a few months after becoming Prime Minister, he rushed into an election in the hope of winning the electorate to tariff reform and protection, lost the Conservative majority, and put in the first Labour government. This electoral catastrophe ensured that there could be no simple retrieval of earlier traditions.

From this point, the tempo in the transformation of Conservative ideology accelerated. The older elements of Conservatism – harmony between classes as one nation, the centrality of race and empire, the stress on 'separate spheres' – were not so much ditched as reworked and integrated into a more liberal and constitutional variant. In effect, the Conservative articulation of people and nation was constitutionalized.

A Hole in the Air

Baldwin himself was Prime Minister in 1923, 1924–29 and 1935–37 and, although Ramsay MacDonald was accredited as premier in the National Government from 1931 to 1935, Baldwin held virtually all the cards. To the Conservative right Baldwin has always appeared a dangerous figure, much too soft on Labour and a crypto-socialist. (His cousin, Rudyard Kipling, firmly believed that 'Stanley is a Socialist at heart.') Churchill and Birkenhead displayed their contempt by referring to the pawns in their chess games as 'Baldwins'. From the left he has consistently been seen as the embodiment of the worst hard-nosed Conservatism, presiding over the General Strike, the annihilation of the miners and mass unemployment. From May 1940 when Churchill (rather half-heartedly) ousted the appeasers, Baldwin's reputation became entirely discredited and oblivion seemed to swallow him up. To Orwell, in 1940, 'one could not even dignify him with the name of stuffed shirt. He was simply a hole in the air.' Even his official biographer, G. M. Young, managed through a judicious combination of innuendo and outright hostility to produce a picture of Baldwin as a

David Low, *Evening Standard*, 12 December 1927. (Baldwin is shown with Austen Chamberlain, W. S. Churchill, W. Bridgeman and Sir W. Joynson-Hicks. A. J. P. Taylor has observed that 'the Stanley Baldwin we remember for his gentle bewilderment is the Baldwin of Low's cartoons, not the ruthless statesman of real life'. Baldwin himself remarked that 'Low is a genius, but he is evil and malicious. I cannot bear Low . . .')

thoroughly untrustworthy, listless and negative politician, the architect of the fashionably designated Wilderness Years.

Baldwin's political skills, however, are beyond dispute. He put an end to Lloyd George's career, he brought Churchill to heel and kept him there for over a decade, he broke up the alliance between Rothermere and Beaverbrook, he dispatched in one move the Birkenhead/Austen Chamberlain constellation in 1922, he won obedience from the Labour leaders and he refused to make a single concession during the nine days of the General Strike. Each confrontation he fought with determination and ruthlessness. (His wife's nickname for him – Tiger – may provide an insight.) The retrospective assessments of his career are more difficult to deal with, for they hide the extent to which, at certain moments in his political life, Baldwin was revered by the dominant sections within the power bloc. For example, in 1936 Bechhofer Roberts published a book with the title: *Stanely Baldwin. Man or Miracle?* (Nor was this admiration exclusively from the right: Harold Laski was at times extremely sympathetic to Baldwin's politics, and could never quite understand how he had ended up a Conservative.) What is of interest, in this context, is not so much how this political hegemony was established but rather its specific forms and discourse.

Baldwin presented himself, and was presented by Conservative Central Office, as the peace-maker, conciliator and consensus-builder. It became his self-appointed task to heal the traumas which racked the body politic, to resolve harmoniously what he saw as specific national and moral crises. A continual reference point in his speeches was the disaster inflicted by the war, and the need to avert conflict and violence remained their touchstone. It was Baldwin's belief that, for the first time in British history, the political conditions had come into existence in which social antagonisms could be peaceably resolved through the due parliamentary process, which since 1918 had become truly representative. Harmony in the nation and constitutionalism together formed his political thought. In abhoring Lloyd George's war-time politics of exceptionalism and playing upon real hopes for tranquility, he consistently elided in his speeches the violence of the trenches with the violence of domestic social conflict.

There were three decisive moments in his career when he was able to intervene pre-eminently as conciliator, as the personification of constitutionalism. The first was the break with coalitionism in 1922, when the language of parliamentary politics could again come into dominance. The second moment occurred in 1925 when Baldwin opposed the majority of his party on the issue of the political levy imposed by the trade unions. Baldwin's support for the levy drove many of his backbenchers to an infuriated apoplexy, but he eventually succeeded in winning them to his position. For this he received unprecedented acclaim from both politicians and press. The third occasion was the abdication crisis of 1936. It is hard to imagine, now, what reverberations this sent through the power bloc. Harold Macmillan – miles to the left of most Conservatives, a young turk courting the radicals in the Labour Party – wrote to Baldwin arguing the 'The slightest weakness now would be a shattering blow to the whole basis of Christian morality, already gravely injured during recent years. May God help you in this painful and difficult time.' With divine help or not, it was mainly through Baldwin, in the closing and triumphant moment of his career, that the moral authority of Church, State and Family was reasserted. All the hierarchical, mystical, imperial rhetoric gushed out – a dulling reminder of the profound conservatism of the ideology of the nation in contemporary British history, mobilized here in a crescendo. To these conjunctural crises should be added the more protracted, organic crisis of the first tentative moves of the power bloc to extricate itself from the imperial jewel of India, and the shift from Empire to Commonwealth – the cause of the final breach between Baldwin and Churchill.

The paradox, however, is that at every turn Baldwin resolutely presented himself as non-political, as the little man thrust unwillingly onto the public stage, talking to others of his type. He spoke as one of the people. The realities of his social position – the silver spoon from birth – are not to the point. Patrician dominance of the governing classes had weakened before the war, with Bonar Law's leadership of the Unionists, and definitively when Lloyd George, the archetypal outsider, assumed the premiership in 1916. But for a Conservative leader and prime minister to adopt so assiduously a popular idiom, as Baldwin did, was unprecedented. Lord Curzon, the main contender for the leadership in 1923, was aghast when he learned that he had been beaten by Baldwin and his first response was to declare, 'He is not even a public man.' It was on this image that Baldwin traded.

It is difficult to tell how far this persona was developed by Baldwin himself, or by his immediate cronies, and how much by the Conservative Party apparatus. The potential of the latter should not be underestimated. In 1925 Conservative Central Office distributed or sold 5,300,000 leaflets and booklets; by 1929 this had risen to 110 million. Links to the leading businessmen in the film companies enabled the Conservative Party to establish a vanguard position in cinema propaganda. In 1926 the party was commissioning films and cartoons. By 1927, the 1922 Committee had purchased one of the earliest sound-film patents in the United Kingdom, and audiences of thousands would have first experienced talking pictures by watching films shown by one of the many Conservative travelling vans.

In May and June 1924, when the Labour government was already weakening, Baldwin delivered ten major speeches on Tory democracy, and apart from receiving extensive coverage from Central Office they were almost certainly prompted and co-ordinated by the party managers. In addition, Baldwin's speeches were collected and published throughout his

The image with two voices. Low, *Evening Standard*, 2 August 1928. (The voices are Churchill and Joynson-Hicks.)

career. Again, pressure may have been exerted from Central Office, for on the publication of a volume in 1928, Baldwin remarked – perhaps with a touch of weary realism or cynicism – 'In years to come this book will probably be forgotten.'[2] Moreover, he wrote comparatively little of the stuff himself. Over half the first volume was written by the assistant secretary to the cabinet, Thomas Jones (a Fabian, ex-ILPer and life-long Labour Party member to boot), and his private secretary, Geoffrey Fry. For his trip to Canada in 1927, it was arranged that a group of academics would busy themselves drafting his speeches. And in the 1930s the chief publicity officer at the Conservative Central Office, Sir Patrick Gower, became Baldwin's main adviser on film and radio, again writing many of the speeches.

It has often been remarked that one of Baldwin's particular skills was the radio broadcast, a medium which he came politically to monopolise. He took great care in preparing his radio talks and ascertaining not only the social composition of his audience but also how they would be listening – whether at home with the family or more publicly, in a club or pub. Apparently Baldwin even persuaded his wife to accompany him in the studios with her knitting to give him a closer idea of his relationship to his audience. The radio was especially suited to his supposedly non-political, low-key chats – just as it was disastrous for Ramsay MacDonald's more rhetorical style of the auditorium – penetrating into the domestic sphere itself. But what has been less noted is the extent to which Baldwin's career as a leading politician coincided with the development of the mass aural and

'Don't forget the tear in your voice, Al.'
Low, *Evening Standard*, 28 February 1929. (J. C. C. Davidson, behind the camera, was Chairman of the Conservative Party.)

visual media. In the 1920s and 1930s radio and newsreel first co-existed with, and then gradually displaced, the mass meeting as the forms in which politicians could reach public opinion. One of the first programmes transmitted by the British Broadcasting Company, in 1922, was the coverage of the election which brought the defeat of the Lloyd George coalition. The same month, the first newsreels showed 'the inside of Number Ten' with the new cabinet assembled. Baldwin himself became a familiar media figure – he even joked, on his trip to New York in 1939 at the age of 73, that 'I might be a film star'. It was with Baldwin, and in the Baldwin era, that the relationship between politicians and electorate, mediated through the elusive category of public opinion, first took shape, and when party managers assumed a decisive role in generating party images for public consumption.

Baldwin's primary response to the successive crises of hegemony of the First World War period was to regulate and define public opinion, by broadening the Conservative discourse of the nation, deepening its reach into the culture of 'the people'. To preserve the nation in crisis was also to insist on the function of the Conservative Party as the representative, not of a class, but of the whole people and of the post-war constitutional settlement. In the 1940s Baldwin looked back to the First War and claimed, 'I tried hard in those confused years immediately following the war to get a reorientation as it were of the Tory Party, i.e., to give it a national rather than a party outlook.'[3] The sentiment echoed Disraeli, but the political task and the ideologies of nation in play were quite new.

Statesman and Englishman

Selections from Baldwin's speeches were published as *On England* (April 1926, reprinted twice the following month – the month of the General Strike), *Our Inheritance* (1928), *This Torch of Freedom* (1935) and *Service of Our Lives* (1937, to coincide with his retirement from the premiership – this was twice reprinted within the following two months.) His Falconer Lectures, delivered at the University of Toronto in April 1939, were published as *An Interpreter of England*. In a note to the third volume the publishers emphasized that these speeches were not the product of mere party politics – 'Throughout this volume he speaks as the statesman and Englishman, not as the party leader concerned with immediate issues' – while the subsequent volume aimed 'to complete the record in book form of his principal public utterances as a national leader.' The speeches themselves, apart from a handful of exceptional cases, were drawn from talks to voluntary and private organizations, and this gave to them a distinctive sense of being ethical and non-political. To Wickham Steed of *The Times* they appeared to be lay sermons and he noted above all Baldwin's ability to communicate directly to the people: 'His "plain speech" goes home'.[4]

The unstated core of the speeches in the early volumes is Baldwin's construction of an implicit opposition between English constitutionalism and Bolshevism. Only in rare moments does this spectre appear explicitly in the text. One example occurs in the first volume. In order to signify the full danger of communism, a parliamentary speech was printed in full – the institutional setting adding weight to the argument of the text:

> 'I am quite certain that . . . there will never in this country be a Communist Government, and for this reason, that no gospel founded on hate will ever seize the hearts of our people – the people of Great Britain. It is no good trying to cure the world by spreading out oceans of bloodshed. It is no good trying to cure the world by repeating that pentasyllabic French derivative, "Proletariat". The English language is the richest in the world in thought. The English language is the richest in the world in monosyllables. Four words, of one syllable each, are words which contain salvation for this country and for the whole world, and they are "Faith", "Hope", "Love" and "Work".'[5]

The trisyllabic *Charity* was clearly inconvenient. That Baldwin – bourgeois to the core – chose to substitute *Work* is no surprise, and in any case his audience appeared not to notice. The discursive polarity was resonant enough, and so deeply did this structure his speeches that frequently it was not even necessary to mention the primary antagonist. Only later, in the 1930s, does Baldwin refer more specifically to Bolshevism, and then only coupled with fascism as a twin expression of that most un-English phenomenon of totalitarianism.

It is this overpowering sense of the socialist threat, condensed in the image of Bolshevism and barbarism but suppressed and displaced in the manifest text, which gives these anodyne speeches their political bite. (When instructing Thomas Jones to prepare a speech for the London School Teachers' dinner, Baldwin gave only this advice: 'So many of the teachers are tinged with Bolshevism – so many cranks about; perhaps you could say something about that, and I will talk about my old school days.') Publicly Baldwin maintained that freedom and liberty were inherently English – 'We are so accustomed to it [our freedom], as to the air we breathe, that we take it for granted.'[6] His conviction could only be half-hearted, however, for he appreciated that this was a situation which had to be *achieved*. It was the precariousness of the constitutional settlement which drove Baldwin into such deep political anxiety. In 1927 he wrote to a friend: 'Democracy has arrived at a gallop in England and I feel all the time it is a race for life. Can we educate them [the mass of the electorate] before the crash comes?'[7] This precipitous development – a curious reading of the protracted and uneven historical process of political reform, but that can be left aside – 'had brought our people and other peoples to a political status in advance of their cultural status.'[8]

Much later, when Baldwin last addressed his Bewdley Unionist Association as their parliamentary representative, he returned to his theme, compressing all the complexities into a superbly inappropriate platitude:

> 'While today you may, I believe, drive with safety on the roads at sixty miles an hour, if this country ever tries to travel in constitutional change at sixty miles an hour the Constitution will be wrecked, and it will be wrecked, as it always has been in those rapid changes, in disaster and in bloodshed. That is one more proof of what I have often said, that we must try not to confuse acceleration with civilisation, because they have really nothing at all to do with one another.'[9]

However simple-minded the metaphor, the problem was clear: it was necessary to raise the cultural level of the masses, to educate the electorate into a fit state for exercising democratic responsibilities, and thereby to avert the 'very great danger that the higher, the more spiritual, the only lasting qualities of civilisation may be submerged in the lower and inferior.'[10] And, as Baldwin explained to the Cambridge University Conservative Association, although it was possible to count on the innate sense of most of the English people, there did exist 'large masses' who might be prey to propaganda of the wrong sort, to 'alien, class hatred'. The political inexperience of women was a particular source of worry:

> 'And who is it gets the heavy end of the stick if Bolshevist propaganda wins out in this country? The women every time . . . it may well be that

they may be more ready to jump at any form of remedy that can be put before them by the smooth and clever tongues of those who propagate heresies in our country.'[11]

In this struggle Baldwin consistently took it upon himself to oppose the unscrupulous 'smooth and clever tongues' of the powerful, defending the poor, the weak and the inarticulate in the name of the rule of law, and what can only be called a sense of fair play – a bizarre moment for this antiquated sediment of English folk culture to enter the dominant political discourse. The powerful and unscrupulous included for Baldwin a spectacular combination of the press barons (for whom he savoured his most venemous, outraged moral onslaughts), Lloyd George (who was 'neither simple, nor English, nor a gentleman', whose influence was 'morally disintegrating', and whose political system 'was poisoning the whole atmosphere of public life'[12]), 'Bolshevists' of all varieties (naturally), and – the moment they showed a hint of spirit – labour leaders.

The persistent identification of trade unionism with Bolshevism was worked into the common sense of the power bloc with such consummate, almost surgical skill by Baldwin that it has provided desperate politicians with a handy cliché ever since. (In this rhetoric, there was little difference between him and Lloyd George, except perhaps that Baldwin was the more adept.) Trade unionism was thus positioned as another vested interest which threatened the community. During the General Strike this ideological work flourished. In the *British Gazette* on 6 May 1926, under Baldwin's name although initially drafted by that cheery social democrat Tom Jones, appeared the following:

> 'Constitutional Government is being attacked. Let all good citizens whose livelihood and labour have thus been put in peril bear with fortitude and patience the hardships with which they have been so suddenly confronted. Stand behind the Government who are doing their part, confident that you will co-operate in the measures that they have undertaken to provide the liberties and privileges of the people of these islands. The laws of England are the people's birthright. The laws are in your keeping. You have made Parliament their guardian. The General Strike is a challenge to Parliament and is the road to anarchy and ruin.'

The Bunyanesque puritanism, the knowing but unprecedented reference to citizens, the neat encapsulation of people's birthright and Baldwin's government demonstrate not only the combination of characteristic styles of those who drafted the statement, but also illuminate a deeper political alliance between social democrats and Conservatives developing in this period. (This is nicely caught in the diligent Thomas Jones *reminding* his Conservative boss to be as tough on the high Tory *Morning Post* as on the *Herald*.) The process of incorporation of a radical language of reform and class resistance, and the re-workings of older traditions, were completed. This enabled Baldwin during the Strike to broadcast to the nation, 'I will not surrender the safety and security of the British Constitution'[13] – and then to sit tight.

The National Character

It can be seen that Baldwin hoped – by activating a sense of national identity – to bring the masses to an appreciation of the liberal-constitutional heritage enshrined in the nation's past, preventing the tumble into political and cultural collapse. Just as he disdained to indulge in propaganda, so he made no attempt to create an 'ugly nationalism' but appealed instead to what he called the 'natural devotion to the land and people of one's birth.'[14] Political salvation lay in the historical and natural formation of 'our National Character.'[15] This construction of the English character depended upon an unquestioned racism (it was, by definition, white and superior) and a rather more ambivalently poised masculinism; it summoned a breathless collection of half-baked abstractions (the English, 'gallicised Scandanavians', inheriting nordic naval skills and the qualities of the Normans, 'perhaps one of the greatest races that has ever lived on this earth'[16]); and it wove together a highly particular reading of English literature, history and geography.

Chaucer, Shakespeare, Bunyan, Scott, Dickens, Ruskin and Morris – all of whom used the language of the common people – defined the literary canon, and commitment to this tradition was expressed as a commitment to a popular rendering of literary values. Great writers yes, but their stature derived from the fact that they listened to the language of the people, and reproduced it in living form as literature. The contemporary debasement of language threatened to engulf literature and the values inscribed within it:

> 'I regret that the dialects have gone, and I regret that by a process which for want of a better name we have agreed among ourselves to call education, we are drifting away from the language of the people, and losing some of the best English words and phrases which have lasted in this country through centuries, to make us all talk one uniform and inexpressive language.'[17]

In this way English literature and the English language were seen as the central component of a historical *tradition*.

It was this extraordinary evocation of tradition and of national past which really became the characteristic of these speeches. Baldwin consciously attempted to build an organic and active relation between past and present, while at the same time suggesting that this relationship was already an integral, constitutive and permanent feature of English culture. Continuity and constitutionalism provided an inheritance which was presented as common to all Englishmen, in a language which was to have a strategic ideological role in the present. Thus the constitution itself 'could never have been created: it is the result of centuries of evolution and native in its growth'[18], and democracy in England, 'growing through the centuries' has its roots 'in our being: we are so used to its free air that we sometimes notice it no more than the air we breathe, and it is only when it is threatened that we realise that without it we would perish.'[19] Magna Carta marks one of the earliest points in the evolution of this parliamentarianism, a parliamentarianism which 'was the natural outcome, through long centuries, of the common sense and the good nature of the English people, who have always preferred committees to dictators, elections to street-fighting, and talking shops to revolutionary tribunals.'[20] Again, however, Baldwin knew only too well that this was not the case: he was terrified that 'street-fighting and revolutionary tribunals' were just around the corner. He resolved such discrepancies by resolutely ignoring the ruptures in the evolution of constitutionalism, by condensing and mystifying specific histories (creating such magical entities as that 'ancient British institution, the policeman'[21]), and by projecting his contemporary fears of crisis back into his reading of the seventeenth century. Not even Baldwin could pass over the history of the seventeenth century without some recognition of the social and political collapse of the 1640s, and he himself drew the parallel with his own times. He claimed that after the civil war 'Englishmen longed for constitutional stability'.[22] Cromwell (the Lloyd George figure) he believed to be alien to the traditions of 'our race', an example of the dangers of too much liberty[23], but at the same time he endorsed the stand of the radicals at Putney – suggesting, perhaps, that Kipling's condemnation of his cousin was not entirely nonsense – appropriating a militant democratic radicalism for his own version of constitutional Conservatism[24].

But to argue in historiographical terms like these misses the point, for Baldwin ultimately transposed history to the natural world, eternalizing the ideology of Englishness. His depiction of England was steeped in an inordinately detailed image of the regional, rural landscapes – a ruralism which signified not only the past-in-the-present but, in his own words, 'the land of childhood and memory'[25]. In his biography of Baldwin, Arthur Bryant (a key figure in this general ideological formation) suggested that 'English history was written for the boy not only in the books he read but in the landscape around him.'[26] And Baldwin himself asserted: 'To me, England is the country, and the country is England. And when I ask myself what I mean by England, when I think of England when I am abroad, England comes to me *through my various senses* – through the ear, through the eye, and through certain imperishable scents.'[27] History, here, becomes literally naturalized. From this starting point Baldwin was able to develop a mystical,

timeless notion of Englishness which, precisely because it was so thoroughly abstracted from history – despite the wealth of historical references –
expanded the range of possible readings of the central sign, England.

In this way Englishness and continuity became condensed through an
invocation of the temporal rhythms of the natural world. The most famous
passage of all:

> 'The sounds of England, the tinkle of the hammer on the anvil in the
> country smithy, the corncrake on a dewy morning, the sound of the
> scythe against the whetstone, and the sight of a plough team coming
> over the brow of a hill, the sight that has been seen in England since
> England was a land, and may be seen in England long after the Empire
> has perished and every works in England has ceased to function, for
> centuries the one eternal sight of England. The wild anemones in the
> woods in April, the last load at night of hay being drawn down a lane as
> the twilight comes on, when you can scarcely distinguish the figures of
> the horses as they take it home to the farm, and above all, most subtle,
> most penetrating and most moving, the smell of wood smoke coming
> up in an autumn evening, or the smell of the scutch fires: that wood
> smoke that our ancestors, tens of thousands of years ago, must have
> caught on the air when they were coming home with the result of the
> day's forage, when they were still nomads, and when they were still
> roaming the forests and plains of the continent of Europe. These things
> strike down into the very depths of our nature, and touch chords that
> go back to the beginning of time and the human race, but they are
> chords that with every year of our life sounds a deeper note in our
> innermost being.'

The recurring images of nature, home, harmony and (less explicitly) of the
continuity of human life carried through the family are packed up in the next
passage and linked to the identity of the English people and their conception
of Empire, in an unusually homely, domestic and unmilitaristic mode for a
Conservative:

> 'These are the things that make England, and I grieve for it that they are
> not the childish inheritance of the majority of the people to-day in our
> country. They ought to be the inheritance of every child born into this
> country, but nothing can be more touching than to see how the
> working man and woman after generations in the towns will have their
> tiny bit of garden if they can, will go to gardens if they can, to look at
> something they have never seen as children, but which their ancestors
> knew and loved. The love of these things is innate and inherent in our
> people. It makes for that love of home, one of the strongest features of
> our race, and it is that that makes our race seek its new home in the

Dominions overseas, where they have room to see things like this that they can no more see at home. It is that power of making homes, almost peculiar to our people, and it is one of the sources of their greatness . . . It may well be that these traits on which we pride ourselves . . . may survive . . . among our people so long as they are a people . . .'[28]

The sentimentality and crass absurdity of this rhetoric should not lead us to underestimate its political impact. Through the 1920s and 1930s there were few ideologues on the right who could match Baldwin. It was Wickham Steed's opinion that: 'As an orator or, if he prefer it, as a "Minister of Public Opinion", he has hardly a rival among contemporary British politicians.'[29] Many of his conservative critics were forced to adopt that same discourse which Baldwin had made his own in order to articulate their attacks: much hinged on Baldwin's claim to Englishness. Bechhofer Roberts opened his survey of Baldwin's career with the statement: 'Like so many representative Englishmen, Stanley Baldwin is a modest and a shy and a very simple Englishman. There is no more thoroughly an English Englishman in the House of Commons.'[30] To John Green, writing in the early thirties, Baldwin represented the decay of the English polity, the obliteration of the traditions by which the common people had lived, the surrender of Conservatism to whiggery and the general collapse into liberalism: but he could comfort himself with the thought that, after all, Baldwin was not really 'English'.[31]

But there is a more serious side to this as well, which takes us out of the mainstream traditions of Conservatism altogether. Baldwin's was a political language which became a mainspring of much anti-fascist populism during the Second World War. Baldwin himself, and the governments over which he had presided in the inter-war period, were reviled in the 1940s. But there did exist nonetheless a direct ideological lineage between Baldwinism and the sentimental nationalism which took a more radical and popular turn in the Second World War – in J. B. Priestley's famous radio *Postscripts*, for example, or, in a more defeated and contained form, in the Ealing cinema after the war. And when, in May 1940, that arch-caesarist Churchill assumed the national leadership of the anti-fascist struggle he was only able to win credibility – as a *Conservative* – because of the ideological work already carried out by Baldwin in the 1920s. Even then, Churchill's imperialist, adventurist and deeply conservative militarism undeniably reordered many of the elements in the Baldwinite discourse. But equally, it was Churchill's commitment to an antiquarian Conservatism which prevented him from accurately assessing the mood of the popular forces, not least in the midst of his defeat in 1945. It may well also have been that some of the most radical political positions of the 1940s, including those self-consciously socialist, became compromised – not necessarily by the identification with the nation as such, but by the cultural dominance of what has been described here as

Baldwinite nationalism. It was the particular strength of Baldwinism that, in adopting and re-working the language of the Englishman's birthright, it was able both to displace and neutralise the antagonism between the people and the state.

Notes

1. N. Pronay, 'The first reality. Film censorship in liberal England', in K. R. M. Short (ed.), *Feature Film as History*, London, Croom Helm, 1982, pp. 125–6. And see J. Ramsden (ed.), *Stanley Baldwin*, Inter University Film Consortium, Archive Series no. 3, 1980, and J. Ramsden, 'Stanley Baldwin and Film,' in N. Pronay and D. W. Spring (eds), *Propaganda, Politics and Film*, London, Macmillan, 1982.
2. T. Jones, *Whitehall Diary*, vol. 2, Oxford University Press, 1969, p. 136.
3. H. M. Hyde, *Baldwin*, London, Hart Davis, 1973, p. 550.
4. W. Steed, *The Real Stanley Baldwin*, London, Nisbet, 1930, p. 140.
5. S. Baldwin, *On England*, Harmondsworth, Penguin, 1939 ed., pp. 66–67.
6. S. Baldwin, *Service of Our Lives*, London, Hodder & Stoughton, 1937, p. 25.
7. K. Middlemas and J. Barnes, *Baldwin*, London, Hutchinson, 1969, p. 390.
8. *ibid.*, p. 530.
9. *Service of Our Lives*, p. 97.
10. *On England*, p. 156.
11. S. Baldwin, *Our Inheritance*, London, Hodder & Stoughton, 1928, p. 35.
12. Jones, *Whitehall Diary*, p. 123; Middlemas and Barnes, *Baldwin*, pp. 97 and 98.
13. Hyde, *Baldwin*, p. 271.
14. *Our Inheritance*, p. 48.
15. See S. Baldwin, *This Torch of Freedom*, London, Hodder & Stoughton, 1935.
16. *ibid.*, p. 18.
17. *On England*, p. 15.
18. Earl Baldwin, *An Interpreter of England*, London, Hodder & Stoughton, n.d., 1939?, p. 36.
19. *ibid.*, pp. 46–7.
20. *Torch of Freedom*, p. 13.
21. *ibid.*, p. 63.
22. *Service of Our Lives*, p. 32.
23. *Torch of Freedom*, p. 26.
24. *ibid.*, p. 45.
25. *Our Inheritance*, p. 81.
26. A. Bryant, *Stanley Baldwin: A Tribute*, London, Hamish Hamilton, n.d., 1937?, p. 20.
27. *On England*, p. 16, my emphasis.
28. *ibid.*, p. 17.
29. Steed, *The Real Stanley Baldwin*, p. 147.
30. B. Roberts, *Stanley Baldwin. Man or Miracle?* London, R. Hale 1936, pp. 9 and 108.
31. J. Green, *Mr Baldwin. A Study in Post-War Conservatism*, London, Sampson Low, n.d., 1933?, p. 23.

Alan O'Shea

TRUSTING THE PEOPLE:
How does Thatcherism Work?

During the winter of 1981/2, the political pundits were predicting the beginning of the end for Mrs Thatcher and her policies. Opinion polls testified to her unpopularity: seventy five per cent of respondents thought she was not in touch with ordinary people. The SDP/Liberal Alliance had high hopes of being the largest party in the next Government. A new era of consensus politics was forseen. This article began its life in that moment, as a warning that such a scenario obscured a more profound achievement of 'Thatcherism' – a more permanent shift to the right in popular common sense, a change in the political culture deeper than fickle shifts in public opinion. The revitalisation of Thatcherism during 1982 and her victory in the June 1983 election have made this case much stronger, and hence less controversial. This has made it all the more imperative to recognise that Thatcherism will not go away by itself, but will have to be criticised and displaced. Part of this process is to understand how Thatcherism is able to penetrate and represent popular experience. Out of such an analysis it should be possible to establish the mechanisms through which popular experience might be re-addressed in more progressive ways.

Analysing Thatcherism

A first stage in such an analysis, and one which has already made some progress[1], is to consider what Thatcherism broke from, and how it was able to mobilise popular support in this process. During the years 1975–79 the elements which make up Thatcherism were consolidated into a unified 'philosophy' which was simultaneously a critique of the social-democratic solutions which, in various forms, had been hegemonic for the previous thirty years across all the parliamentary parties, including the Conservative Party.[2] Economic and social crises may have caused the social-democratic repertoire to totter under the weight of its own internal contradictions, notably that of attempting to represent the interest of working people and the national interest as if they were one and the same thing. Nevertheless, the radical right had been able to hasten its collapse by exploiting its failure to address popular experience of crises, and by expressing these experiences, frustrations and anxieties within a reactionary framework. It has been a remarkably successful attempt to rework the totality of popular experience, to introduce new forms of social identity, and to discredit those summoned up within the social-democratic ideologies which it displaced.

The grievances addressed within the discourse of the new right are by no means illusory. The organisations of the Welfare State, for example, have been widely experienced as depersonalised, oppressive and interfering. The trade union bureaucracies, the nationalised industries and other public sector bodies have also come under selective but consistent attack. These feelings were not simply manipulated, but sprang from concrete restrictions on autonomy and democratic participation.[3] Another sphere of frustration was inner-city breakdown in its various forms: deteriorating housing, street violence, vandalism and theft are not inventions of the hard right. But instead of these experiences of powerlessness being yoked to a movement for popular participation led by the left, they were successfully articulated in Thatcherism to reactionary panics over immigration, to the 'rising tide' of youth crime, to the 'welfare scroungers' and to 'crippling' taxation and rates.

What is striking is Thatcherism's ability to address such varied issues in a way that appeals to diverse sectors of society through a simple, terse and fundamental discourse:

> 'For what is the real driving force in our society? It is the desire for the individual to do the best for himself and his family. There is no substitute for this elemental human instinct . . .'
>
> (Margaret Thatcher, speech at Cardiff, 16 April 1979)

Again and again Mrs Thatcher's audience is offered this identity: the individual consumer protecting his (sic) rights of privacy. This identity suppresses other possible modes of address. It also makes it possible to conflate state intervention in its welfare form with state intervention in the economy – with support of ailing firms in the interest of full employment, with taxes on capital gains and with the repression of incentive. This defence of individual freedom is thus able to provide a link between the poorer sectors of society and particular fractions of capital. Attacks on the freedom of capital are implicitly presented as being criminal in the same way as attacks on property (by vandals) and on persons (by muggers). Thatcherism attempts to make various fragments of lived experience more coherent. It articulates a variety of identifications – aggrieved council tenant, overtaxed businessman, disgruntled trade unionist – into a relative unity. This then seems to be the expression of a single, coherent subject – the ordinary individual protecting his sphere of freedom.

We have to be careful here. Some commentators have seen this dependence on the rhetoric of possessive individualism as a return to

classical Liberalism. This view is encouraged perhaps by the attempts by Tories like Mrs Thatcher and Sir Keith Joseph to place themselves in the tradition of nineteenth-century *laissez-faire* policies or even further back in the struggles of the 'free-born Englishman' for political and legal rights in the seventeenth century. But it is an oversimplification. Thatcherism draws on a number of identifications. These elements may be fused into the figure of the free, consuming individual, but Thatcherism is more than the sum of its ideological parts. Each element (such as the idea of 'freedom of the individual') has its own history which sets limits on how it can be employed. But this does not mean that they have a fixed, pre-given social reference or class connotation.[4] How they become part of popular common sense is an empirical historical question. A second approach to Thatcherism sees it not as a return to *laissez-faire* but as a set of policies added together – monetarism plus law-and-order plus free exchange rates plus restricting the powers of the unions and so forth. If these policies are analysed as anti-working-class, then it seems obvious that Thatcherism will eventually be seen for what it is and topple. Such assumptions fail to account for the popular appeal of Thatcherism because they ignore how these policies are represented and inflected in its discourse – the apparently incidental forms through which the project is expressed. It is these that I shall be analysing in this article, concentrating particularly on those aspects which address us not merely as free individuals, but as members of 'the people' or 'the nation'.[5]

The People

What is decisively new about Thatcherism, what constitutes a break with the mode of address of the previously dominant fraction of the Conservative Party as well as with that of the Labour Party, is its populism.[6] This term has caused some difficulties. Was not James Callaghan equally populist during the 1979 election campaign? He too argued on the basis of what the people want and in simple, grassroots terms. In the derogatory sense of populism – the use of demagogic rhetoric, speaking down to the people and playing on emotions in an exploitative way – there is no doubt that both Callaghan and Thatcher have used a populist address; so too have the versions of Thatcherism in the popular press. But populism is being used here in a more precise sense developed by Ernesto Laclau: that of constructing an antagonism of 'the people' *against the existing power-bloc*, mobilising certain *anti-statist* feelings and forces. This enables us to distinguish between the electioneering rhetoric of Thatcher and Callaghan. All such discourses will take a combative form. In social democratic discourses, this contestation has centred on the question of 'who manages best?' Thatcherism breaks fundamentally with this strategy and harnesses popular grievances against economic and social management as such – against statism. Mrs Thatcher argues that people want to be 'free from the apron-strings of the governess state' (reported in *The Guardian*, 30 December 1978). This form of address meets the requirements of Laclau's definition of a populism of the dominant classes.

> 'When the dominant bloc experiences a profound crisis because a new fraction seeks to impose its hegemony but is unable to do so within the existing structure of the power bloc, one solution can be a direct appeal by this fraction to the masses to develop their antagonism towards the state.'[7]

It is this sort of populism that was new – although it is also clear that by 1979 Callaghan had moved closer to Thatcherism, and had indeed taken on many of its elements. This suggests how deeply it had penetrated. Like 'social democracy' before it, Thatcherism is not just the policy of one parliamentary party, but represents a shift in the whole political culture and will be embraced, or at least negotiated, to differing degrees by all the parties. Thatcherism does not consist only of the pronouncements of Margaret Thatcher and her clique, though these remain powerful initiators. It has now become the very agenda which constrains the terms in which issues are to be discussed. This agenda was constructed gradually between 1968 and 1979 out of themes drawn largely from the old right of the Conservative Party – the rule of Law, standards, the family as the source of moral discipline, standing on your own two feet, national pride, and so on – but it also incorporates a particular economic theory – monetarism. The partial installation of Thatcherism as the new political common sense by the late 1970s is evident in a speech delivered by Callaghan in Cardiff in April 1979. He first sets himself up as the protector of individuals against vandals and criminals and then goes on to assert:

> 'Council tenants are entitled to ask the question: why should the town hall bureaucrats tell them how to run their houses?'

Nevertheless, this anti-statism is highly tentative and contained. Callaghan does not break cleanly with the idea of government as management. Although Thatcherism goes further than this, the antagonism between people and power-bloc is still developed within extremely circumscribed limits. Certain spheres of the state – the repressive aspects of the judiciary and the police, for example – are not to be rolled back but strengthened. That is why it has been designated an *authoritarian* populism. But even to describe Thatcherism as an authoritarian, constitutional populism does not exhaust its relation to the popular. There are two ways in which the analysis needs extending – first, into a range of variations on the popular address, which provide a highly condensed and complex 'national-popular' identity (and which incidentally involves rewriting British history); and, second, into the language of Thatcherism, its imagery and tone, the forms of its address.

The complexity of Thatcherism's construct of 'the people' is apparent in a speech made to the Conservative Trade Unionists' Annual Conference in November 1979. 'We are a practical people, we judge ideas by their results,' it begins. This immediately asserts a unity at the level of a national characteristic, and pulls it into a pragmatic-empiricist, commonsensical epistemology. This 'we' then turns to look at the trade unions.

> 'The purpose of trade union activity is to improve . . . the general well-being of working people. When we look at the unions today, we ask: have they achieved their own purpose? How have they affected the lives of their members and the nation at large? This is the natural question for trade unionists to ask themselves.'

The 'natural' concern of trade unions is here quietly extended from that of defending working people to benefiting 'the nation at large.' This attempt to disarticulate trade union activity from sectional interests and to articulate it to the national interest is developed through the rest of the speech. Mrs Thatcher notes that as workers we have sectional interests, 'but we are all *consumers* and as consumers we want a choice. We want the best value for money.' Hence 'the same trade unionists, as consumers, want an open market' – and thus no protectionism. This is what Nicos Poulantzas has called the isolation effect: antagonistic social groupings (in particular, classes) are broken down into individuals, consumers, families – non-antagonistic groups, sharing common concerns and interests. It should be said that, in seeing this process as the masking of class domination, Poulantzas tends to assume the unreality of the category 'consumer'. But this appeal by Mrs Thatcher is not a confidence trick. Being a consumer has distinct material effects. As Paul Corrigan puts it:

> 'Working people may experience the importance of collectivity, but they also experience the individualised experience of the market every single day. Thus whilst they may believe in collectivity, they also *have* to believe in capitalist social relations. Thatcher's major argument around incentives is one that is backed up and given validity in the lives of nearly every working person every day.'[9]

Many of the left have assumed (or at least hoped) that membership of a trade union makes a person a solid trade unionist, identifying primarily with that role and all that is assumed to be tied to it – such as becoming an activist and a socialist. This picture tends to regard all other identities or positionalities as somehow less real.[10] But, as Gramsci has argued, 'the personality is strangely composite' – and *has* to be in order to negotiate the different identities generated in a variety of institutional contexts and social relations.

Mrs Thatcher's speech aims to subordinate the 'trade unionist' identity to that of 'consumer', which becomes apparently more natural. But it is not simply the displacement of one identity by another. 'Consumer' and 'trade unionist' never appear in the abstract – their connotations are always specific to a particular context. Take this example:

> 'Our belief in the secret ballot stems from our trust in the good sense of the twelve million British people who are members of trade unions.'

Here is a combination of displacement and condensation. The individuals are addressed primarily as 'British people' – this is what they are funda-mentally. Secondarily, they happen to be in trade unions. And it is as British people that they can be trusted with good sense, not as trade unionists. In this displacement of 'trade unionist', there is a double condensation, which secures 'the people' to particular connotations. 'The people' are not articu-lated here as popular classes against ruling classes, or against the state, but to *Britishness*, to a national identity. Nor are 'the people' identified simply as a collectivity: they constitute twelve million *individuals*.

These passages do not employ a strictly populist mode, in Laclau's sense. They have a non-antagonistic, consensual appeal. This part of the speech offers a common identity which, as we shall see, can then be posed as threatened by alien forces against which a populist indignation can rage. Thatcherism subtly combines both antagonistic and consensual definitions of 'the people.'

The Nation

The connotations and resonances attached to the term *British* by Thatcherism are distinct from those provided by the Labour Party or by wet Conservatives. It resurrects the traditional patriotism kept alive in political circles by the old right, but also available in popular forms – the nostalgia for the Dunkirk spirit, for example, revived with a vengeance during the Falklands campaign, and the channelling of the search for Britain's greatness into international sporting achievements. The national interest was defined by the 1974–9 Labour Government primarily in terms of a social contract in industry: this offered economic rewards if only we would all pull together. Thatcherist nationalism involves a more competitive economic strand: 'And yet, while other countries in the free world have gone ahead, we have stood still or even slipped back.' But this is not the primary concern. As Mrs Thatcher insisted in a speech in Berwick in July 1978, she considers things 'not just from the economic point of view, important though that is . . .'

In the Berwick speech she broadened economic problems about public spending into questions of national pride and morality: 'Now you don't build a great nation like that, and you don't build a great people like that.' This goes beyond mundane economic health and into the realm of national spirit, morale and pride. The greatness she invokes here is a recurrent theme in Mrs Thatcher's speeches. It requires British history to be rewritten so that Thatcherism emerges as the bearer of the torch of our national spirit. First some dismantling of alternative histories is necessary, as in this speech to the 1975 Conservative Party conference:

> 'We are witnessing a deliberate attack on our values, a deliberate attack on those who wish to promote merit and excellence, a deliberate attack on our heritage and our great past. And there are those who gnaw away at our national self-respect, rewriting British history as centuries of unrelieved gloom, oppression and failure – as days of hopelessness, not days of hope.'

The confidence of such a contestation is remarkable. She could have chosen to give her own version of history as if it were the only conceivable one; instead she goes out of her way to admit an alternative and then throws down an open challenge to it. In her version of history, 'Britain' turns out to stand for the 'free individual' we have already encountered:

> 'Our defences *within* are vital if our nation is to prosper, if the weakest are to be cared for and if true liberal values are to prevail. But our defences *without* are just as vital. A defenceless nation which thinks itself free is living in a bubble of illusion. Any day, at the will of others, that bubble can be pricked.'
>
> (Birmingham, 19th April 1979)

As in all nationalisms, the alien forces – the Other – have to be specified:

> 'The real difference between the Soviet system and the systems of the free world is not that we are materially more prosperous and our standard of living is higher (though it is). The essential difference is that in the West we believe in the liberty of the individual, freedom of expression and the right of every man to help choose for himself the system under which he is governed.'

By making the important feature of the alien its anti-liberalism, Mrs Thatcher is able to secure an important effect: the enemy *without* can be fused with the enemy *within*. This is identified as our own collectivist elements. These include the wets in the Conservative Party, but are to be found principally in the Labour Party, for this too is infiltrated by the foreign body of Marxism:

> '. . . the voices that seem anxious not to overcome our economic difficulties, but to exploit them, to destroy the free enterprise society and put a Marxist system in its place. Today these voices form a sizeable chorus inside the Parliamentary Labour Party . . .'
>
> (Conservative Party Conference 1975)

These connections illustrate the specific nature of Thatcher's populism. Because the non-antagonistic appeal to the idea of 'One Nation' is so central to her discourse, it is difficult to sustain at the same time an antagonism to the national power bloc. Because the British people are so full of good sense, this power bloc has to be a foreign implantation – or rather, it has to be able to slip between being foreign and national. It is this that gives the populism its muted, circumscribed quality.

This omnipresent enemy is seen as attacking the liberal values of the free world. These values may be Western but they are quintessentially British:

> 'I say "in the West we believe". But nowhere has this belief been more treasured, more jealously guarded, more subtly protected than on this island of ours. That was always our glory – not our wealth, although that was great – not our Empire, although that was the greatest ever seen – but our constant insistent commitment to the fundamental liberties which alone allow the human spirit to grow and a free nation to be governed with tolerance, decency and compassion.'
>
> (Birmingham, 19 April 1979)

Here, liberalism is no mere market system to be evaluated in terms of productivity and material goods, but an absolute moral principle. It explains why in an interview on *Public Eye* in February 1982, with over three million people unemployed, Mrs Thatcher could still say, 'Ours is not the easy way, but the successful way, the *proud* way'. Two other features of Thatcherist

nationalism should be noted here. First, from her early years as Conservative leader, Mrs Thatcher has presented herself as the personal torchbearer of the tradition Thatcherism has re-constructed, of this 'force for freedom – muted, even weakened in these last few years, but still with the fires burning deep within us ready to drive forward again.' She takes up this torch from Churchill:

> 'I know you will understand the humility I feel at following in the footsteps of great men like our leader in that year, Winston Churchill, a man called by history to raise the name of Britain to supreme heights in the history of the free world.'
>
> (Conservative Party Conference, October 1975)

And, secondly, despite rolling out 'the Empire' only to disavow it as 'our prime glory', both the themes and the tones are close to the popular imperialism of the beginning of this century – a legacy indelibly marked by racism. Pride in our 'special mission' and the sense of superiority it gives have shaded into the fear of being 'swamped by alien cultures'. Such tendencies were muted in the speeches of the 1979 election period, and the National Front was denounced. But British racists knew where they stood with Mrs Thatcher, and so did the ethnic minorities – they were able to recognise the cultural alliance offered in this imperialist rhetoric.

In such ways, the connotations of 'the national interest' had already been thoroughly reworked within Thatcherism by 1979, although most analysts paid little attention to these aspects of its repertoire until forced to do so by the Falklands campaign. Within Thatcherism, the 'us-them' antagonism is neither a clear 'people versus power bloc' polarity, nor 'British people versus foreign threat'. It is a subtle combination of the two which incorporates all the accretions and associations discussed above. *British*, for example, is simultaneously constructed as a metonym for *Western* and hence *liberal*, so that the 'ugly impersonal order' in which 'the weak go to the wall' appears simultaneously as eastern and on our own doorsteps:

> 'Let us not forget. The left opposes any extension of the secret ballot. For the left, democracy means the mass meeting marshalled by the bully boys . . .'
>
> (Nottingham, 17 November 1979)

Labour has to be seen to be harbouring 'the bully boys of the left' in order for Thatcherism to be represented as protective and caring – to pre-empt a revival of the common sense of thirty years ago that it is social market economics that operate by 'letting the weak go to the wall'.

An effect of these rhetorical devices is to make *socialism* into a dirty word. It becomes part of the popular common sense to which Mrs Thatcher appeals with such aggressive confidence. The reason she is able to speak out for secret ballots is because:

> 'The left knows that the majority are not Marxist and will not support Marxists. Conversely, for us Conservatives, an extension of trade union democracy is simply a new version of an old Conservative maxim. Trust the people. Trust the rank and file trade unionists.'

Of course, Thatcherism cannot just decide to develop a populist discourse without calculations being made about the extent to which popular grievances are conducive to representation by the right. In this quotation, for example, she plays on real splits in the Labour movement. She attempts to reconstruct the splits in such a way that Trade Unions have to be either 'Left/bully boy/Marxist' or 'moderate/sensible/like us' – either Marxist or Thatcherist, in short. She also exploits the existence of undemocratic structures within the trade union movement which the leaderships have been slow to face up to. And she can afford to 'trust the people' because she knows that secret ballots will shift the unions, or at least specific unions, rightwards.

The slogan 'trust the people' could equally successfully be applied by the right to a referendum on the reintroduction of hanging. And in 1978, George Gardiner, a grass-roots right MP, was able to warn Tories against approving sanctions against Rhodesia in strong populist terms. The *Sunday Times* of 2 February reported his speech:

> 'Recalling Mrs Thatcher's words when she became leader that the

greatest fault of Edward Heath's government was that it did not listen to what its supporters were saying, Gardiner commented, "We must not make that mistake again." "Trust the people must remain a Tory theme," he said. So-called expert advice on sanctions, education and the right way to deal with criminals "must be ignored".'

The implications of the need to ground populism in existing common sense will be pursued further. First, though, two other features of Thatcherism's construction of 'the people' need to be examined. One is the *moralism* which permeates its every theme, whether crime, economic policy, industrial relations or foreign affairs. The other is the *anti-intellectualism* manifested in its rejection of 'expert advice'.

Morality, Common Sense and the Family

In 1978 an official Conservative publication attempting to 'pinpoint the underlying reasons why so many young people were involved in criminal activity' concluded that:

> 'The Working Party was convinced that the decline in discipline in many schools combined with lower moral and religious standards had eroded the sense of personal responsibility, individual self-respect and self-discipline that has formerly been the cornerstone of society.'

These fears have long been expressed by the law-and-order lobby, and they provide Thatcherism with its strongest connection to the old right. Schools may be condemned for their declining standards, but the pivot of this moralism is the family.

> 'It was stressed that a child's prime need was for a stable home, coupled with loving care and training for future life . . . In many cases where parents have opted out of their responsibilities, discipline was not exercised in the home, and such parents seemed unable to understand that it was possible to combine love and discipline. A number of people who were questioned believed that reliance on the state had led to a lack of care and to indifference on the part of parents regarding the whereabouts and activities of their young people.'

This report weaves together the hard and soft variants of Conservative moralism – 'loving care' *and* 'discipline'. Often this is achieved by treating 'discipline' and 'self-discipline' as if they were the same thing. Mrs Thatcher's moralism is closer to the authoritarian pole, but it does not simply take up the old themes. It also reworks them and gives them an extended field of reference. What is interesting in the quotation above, for example, is that the (interventionist, welfarist) state is blamed for the disintegration of the family. This moral authoritarianism is tied up with nationalism and anxieties about Britain's fall from greatness. The welfare state is, in Rhodes Boyson's terms, 'sapping the moral fibre of the nation.'[13]

I have already noted that the sanctity of the family is incorporated into economic ideas, through the axiom that the 'elemental human instinct' is to 'do the best for oneself and one's family.' This can be presented in an anti-statist form: 'people want to work for their families not for the Chancellor of the Exchequer.' The position was expressed clearly in a letter to the *Guardian* during 1978:

> 'I don't want anyone to tell me what my needs are – I'll decide them for myself thank you. I'll work to fulfil my needs, and those of my wife and children, and, if there's any left after that, for my parents and parents-in-law. . . .'

Even in the sphere of economic planning, policies are not argued for in terms of economic calculation, but through moral precepts whose imagery is derived from the family budget – keeping out of debt, paying your way, living within the budget. Using these metaphors of good housekeeping opens up the possibility of appealing specifically to women. On *The Jimmy Young Show* in April 1979, Mrs Thatcher asserted that 'men understand this less than women – they are used to living within a budget'; she backed this up during the 1979 election campaign by ostentatiously buying the family joint before assembled reporters. A gendered discourse also operated during the Falklands campaign – women know how to get things done, men just talk . . . Women are nevertheless assigned a supporting role: 'the individual' is always male and working for *his* family. Women are addressed from time to time, their common sense is appealed to – indeed, their experience is the source of Mrs Thatcher's common sense. But this refers only to their experience and skill as housewives, which subordinates them to the male breadwinner.

This domestic economic imagery – the equation between inflation, public spending and borrowing, and 'getting into the red' – was present before the full development of Thatcherism. It is manifested in embryonic form in a remarkably tortuous statement in the Conservative Manifesto of 1974:

> 'Every reasonable person knows that if we pay ourselves higher wages than we can afford, sooner or later we shall have to pay ourselves higher bills than we can afford.'

Thatcherism reworks such a position in two ways. The statement clearly bends over backwards to be non-antagonistic, to gloss over social divisions in its clumsy use of 'we'. The fully-fledged Thatcherist voice is more confident and combative, not afraid to point the finger at particular social sectors. In 1974, also, such arguments were attached (by both major parties) to policies of direct control over wage increases. As the monetarist solution gained ground, so the 'borrowing-is-sinful' theme has become stronger.

This sweeping moralism is not present only in Mrs Thatcher's broad strokes of the brush, but can be found in economic policy statements by the Chancellor of the Exchequer. Sir Geoffrey Howe's mid-term review in 1982 of the Government's economic policies avoided discussion of the mechanics of monetarism or any quantification of the effects of his policies. Instead, he asserted that 'inflation is a great moral evil' and that his solution is the only solution. In such ways, economic considerations have been subsumed into moral ones. The restoration of free enterprise and profitability will follow from the restoration of 'human values'. According to Mrs Thatcher at the 1975 Conservative Conference:

> 'Our capitalist system produces far higher standards of living because it believes in incentives and opportunity and because it is founded on dignity and freedom.'

Such moral absolutes become the limits of truth; they determine what counts as evidence. There is no need to analyse all those statistics in order to judge economic performance. Moral certainty replaces data. When Mrs Thatcher calls herself a conviction politician, it is no empty phrase. Her epistemology does indeed fuse *conviction* with *evidence*.

This emphasis on moral certitude and conviction slips into a general mistrust of experts and their jargon. Again, this operates both as an explicit contestation of the managerialism of social democracy and as a celebration of common sense. In a feature in the *Sunday Times* Colour Supplement on 20 August 1978, Mrs Thatcher is reported as saying that the people she likes best, her friends, are:

> '. . . down-to-earth-people. Men who call spades spades and don't talk in convoluted jargon. Someone said to me the other day, "You must keep a low profile" or something or other, and I said, "You mean I mustn't talk about it very much." Jargon is often used to cloak ignorance rather than act as an elucidation of issues.'

Curiously, what purports to be a rejection of jargon, of the specialised language of experts, turns out here to be something rather different – the refusal of a cliché of a specific middle-class culture. In an effort to be down-to-earth, the rejection of jargon is conflated with an attempt to be 'ordinary' in class terms, to belong to 'the people' as distinct from middle-class élites. This conflation is very revealing. It has a material basis in the class character of groups who have come to be regarded as experts in our society, and will resonate with the double sense of unease which professional people produce in working-class clients – the sense of ignorance and the sense of inferiority. This stance has political bite because, as I have

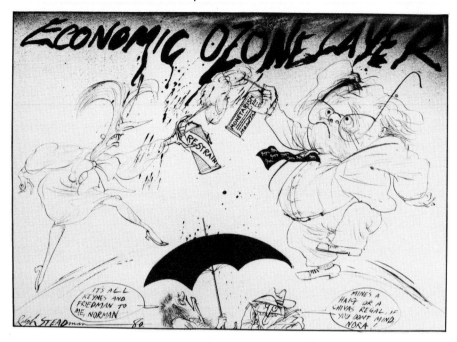

noted, political debate over the past thirty years has been couched in terms of who manages the nation's affairs most competently. The Labour Party, in particular, staked a great deal on employing experts to solve problem on behalf of the people, in every sphere of their lives. When such provision is experienced as bureaucratic, oppressive or patronising, Thatcherism is able to represent this experience not merely through an overt anti-statism, but also through the down-to-earth nature of its language.

The situation, however, is more complicated than it first appears. The Thatcher régime does of course employ experts and intellectuals. It has been closely associated with a revival in recent years of theory and research on the political right – in institutions like the Centre for Policy Studies and the Institute of Economic Affairs, for example. Mrs Thatcher's advisers are just as academic as Mr Foot's. Further, politicians of all parties profess to treat ideas and theory as suspect, preferring to invoke the personal, the concrete and the empirical. In an election period, the parties vie with each other in presenting themselves as the most responsive to circumstances and the most experienced in government. They accuse their opponents of blinkered ideologies which have no grip on the practicalities of government; experience of life is given greater legitimacy than research or argument. It is not a question of which party draws most heavily on theory – what is at stake is a struggle over whose ideas and policies can be constructed as 'common sense' and whose as 'dogma'. Given this, Thatcherism had some difficulty between 1977 and 1979 popularising the new monetarist policies. This ideological work could be detected in the press during 1978. For a *Guardian* editorial on 3 November, wages policy was common sense. A *Times* editorial on 28 November therefore found it necessary to debate the 'fallacies of common sense':

> 'The country has a natural tendency to believe in incomes policies because such policies appeal to common sense. Common sense always tells people in economic matters that they should interfere. If wages go up, stop them! If prices go up, stop them! If interest rates go up, hold them down! Common sense is very dirigiste. It is also notably lacking in humility since it believes in its own capacity to interfere successfully in matters that it hardly understands at all. The history of libertarian economic theory – which can no longer be called liberal for fear of confusion with the party of the same name – is one of explaining that the common sense answer leads to the opposite of common sense results.'

The naturalising of monetarism has involved two manoeuvres. In the first place, it was presented as a radical solution, getting to the root of the problem in ways the alternatives had failed to do; although it was usually quickly stressed that this radicalism was not imported or esoteric, but a return to the certainties of 'our British inheritance'. The other strategy has been to recast monetarism into a language we all understand: that of the family budget. The effect has been to redefine popular conceptions of the economy. This represents not the replacement of one discourse by another, but rather a *dis*placement. The issue of wage-restraint does not disappear, but it is subordinated to and re-inflected within a 'cash limits' rationale.

The power of Thatcherism to present itself as traditional British common sense – both in what it says and how it says it – is exemplified in the 1978 *Sunday Times* interview:

> 'At the very heart of her convictions is a belief in an order of life, and values, strictures the rest of us know we should be dinning into our children, but feel too guilt-ridden to spell out. "I want decent, fair, honest, citizen values, all the principles you were brought up with. You don't live up to the hilt of your income; if someone gets the bills wrong you tell them, you don't keep the extra change; you respect other people's property; you save; you believe in right and wrong; you support the police. You believe the innocent shall go free and the guilty be convicted. I myself do believe in capital punishment but not to be used very often. We were taught to help people in need ourselves, not stand about saying what the government should do. Personal initiative was pretty strong. You were actually taught to be clean and tidy, that

cleanliness was next to Godliness. All these ideas have got saddled as middle-class values, but they're eternal."'

This text illustrates a number of key features. Note, first, how the writer of the article interposes a sympathetic reading of Mrs Thatcher's comments, suggesting that although we may have adopted fashionably progressive approaches to child-rearing, we really harboured more fundamental values in our hearts all along. Secondly, Mrs Thatcher manages to introduce monetarism ('you don't live up to the hilt of your income'), juridical liberalism, welfare policy and the moral principles which sustain all these without stepping outside a mode so familiar that they have the force of truisms. The syntax itself – not 'You ought to save . . .' but 'you save . . . you believe . . . you support . . .' – reinforces this moral absolutism. It's a morality which does not really need to be preached – it's what people do 'freely', because it's in their nature to do it. To restrict this freedom (and, incidentally, to resist the concrete policies which have become attached to it by the New Right) is not just a political error, it is contrary to human nature itself. This axiomatic fatalism about the way people are – you can't change human nature – is turned against Labour's claims to be the natural party of government. Labour had sought to smother this 'elemental human instinct' with collectivist alternatives smuggled in from the 'inhuman' region of the Eastern bloc – 'the ugly, impersonal order in which responsibility withers and in the end nobody cares.'

Responsibility, *care* and *decency* are all constant themes. Talking of the Shrewsbury pickets and the rebel councillors of Clay Cross in 1975, she commented: 'No decent society can live like that and no responsible society can condone it.' There can be no debate about what constitutes decency: it goes without saying.

'We Conservatives do things for others, not because any government told us to, but because that is the best way to live – that's the way we go about things.'

(Berwick, 30 July 1978)

The terminology of 'decent, honest, citizen values' is boldly applied across the spectrum of political themes. In 1982, for example, Mrs Thatcher was still arguing that 'countries that have run on a sound, honest basis have done well' (interview on *Public Eye*, February 1982). She contrasts 'sound, honest, honorable money' with 'dishonest money' – that which would have to be borrowed for reflationary purposes. A final notable feature of the *Sunday Times* homily is its reliance on personal experience – 'we were taught . . .', 'the principles you were brought up with' – and the shifting use of personal pronouns, '*we* were taught . . .', '*I* want . . .', '*You* save . . . *you* don't . . .'. This generalises the experience and converts it into a moral absolute – a syntactic soldering of experience to *conviction*.

Thatcherism

So far I have relied almost exclusively on Mrs Thatcher's own pronouncements to characterise Thatcherism. The advantage of this is that it emphasises that Thatcherism is not just a set of policies, but refers to politically
effective discursive strategies. The danger is of slipping into a cult of the
personality, or a study of Mrs Thatcher's rhetorical style as if the linguistic
forms were no more than the vehicle for transmitting an already defined
ideology. My point is that discursive forms – Mrs Thatcher's unique mode of
address, for example – actually help to construct the terms and the boundaries of the way we can think about a particular topic. Many elements of
Thatcherism undoubtedly existed already in various forms of popular
common sense,[14] but in an inchoate way. They had yet to be integrated into a
popular, chauvinistic and morally righteous discourse with a particular set
of referents – and this work has been dominated by Mrs Thatcher's own
pronouncements and self-presentation. Complex policy issues are boiled
down to absolute moral precepts, as when in 1982 she rejected American
requests to boycott the Russian pipeline project because 'our word is our
bond'. Such great simplicities lend themselves to the style of popular
headlines and editorials as well as to common sense. They constitute the
'voice' of Thatcherism – which is not an expression of one woman's soul, but
part of the process of constructing 'Margaret Thatcher' as an ideological
figure. This has indeed involved vocal training, but, more importantly, it has
meant constructing an *identity*. Her speeches, for example, are a collective
production. Although they do rely on Mrs Thatcher's personal capacities,
style and beliefs, they remain calculated creations. (Fittingly, their chief
architect is Sir Ronald Millar, a show-business impresario and dramatist.[15])
But it is not necessary to know of these calculations. Thatcherism is more
than Mrs Thatcher. Its concepts did not originate in any one person, and
they circulate independently of her, to be taken up and rearticulated in
various ways by different individuals, groups and institutions.

Whether Thatcherism has effectively displaced alternative discourses
(either inside or outside the Conservative Party), in the sense of establishing
its concerns as the implicit basis for political debate, cannot be established
through statistical research into public opinion. The figures will not tell us
whether the political agenda has shifted, but such information can be
derived from the kinds of questions asked. A poll in November 1979 found
that half of its survey considered Mrs Thatcher 'the right person to protect
the British taxpayer'. What is interesting is not the percentage, but the
assumptions of the question. It did not ask who would protect the British
people, the British citizen or the British workers. Quietly and unemphatical-
ly, 'the British taxpayer' had become the obvious identity to offer people. A
more forceful piece of evidence that a new political agenda had been set by
1979 came in an interview that James Callaghan, then still Prime Minister,

gave on *The Jimmy Young Show* on 30 April, just before the election. Not only did he fail to protest that most of the questions embodied the assumptions of the New Right – should the trade unions be curbed by law? Are extremists taking over the Labour Party? How can we stop standards deteriorating and violence increasing? He also responded enthusiastically in kind, producing evidence of increased police numbers and stronger penalties against hooligans. There was little trace of the social-democratic concerns with full employment, standards of living, welfare provision and social justice.

1982

At the end of 1982, the Thatcherist agenda still seemed firmly in place. The Falklands war had seen its nationalism amplified in sections of the popular press – by *The Sun* on 21 May, for example:

> 'The battle has begun. Our lads are going in ready to lay down their lives for the principles that have always made Britain great. Love of country and love of freedom.'

In its coverage of the war, *The Sun* added to this chauvinism the clichés of sports reporting: '. . . in a crunch battle yesterday, the jittery Argies lost their nerve and beat a hasty retreat . . .' (15 June). Without going into the discursive work around the campaign in any detail, it is worth noting how confidently Thatcherism was able to define and orchestrate the popular response to the war. Partly this was because no articulate opposition was developed.[16] But it was also because Argentina could be presented in crudely xenophobic terms as both *fascist* and *dago*. (Again, this became tied up with the nationalism of soccer – should the Argentinian Ricardo Villa play in the FA Cup Final? Should England or Argentina withdraw from the World Cup?) In this jingoistic climate, qualms about the war could be represented as treachery.

It is important to stress that the Thatcher Government did not owe its remarkable mid-term popularity solely to the accident of the Falklands. For a start, the opinion polls indicate that its revival *preceded* the campaign and showed no marked increase after it.[17] This supports my argument that Thatcherism has successfully persuaded 'the people' that the old Keynesian solutions don't work, that they must tighten their belts for a decade of resettlement and that the steadfastness and resolve of Margaret Thatcher is uniquely placed to take them through to a better future. Mrs Thatcher's speech to the 1982 Conservative Party Conference certainly drew on the Falklands victory for a reconfirmation of her nationalism ('The spirit of the South Atlantic was the spirit of Britain at her best . . .'), but throughout the conference this was subordinated to themes of constancy and resolve. There was an unwavering commitment to long-term solutions which would carry us through these difficult times – 'we are in the business of planting trees, for our children and grandchildren . . .'. The economic and administrative practice of Thatcherism has not (yet) been as fundamental as its ideologies. The public sector has not been cut so severely as threatened, nor have cash limits always been strictly imposed. The Government has drawn back from a frontal attack on the trade union movement. But its language of inflexible toughness has sustained its popularity and has shifted debate to the right in a number of key areas.

In the sphere of law and order, demands for greater police powers, led by the Police Federation and the Chief Constable of Greater Manchester, may have met some opposition, but they also have support from a number of constituencies – the increasingly active hanging and birching lobby, for example. More importantly, they have succeeded in reorganising the terms of the debate on a more authoritarian basis, so that even when Mr Whitelaw introduced new riot-gear for the police and a new stop-and-search bill, he could still be represented as 'wet'. John Alderson, a supporter of community policing, eventually decided he could no longer hold the line in a police force moving politically to the right. He resigned as a chief constable to pursue his campaign through Parliament. Racism, too, seems to be increasing. In February 1981 a poll found that forty one per cent of people believed that 'the Government should send back coloured immigrants to their own country': the figures increased after the riots during the spring and summer.

Even the new Social Democratic Party seems to accept Mrs Thatcher's view that competitive individualism is an elemental human instinct. It too emphasises enterprise and effort, market incentives and consumer sovereignty: it makes the same attacks on over-government and lame ducks.[18] Although the spread of Thatcherist assumptions is still far from total, it does now provide the terms for general political debate. It can claim to represent popular feelings even as the policies of Mrs Thatcher's government corrode the living conditions of many sectors of the population. Underestimating Thatcherism's mobilisation of traditional popular sentiments, predictions that economic oppression would provoke overwhelming popular resentment remain unfulfilled.

Political Lessons?

This article has been confined, by and large, to looking at competing political discourses. I have said little about the Thatcher government's policies, about Britain's economic and political position in relation to the rest of the world, about the struggles within the major parties, or about existing initiatives against Thatcherism. All these would have to be looked at in a full conjunctural analysis, of course, but my main concern is with what forms of mobilisation might be able to displace the present balance of ideological forces. The outlook is undeniably gloomy: the most optimistic slogan seems to be that the left faces a long haul.[19] But the rise of Thatcherism does offer some pointers about what might be involved in this uphill struggle.

For a start, Thatcherism itself has been a long haul. It has been concerned not just with short term electoral success, but with redefining the terms and the terrain of political struggle for a decade or more. Equally, any radical shift to the left is not an immediate prospect, but requires a medium-to long-term analysis which can reconceptualise the nature of political representation as expressing the 'collective will'. As Gramsci, a major influence on that project, puts it:

> 'If the relationship between intellectuals and the people-nation, between the leaders and the led, the rulers and the ruled, is provided by an organic cohesion in which feeling-passion becomes understanding and thence knowledge (not mechanically but in a way that is alive), then and only then is the relationship one of representation. Only then . . . can the shared life be realised which alone is a social force – with the creation of the "historic bloc".'[20]

This vision may be strikingly at odds with the apparent apathy of British politics. But one reason for the grudging respect shown towards Thatcherism by the left (and in this article) is the recognition that it has tackled a widespread political cynicism and attacked anti-democratic, mechanical forms of representation. In this – if only in this – it seems oddly in tandem with the new left's critique of the structure of the Labour Party and the trade unions and with the feminist critique of the masculine nature of hierarchical and bureaucratic organizations.[21] Whereas Thatcherism's populist expression of this cynicism has contained any demands for new forms of representation, however, it is through this widespread rejection of existing forms of politics that left intellectuals may be able to re-establish contact with popular common sense.

In building such a popular movement, there are lessons to be learnt from the moral and ethical dimension of Thatcherism – its ability to unite 'feeling-passion' and understanding. Before 1945, according to Trevor Blackwell and Jeremy Seabrook, the left's critique of capitalism was presented largely in moral terms.

> 'The Labour Party had lived on the ideas of sacrifice, martyrs, unity, courage in the face of adversity and persecution, the lone voice in the wilderness, the day of reckoning, the awakening, the struggle, being led out of captivity, exploitation and bondage.'[22]

Now, they argue, Thatcherism has moralised Toryism and, in the same process, demoralised socialism. Capitalism has itself been made into the moral critique. Attempts by the left to counter this, most notably by Tony Benn, have not met with much success as yet. Popular anti-Thatcherism is as often marked by amused incredulity as by moral indignation. Perhaps the unfashionably Christian tones of Benn's moralism are not the ones to mobilise it, and his effective discrediting both within the Labour Party and in the popular imagination are an additional handicap. Nevertheless, the basis for a sense of moral outrage against the harshness of Thatcherism certainly exists: it awaits the right *voice* to articulate it.

Similar difficulties arise for attempts to appeal to the interests of 'the British people' while nationalism seems to be monopolised by the right. Two possibilities present themselves, each with attendant difficulties. One strategy is to rescue national identities for the left. Although for most of the past two centuries patriotism has been imperialist and xenophobic in its connotations, there have also been moments of radical patriotism.[23] The radical populism of the Second World War had at least an ambiguous relationship to nationalism, for example. Nevertheless, recent attempts to recapture 'the nation' and nationalism from the right – most notably by Robbie Gray and Eric Hobsbawm[24] – seem to have been understandably overwhelmed by the immensity of the task and even uncertain about quite where to begin. The second strategy would be not to rework 'the national', but to displace it. There is no inevitable reason why social groups and individuals should define themselves in terms of a national identity. The situations and institutions people pass through position and address them in a variety of contradictory ways – as consumer and producer, as rate-payer and claimant, as voter and trade unionist, as mother and worker, and so on. Thatcherism has woven certain of these contradictory elements into ideologically integrated points of identification: the left too can attempt to produce new coherences out of popular identifications. National-popular identities may have been cornered for the moment by the right, but popular-democratic ones could provide the principle of coherence for an opposing 'collective will'. Such a movement would have to address all forms of powerlessness, and would sometimes mean disengaging from the traditional leadership of Labour and the trade unions. Such polarisations are already taking place. In campaigns against the cuts in Barking, for example – a London borough not noted for its political activism – mass meetings of several thousand people including parents, teachers and other public employees have been joined by constituency Labour Parties *against* the Labour Council which was perceived as part of the Thatcherist power-bloc in imposing the cuts. Thatcherism, then, can only adopt antagonisms between people and power-bloc in certain instances. It can endorse demands for more direct participation in trade unions, on the assumption that they would be weakened by breaking centralised control, but vigorously resists calls for increased community control over the police. The immediate future may look bleak. But it could be that Thatcherism, whatever havoc it wreaks, may have developed an antagonism which will in the long term stimulate the rearticulation and revitalisation of popular-democratic forces in Britain.

Notes

1. See for example S. Hall et al., *Policing the Crisis*, London, Macmillan, 1978, and many articles in *Marxism Today*, 1979 to 1983.
2. See especially S. Hall, 'The Great Moving Right Show', *Marxism Today*, January 1979.
3. See P. Corrigan, 'Popular Consciousness and Social Democracy', and P. Leonard, 'Restructuring the Welfare State', both in *Marxism Today*, December 1979.
4. See E. Laclau, *Politics and Ideology in Marxist Theory*, London, New Left Books, 1977, p. 99.
5. The paper is part of a larger group project, as are many of its ideas. It is indebted in particular to Alan Clarke, Ian Connell, Richard Drain, Tony Fitzgerald, Stuart Hall, Colin Mercer and Adam Mills.
6. See especially S. Hall, 'Popular Democratic vs Authoritarian Populism' in A. Hunt (ed.), *Marxism and Democracy*, London, Lawrence and Wishart, 1980.
7. Laclau, *op. cit.*, p. 173.
8. N. Poulantzas, *Political Power and Social Classes*, London, New Left Books, 1973, p. 130ff.
9. Corrigan *op. cit.*, p. 14.
10. See, for example, Mick Costello, 'The Working Class and the Broad Democratic Alliance', *Marxism Today*, June 1979.
11. Conservative Women's Advisory Committee, *Delinquents at Large*, 1978.
12. *ibid*. p. 5.
13. Quoted in *Policing the Crisis*, p. 314.
14. See R. King and N. Nugent, *Respectable Rebels*, London, Hodder and Stoughton, 1979.
15. See *The Times*, 4 November 1982.
16. See A. Barnett, *Iron Britannia*, New Left Review no. 134, 1982.

17. See Peter Jenkins's column, *The Guardian*, 6 October 1982.
18. Raphael Samuel, *The Guardian*, 5 April 1982.
19. See the articles by R. Gray and S. Hall in *Marxism Today*, November 1982.
20. Antonio Gramsci, *Selections from the Prison Notebooks*, London, Lawrence and Wishart, 1971, p. 418.
21. See, for example, Sheila Rowbotham et al., *Beyond the Fragments*, London Merlin, 1979.
22. Article in *The Guardian* (date lost).
23. Hugh Cunningham, 'The Language of Patriotism', *History Workshop Journal*, no. 12, 1981.
24. See R. Gray, *op. cit.* and E. J. Hobsbawn, 'A requisition order on patriotism', *The Guardian* 20 December 1981.

Patrick Wright

A BLUE PLAQUE FOR THE LABOUR MOVEMENT?
Some political meanings of the 'National Past'

> It was interesting to note how in the early, wild and enthusiastic days of the Revolution the characteristic costume was a great-coat flung over, a hat askew, a hand spread outwards; later the representations of leaders became identified with neatly buttoned uniforms, well set caps and firm salutes, and only the Cossacks, as in Tsarist times, had been allowed to display a certain freedom. . . .
>
> Michael Moorcock, *The Entropy Tango* (1981)

Irritated commentators don't seem to have been sure whether it was exactly a dufflecoat, with its early CND connotations, or a donkey jacket, resonant of sullen proletarianism, but it was certainly green rather than black, untailored and – as many people will doubtless still remember – distinctly out of place on the back of the Leader of the Labour Party during the solemnities at the Cenotaph on Remembrance Day 1981. Among those black columns of uniformed men Michael Foot's garb was taken as giving his appearance over to the ordinary, the casual and even, in an intellectual CND sort of way, to the popular.

Walter Johnson, Labour MP for Derby, started the fuss by accusing Mr Foot of looking like an out-of-work navvy on the way to a demo. The following morning, on 9 November, a *Daily Telegraph* leader described Foot as 'an old man'; he looked like 'a bored tourist at a bus stop' and he laid his wreath 'with all the reverent dignity of a tramp bending down to inspect a cigarette end.' The effect of these objections was to sharpen debate on Foot's efficacy as Leader of the Labour Party; the coat was taken up as another of those 'last straws' which assume such powerful metaphorical presence in public debate. Here I am not concerned with Michael Foot himself or his private sincerities and intentions, but with the publicly constructed *image* of the man which was articulated around Remembrance Day. As he was drawn into the public eye on that day Foot *was* taken to be 'demonstrating' in a mild way against the customary proprieties of what the offended Labour MP thought should be 'a solemn act of respect and remembrance.' Foot was to comment afterwards that 'respect for the dead isn't a matter of the clothes you wear.' His defenders also showed little concern for appearance, invoking the invisible authenticity of what is felt at heart, opposing this to the relative triviality of dress and, in some cases, to the military rigidities of the Establishment on parade.

Some sections of the press staged this as a matter of informality versus formality – as if Foot were merely a slob who needed to 'pull his socks up' (*The Standard*'s phrase) – but the real significance of the incongruity of his appearance was that it represented a clash between opposed modes of public remembrance.

The Establishment mode of remembrance is both militarist and nationalist. Remembrance is a state occasion structured through regimental history and parade; retired generals and admirals speak in grave tones on the BBC World Service. The interest of this mode does not lie primarily in any selectivity which it may bring to bear on previous events – its concern with glory rather than gore. Remembrance of this kind is not merely obliterative of the 'realities' of war. Its essence lies instead in the *transfiguration* which its ceremonies bring to bear on past war, introducing order, calm, solemnity and meaning where there was chaos, disorder and loss. Acts of commemoration *re-present* the glory of war, its transmutation of destruction into heroism and, above all, nationhood. In its contempt for peace, establishment remembrance tends to accuse the post-war present of mediocre survival, of ending up spineless and bent over a stick. These attitudes were implicit in the way the *Daily Telegraph* derided Foot as 'an old man'.

In his green coat, brown shoes and plaid tie Michael Foot stood out from all this. Instead of transfiguration, Foot's image presented a spectacle of peaceful *solidarity*. Not the uniforms, the ranks, the regiments, nor the specious ceremoniousness: all this was antithetical to Foot who appeared to stand in homage to the ordinary, to the civilians of no particular distinction who were caught up into war, militarised and destroyed, to people whose drive generally was towards justice, socialisation and democracy. The people of the United Kingdom, perhaps, but especially, as some of the press implied, the people of the labour movement – people who might also have lived to find very mixed feelings at heart on Remembrance Day. The sentimentality tends to be part of the image.

Both these opposed modes of remembrance invoke the authenticity of history and tradition. In the establishment mode history *is* tradition. That is what redeems it. As for authenticity, this is something to be *made*: it is the sacramental effect or goal of traditional ceremonies, what the public act of remembrance is meant to bring about. Traditional authenticity exists in the present: it is bestowed upon the dead in ceremonies through which the present also reaffirms its continuity with the past. The dead are authenticated through measures which recuperate them to the traditional rituals of church, army and state. Establishment remembrance raises the dead ritualistically in order to reposition them at the heart of what it simul-

'Don't worry, Michael, I says . . . I'll find another job for you!'
The Sun, 10 November 1981.

taneously reaffirms as the 'nation'. In this way it calms the contradiction between their historical diversity and the single unity of the nation to which they are assimilated.

As it was presented in Foot's image, however, authenticity is not merely a necromantic and ideological effect of public ceremony, but involves a more direct and partisan *identification* with some especially among 'those who have fallen.' In these terms it is a question of *where* one stands rather than the ceremonial steps one might go through. Foot stood there as bearer and manifestation of the history of the common people, of the aspirations, consciousness and courage which have produced and sustained the labour movement. It was the appearance of this oppositional history that discomforted the traditions of Church, Army and State. The two different articulations of history and tradition share no neutral ground on which they can achieve equal public visibility in order to compete. Remembrance Day 1981 indicated the extent to which the public field of meaning is *already* occupied and structured by some traditions to the exclusion and mockery of others (and by some ways of *understanding* those same traditions as opposed to others.) Faced with the ritualised and spectacular ceremonies through which the Establishment lays claim to the traditions of nationhood, the

The Daily Telegraph, 10 November 1981.

history with which Foot stands associated was open to lampoon. On 10 November, both *The Sun* and *The Daily Telegraph* caricatured him as Worzel Gummidge, the scarecrow hero of a popular children's book and television programme. *The Daily Mail* presented a centrefold of Foot as a cut-out doll and offered the reader costume options (including cloth caps and CND badges): 'Dress Your Own Michael Foot', read the caption. As for the *Daily Express*, it showed what Ronald Reagan's British born 'groomer' would have done for Foot: a composite picture showed 'Rt Hon Scruff' looking no longer like a 'lecturer' but smooth with haircut, streamlined glasses and a business suit.

Foot was open to being taken as a personification of a history and traditions which have only the most inadequate if not simply subordinate public status. Everything he might have invoked as support could thus be articulated back into identity with the frail and scruffy appearance of this 'old man'. By identification with Foot the labour movement was staged as a worn out relic. It was mocked as having only an archival existence: something that most working class people have long since forgotten or disowned, and which Foot, known to be a historian of the labour movement, will therefore be among the last to know about. The Conservative press was able to flaunt the difference between spectacular public tradition and that mere history which it identified with the esoteric antiquarianism of a 'decrepit' intellectual nonconformist. Foot's coat left him open to a critical attention; his supporters, both in Parliament and Fleet Street, continued the personalisation by talking about authentic feelings felt sincerely at heart. The Conservative press did the rest: it used the image of Foot to blow the history of the labour movement off the stage, and it did this in the name of national tradition.

'The National Past'

> In times when history still moved slowly, events were few and far between and easily committed to memory. They formed a commonly accepted *backdrop* for thrilling scenes of adventure in private life. Nowadays history moves at a brisk clip. A historical event, though soon forgotten, sparkles the morning after with the dew of novelty. No longer a backdrop, it is now the *adventure* itself, an adventure enacted before the backdrop of the commonly accepted banality of private life.
>
> Milan Kundera, *The Book of Laughter and Forgetting* (1982)

Other events besides Remembrance Day 1981 could open discussion of national tradition and its place in current strategies of legitimation – most obviously the efflorescence of confused nationalism, vindicated nostalgia, aggression, incredulity and make-belief that accompanied the killing, maiming and official secrecy of the Falklands adventure, but also the momentary ruffling of relations between the Tory government and the Church of England or the continuing popular obsession with the public rituals and domestic tittle-tattle around the Royal Family. Major events and ephemeral incidents follow hard and fast on each other, but perhaps more significant have been the developments, and also the fundamental continuities, in the way such occurrences are articulated and assimilated within public opinion. We hear news of this or that particular event through a *thematisation* which encourages us to understand these events (and our relation to them) in the accumulating terms of national identity, culture, history and tradition. The address varies, mobilising hopes, fears, memories, rationality, prejudices, confusions and just plain ignorance as it will. Sometimes it explicitly opposes its 'British' sense of balance to the emotionalism, deviance, bigotry or aggression of others ('Foolish Europe' has recently been modulated to 'Bloody Argies'); at other times it moves in the safe assumption that we – the public – already share the values of the presentation, and at still other times it marshalls us more manipulatively (during the Falklands adventure *The Sun* was spewing out a rhetoric of 'treason') to what it hails as the consensual measures of public opinion. It is at the level of this public thematisation of events that the 'nation' has been posed so thoroughly of late. Indeed, during

1982 this nationalist thematisation of British life seemed to enter the news not just as a formal characteristic of its presentation but increasingly at the level of content itself; it seemed to become so strong that it was actually capable of generating events.

So the 'nation' has become a key figure in British politics, one that must be understood and carefully negotiated if we are to move beyond the passive experience of deadlock to an active public engagement with the issues determining our situation. To a considerable extent this upsurge of public nationalism reflects the crisis of a social system which, while its development is leading directly to the destruction of traditions and customs (many of them locally based), at the same time demands an ever deepening source of cultural meaning to legitimate itself. In this situation tradition appears as artifice, articulated not in particular or essential connection to people's experience, but at the *generalised* and diffuse level of an overriding 'national' identity.[1] The 'nation' of this concern therefore has no easy relation to the existence and historical development of the nation-state; it is instead a structuring of consciousness, a publicly instituted sense of identity which finds its support in a variety of experiences, and which is capable of colonising and making sense of others. Among its most fundamental elements is a historically produced sense of the past which acts as ground for a proliferation of other definitions of what is normal, appropriate or possible. This mutual construction of a sense of the past and of a national identity was invoked in press caricatures of Foot at the Cenotaph on Remembrance Day 1981. He was not lampooned just for being slipshod and scruffy, but for representing a recalcitrant and perhaps even oppositional sense of history. That is why the event introduces the central questions for this article. How might a critical and oppositional use of history contribute to political struggle in the contemporary UK? How might it negotiate those overriding and 'deranging' feelings of national past and identity which have been generated in large part by the huge destruction of traditions and transformation of social relations following the post-war development of capital and state?

Far from being somehow 'behind' the present, the past exists as an accomplished presence in public understanding. In this sense it is written into present social reality, not just implicitly as residue, precedent or custom and practice, but explicitly as itself – as History, National Heritage and tradition. Any attempt to develop and assert a critical historical consciousness will find itself in negotiation if not open conflict with this established public understanding of the 'past'. It is therefore important to understand what it is that functions as the 'past' and to distinguish it from history. J. H. Plumb provides a good starting point by describing 'History' as an intellectual process – the endeavour to establish the truth of earlier events – which is pitched against the 'past', conceived as a more mythical complex inherent in the present as a 'created ideology with a purpose'.[2] Many socialist (as well as liberal and social-democratic) historians have worked along comparable lines, holding that a developed historical understanding will help cut through the ideological mists of the 'past' and in this way contribute to changing the political agenda in the present. While much has been achieved in this way over the last fifty years or so – indeed, the 'past' has been substantially rearranged so that it now contains a wider acknowledgement of, for instance, women and the working class – this achievement has been won against considerable and undiminishing resistance. Plumb's 'History' is not a corrosive sublimate capable of burning the 'past' away, for the 'past' is neither free-floating ideology nor illusion. It is an established public *institution*, with all the historical materiality which that word implies.

The inertia of the past – its ability to survive the advent of 'History', for example – reflects its entrenchment in the public field of meaning.[3] The past is not just implicit in the present as the kind of historical continuity – paradigmatic or otherwise – which might more accurately be called tradition. Beyond tradition is a cultivated sense of the past which is reproduced through a variety of public agencies (schools, television, political debate, historical fiction etc), and which stages the past explicitly as itself. This public staging of the past, which I shall here be calling the 'national past', is relatively heterodox (even though it features heavily dominant tendencies) and it works in close and intricate connection with that rather less definable area of experience which Agnes Heller calls 'the sense of historical existence' and attributes not to any special knowledge of history and the past but to the everyday consciousness of 'practically everyone who reflects upon his/her life experience in our world.'[4] So while there are problems of representation, say, to be addressed at the first level there are others concerned more directly with lived experience (memory, disappointment, the persistence of childhood into adult experience and so forth) in the second. The concerns of this article are with the 'national past', but because the 'national past' works most powerfully in the context of everyday consciousness the related set of problems concerning the 'sense of historical existence' will never be far away.

The Past as Interpretation
The past owes much of its public status to the work of nineteenth century historiography which, as Edward Shils has recently argued, sought to order 'antiquities' and also to develop records which would provide a basis for systematic study of national institutions. This historiographical activity was accompanied by developments in the schools as the study of history gained prominence. The national past was recognised as possessing a legitimising capacity and, as Shils has written with perhaps more specific regard to the US than to Britain, 'the promotion of a belief in continuity and identity with

the national past, reverence for national heroes, the commemoration of great national events . . . were among the tasks laid on the teaching of "national history".'[5] There is little existing analysis of the educational uses to which history has been put in Britain, and many of the important questions presumably remain unasked, to say nothing of any answers. Valerie Chancellor's *History for their Masters* shows some of the possibilities open to a reading of school history texts, even though her study, which confines itself to nineteenth-century texts (all of which were published before the study of history was in any sense mandatory on any school curriculum), also indicates the difficulty of differentiating what is written from what is read and taken to mind.[6] To my knowledge the most useful analysis of school history is Frances Fitzgerald's *America Revised*, a study which tells a quite fascinating story of books which are 'managed' and 'developed' rather than written, of publishing houses which function as 'Ministries of Truth for children', and of a miraculous text-book industry which enables famous US historians to revise books they have 'authored', even including discussion of events which have occurred after their own deaths.

Things also happen at the more thematic level of the 'content' of school history. When 'conflicts' become too embarrassing the day of the 'problem' dawns: Imperialism, for example, can be staged as a world literacy campaign. Similarly, and in terms traditional to portraiture, the dramatisation of history around character can reduce a multiple society as complex as India to a 'country', and then to a measure of ground under the hooves of Clive's horse. If character is not the principle organiser of a historical account then institutions are likely to play that role: thus Parliament can appear as the institution through which democracy was accomplished (which puts a date and an end to that particular struggle). While the fact that these are easy points to make does not discredit them, it is important to remember not just that the problems of devising a more adequate school history are complex (it is no good just trading one bias for another, for example), but also that people play a very active part in making, or failing to make, their own sense of the information and analysis presented to them. As Frances Fitzgerald puts it:

> 'Rabbits, it is said, cannot remember pain or fear for more than sixty seconds. Perhaps human beings cannot remember things that bored them. Memory has its own antidotes.'[7]

While it is essential, therefore, to acknowledge that the education system certainly does not implant any single, or even particularly coherent interpretation of the past into public consciousness, one must, I think, acknowledge that its influence does remain largely interpretative. People may not remember whatever detailed analysis was developed for them as schoolchildren, but certain models or 'general sketches' (to use Agnes Heller's phrase) do remain, and they inform everyday thinking closely, especially as they are exercised over and again by politicians and the media seeking to make public sense of current events.[8] If an example is needed to make this clearer one can be found in the special place occupied by the Second World War in public consciousness in Britain and, more particularly, in Margaret Thatcher's increasingly deliberate manipulation of Churchillian sketches over the period of the Falklands crisis. The educational apparatus, therefore, contributes largely to the formation of the 'national past', but it works not only in loose connection with other agencies of public meaning (the press, television, historical fiction, advertising, the conventions of political rhetoric and the culture of national tourism) but also in close relation to memory and the 'sense of historical existence'.

The past as presence

To say that the 'national past' has an achieved public presence is not just to speak figuratively: recent decades have seen an increasing stress on the past as something that is *actually* present. National Traditions like Remembrance Day are certainly involved here, but so are those other phenomena which together make up the National Heritage: landscapes, old buildings, monuments, folkways, skills and exhibitable objects. If the various agencies of public meaning tend to reproduce a 'national' understanding of the past which includes 'reverence for national heroes' and 'the commemoration of great national events', they also ground this understanding in the concrete, unarguable existence of a National Heritage which stands in need of preservation, deference and respect. While this National Heritage may initially have been assembled under the bourgeois academic signs of 'Beauty' and 'Culture', the post-war years have also seen a significant expansion in its repertoire. While it maintains its attention to phenomena of overriding 'national' significance (and also especially still to Art and Architecture), the National Heritage is now also organised in relation to an industrial archaeology, traditional working-class culture and skills, local forms of conviviality, the countryside (increasingly projected as an image of nationhood) and the family.[9]

As a public presence, therefore, the 'national past' tends to institute as fact its thematic generalisation of history, and it presents this interpretative work in the concrete terms of what at the same time it stresses as the National Heritage. The dovetailing of these two aspects means that an urgently *preservational* emphasis characteristic of National Heritage can slide over to provide cover and substantiation for the interpretative account forming the other part of the 'national past'. This dovetailing is evident at a structural level between the two main foci of television history, where a 'documentary' treatment of the sites and objects of National Heritage tends to corroborate, and in some cases is deliberately used to authenticate, fictional dramatisations of the past.

Public philosophies of history

The 'nation' forms the primary perspective of the 'national past', which postulates a collective subject: it presents the 'nation' as the place and state in which 'we' live. In this sense the 'national past' can be thought of as a controlling attribute of citizenship: something that at a generalised level enables citizens to find a unity (as contemporary racism shows all too clearly out-groups are produced in this process) between themselves and to override unresolved socio-political contradictions and differences. It occupies the public stage as 'ours', not just the possession and right of a few. Within this overriding 'national' perspective there is accommodation for both interpretative representations of history and the concrete presence of the National Heritage.

The 'national past' seems also to institute several distinct ways of conceiving the past *in relation to* the present. These past-present *alignments* have histories of their own which show that while such alignments have specific origins they do not continue to exist in simple identity with particular social or political interests. Indeed, they have a significant degree of autonomy and can be variously overdetermined and used by very different and even opposed interest groups. These alignments are not dependent on

My grandfather was bourgeois. My father was bourgeois. I am bourgeois. One day, my son, you can be bourgeois!

A. KRAUZE '83

any great understanding either of past or present, and in this sense they may be considered public philosophies of history.[10] They deal instead with a rather vague and invocatory sense of 'pastness', and their abstract generality appears to contribute to the strength of their operation. Unlike school history and the National Heritage, these past-present alignments do not work to secure and stabilise a national account or representation of the past, but rather to mobilise a legitimising but abstract sense of 'pastness' or 'history' around present social and political events or issues. At this stage it seems worth trying to differentiate three such alignments, each of which has made its entry into the 'national past' through bourgeois culture, and all three of which were evidently in play during the public response to Remembrance Day 1981. I shall call the first one *the complacent bourgeois alignment*. This alignment makes it possible to think of historical develop-ment as complete, a process which finds its accomplishment in the present. Historical development is here conceived as a cumulative process which has delivered the nation into the present as its manifest accomplishment. Both celebratory and complacent, it produces a sense that 'we' are the achieve-ment of history and that while the past is thus present as our right it is also something that our narcissism will encourage us to visit, exhibit, write up and discuss.

But in contemporary political terms the nation is frail and far from being fully achieved, and there is consequently a darker sense that historical development, far from finding its completion in the present, might actually be 'over' – that its hold on the present is increasingly weak and likely to be lost as society becomes more fractured and discontinuous with the past. This

introduces a second past-present alignment, one that I will call *the anxious aristocrat alignment*, which is organised above all around a sense of *betrayal* – a sense that history has somehow been sold short or cut down in its prime, so that the national unity which it bears as its goal or promise may never be fully realised. According to this second alignment citizens are always on the brink of collapsing into barbarism again (reverting to fragmented class cultures perhaps, or to inappropriate coats) and historical development of becoming entropic, its unfulfilled promises now lying as fragile traces which threaten to slip away 'behind' the present rather than being realised within it. In this second alignment 'we', like the monks of Lindisfarne during the Dark Ages, are the 'trustees' or custodians of the past.

These two past-present alignments have served different political interests at different times, and in their public existence they are often now found in combination with one another. This combination is clearly evident in the connections which the 'national past' makes between elements of interpretation and the celebration and display of a concrete National Heritage. There is, for example, an interesting coalescence between the complacent bourgeois alignment, in which historical development is seen to find its culmination in the present, and the physical existence of those buildings, artefacts and traditions comprising the National Heritage. Through this coalescence the past becomes physically present in the sense that it is 'there' to be venerated as tradition, monument, pageantry, spectacle and display. But because the National Heritage is also in danger and therefore dependent on measures of preservation it also makes connection with the anxious aristocrat alignment. In this second connection the very precariousness of the National Heritage comes to witness the precariousness of historical continuity. 'Preservation' thus has an ambivalent and complex meaning: it applies to the maintenance of old buildings and the like, but at the same time it can be implicitly and in a displaced way about preserving those social relations which are taken for granted and legitimised by the public rendition of our history as the 'national past'.

Over recent years this combination of a bourgeois interpretation and philosophy of history with the concrete phenomena of National Heritage has been apparent in the public statements of so-called 'wet' Tories like Patrick Cormack and Norman St John Stevas who have campaigned heavily for the National Heritage.[11] Towards the end of 1981, however, a different formation began to emerge. A fissure in the government saw St John Stevas, main proponent of the National Heritage Act (1980), moved out from the inner circle of power. With the marginalisation of Stevas and the constitutionalist Ian Gilmour, a more traditionalist and even 'cultural' one-nation Conservatism lost out to a hard-nosed and extremist monetarism. In the particular terms of National Heritage this led to some fairly immediate developments; the National Heritage Memorial Fund, established by Stevas' Act, had its

annual allocation of funds somewhat reduced, and Michael Heseltine through the Department of the Environment even went on to float plans for getting shot of the National Heritage altogether by the familiar process of 'commercialisation'. More generally, however, this turning of the screw within the Conservative government included an abandoning of the idea of historical and traditional continuity which Stevas and Gilmour, among others, had been promoting quite assiduously. In this respect the change was informed by a third past-present alignment which, although itself vehemently anti-traditional, forms a key tradition in Tory thought. In this third alignment, which I shall call *the anti-traditional technicist alignment*, the past continues to exist in the present, but it does so in *discontinuity* with modern social reality. Disjunction is the crucial term here; the past exists, but it is 'other', not as something which has been betrayed but as a true swamp of backward traditionality with which 'we', the bearers of modern rationality, want nothing to do.

All three of these alignments depend upon a sense of the past as present, and they consequently need material supports in the world. With both complacent bourgeois and anxious aristocrat alignments the National Heritage provides such material support. With the anti-traditional technicist alignment, however, the presence of the past is somewhat different. As an 'other' the past may indeed be exoticised as a place for tourists and school children to visit, or as a site of lost romance and betrayed glory, but it can also serve a rather more rhetorical purpose, as it did over Remembrance Day 1981, as a kind of dump into which the supposed causes of present social disorder may be thrown. In this latter and far less romantic use, the past becomes an accusation and to be identified with it is to be consigned to a junkyard cluttered with antiquated apparatuses which persist in the present either as pathetic relics or as more demonic engines of social inertia and stress. In the anti-traditional technicist alignment, therefore, the past is characterised not by castles and customs but instead by such things as the trade unions which, under the Thatcher government and also in SDP thinking, are prime targets of this kind of attack (the onslaught against the closed shop and picketing which formed the background to Tebbit's Employment Act made much of their 'antiquatedness'). This sort of accusation by attribution is simple enough: to be 'historical' is not to be part of the national glory so much as it is to be 'old-fashioned', and to be 'old-fashioned' is to be an impediment to social recovery. In the Conservative government of triumphant monetarism, therefore, the past is not just a heritage or trust in need of reluctant, because costly, protection. Neither is it just a convenient camouflage for preserving relations of domination under the guise of national identity and interest. It is also the oblivion which stands there as the rightful abode of all those forces which resist the 'rationalisation' of social relations around market forces.

The anti-traditional technicist alignment brings us firmly back to Remembrance Day 1981. The pillorying of Foot certainly provided a reminder, if one were needed, that the public field of meaning is loaded against assertions of class to the same measure that it promotes feelings of nationhood. Foot's appearance was presented as signalling identification and an intended historical solidarity with the working-class movement. *The Daily Telegraph* mocked this solidarity as spurious and imaginary, implying that in his sentimental concern with 'history', Foot had fallen out of line with the present-day working class – people who are now fully qualified as citizens and capable of honouring the 'national past' as well as of paying their respects to the dead. As a leading article on 9 November put it, 'No member of the working class, which Mr Foot believes he represents, would have worn his working clothes for such a solemn occasion, quite out of the run of ordinary life.' This criticism was made not just in the knowledge of Foot's standing as a historian but also in smug awareness of the crisis besetting the Labour Party and of the increasing difficulties facing attempts to express and develop working-class solidarity, especially those which appeal to an historical dimension. In a nation of citizens working-class forms are not just unfashionable, they are presented as being positively archaic. Hence the blue-plaque operation in which Foot was credited with 'history' so that he, and by implication the entire labour movement, could be all the more easily consigned to the scrap-heap of a very different public rendition of the past.

The Labour Movement and the 'National Past'

While the labour movement faces problems negotiating the loaded inter-pretation of the past which is instituted within the public field of meaning, there are also serious difficulties of a different sort bearing on the apparently unequivocal *presence* of the 'national past'. In order to clarify this second area it will help to introduce a fourth alignment of past in relation to present, and this one might as well be called *the marching proletariat alignment*. This alignment, which sees historical development as a slow but continuous process of struggle through which the working class 'wins' the present, has played a key part in organising the understanding and use (both analytical and also gestural in the use of slogans), that the labour movement has made of history. This, of course, is the Forward March of Labour, and as we know it is a procession which is experiencing some difficulties at the moment. Many of the marchers seem to have scattered from the road, some of them have definitely defected to the other side, and there have also been serious problems with what limited 'winning' of the present has taken place. While the post-war years have indeed seen some realisation of egalitarian and democratic ideas, an overwhelming greyness has also crept over the picture – the bureaucracy, the waiting lists, the destruction of communities and traditional forms of self-understanding, the reduction of ideas of change, social responsibility, emancipation and development to the pallid and reformist state practices of 'nationalisation' and 'planning'. If an earlier time saw the making of the working class, the events of the post-war years have lent great strength to those interests which now benefit from its unmaking.

There has been a greatly disappointing recent history, but it still seems to me that socialist claims in relation to the 'national past' or to historical development face a prior problem which is of a fairly *formal* kind. Because, socialism does not conceive of historical development as a process which is in any full sense achieved or accomplished in the present as we know it, it cannot work up an easy public *presence* for its sense of history. Socialism is so evidently *not* present (except through its mistakes or by negative ascription from its opponents as bureaucracy, union intransigence, East Europe and so forth) and its relation to the present remains one of critical challenge. It still exists, in other words, as an *idea*, and as one which is increasingly difficult to define in traditional class terms. Recent events (including Remembrance Day 1981) suggest that socialism cannot match Conservative claims to the 'national past' and tradition. The Conservative interests have an easy time in this area, resting their case not so much on any *idea* as on the overwhelming *presence* of the 'national past' – its Traditions, Monuments and Institutions. It is a relation of *identity* rather than criticism that is assumed here; manipulative, certainly, but it has been remarkably successful in making even an extreme monetarist Conservatism seem like an emanation from the national interest, and therefore a 'natural' guardian of the national identity.

Faced with this problem in its ability to develop a public image, the labour movement has often responded in ways that appear to entrench it further into the mire by reinforcing exactly those public overdeterminations which are against it. It is worth giving two examples of this kind of response. The first consists of a simple laying of claim to those public presences – institutions, ceremonies and customs – which exist in such apparently easy allegiance to the dominant interests. A strategy of this sort was evident in Michael Foot's initial and outraged response not to any Tory but to the appearance of the ill-starred Peter Tatchell in the until recently rotten borough of Bermondsey. Ostensibly this argument concerned Tatchell's alleged allegiance to 'extra-Parliamentary' activity. It was also significant, however, for what it revealed about Foot's relation to the institutions of Parliament. In true constitutionalist style, Foot laid claim to Parliament as the institution through which democracy had been accomplished and through which further political change should be secured. He identified the Labour Party's historical development and mission with Parliament. The problem is that it is not possible just to 'lay claim' to national institutions such as Parliament unless one is prepared to accept on the recoil their overwhelmingly powerful definition of one's own cause. It may indeed be historically inaccurate to identify the development of Parliament with the struggle for democracy, but additional difficulties follow from the fact that the institutions of Parliament *are* indubitably present. More than this, their physical presence in Westminster is encrusted with a powerful national symbolism which establishes them as fetish-objects rather than institutions of political change. If the presence of the House of Commons is claimed as witnessing the achieved presence of the labour movement, then the way is also opened for the conclusion that the struggle for democracy is over – a thing of the past, perhaps even part of the national heritage. The reality, of course, is different. Evidently, then, it is not possible to treat national traditions and institutions as if they were merely contested items in a claim over inheritance. They have no such singularity and come with whole philosophies of history attached.

The second problematic response to the crisis in the labour movement's public image has been a tendency to fall back onto the historical style – the gestures and vocabulary – of a time when solidarity and progress did seem intact, a time when the presence of socialism seemed positive and growing, and when the road did indeed seem to stretch out in front of the marchers. So we speak of 'comrades' again, of 'the people', of 'solidarity' and 'fraternity', and we use hackneyed images like the Forward March of Labour to comfort ourselves. Alongside this there is a related tendency to support and define present activities by aligning them with the more controllable terms of a nostalgically organised 'past' of the labour movement's own. To the extent that it was formed in the imagined mould of Jarrow, the People's March for Jobs (1981 and again in 1983) can be instanced as an example here. A similarly retrospective appeal to solidarity seems to characterise Tony Benn's more resurrectional invocations of the English 'people' with their own premarxian drive towards socialism: peasant's revolt, Robin Hood and all.

That this way of gesturing with past resonances works is not in doubt: it works to the extent that it provides some sense of coherence and identity, a vocabulary and *some* sort of public profile for those already embarked on the forward march. But there is surely now overwhelming evidence to suggest that the labour movement is only achieving this focus of its faithful by alienating an increasingly large number of people for whom all this reeks of 'history' in the worst publicly sustained sense of the word – the 'past' as that swamp from which 'we' moderns are struggling to escape. This response can't be treated with contempt or simply written off as middle-class or anti-traditional technicist ideology either, for it is only partly attributable to the dispensation of power biassing the public field of meaning and the media in particular. If the agencies of public meaning can sustain a 'national past' which functions to disorder, petrify and contain the labour-movement, they can only do this because the labour movement itself has a tendency towards the comforting simplicities of an evocative and sentimental nostalgia: in its current uncertainty, it *does* tend to fall back on the vanished solidarities of a time when a coherent and unified working class was properly resistant, conscious and oppressed (a time – imaginary or not – when the class struggle was pure and simple), or to hanker after a world which corroborates its more exhausted conceptual machinery such as the theoretical cleaver which still divides mental from manual labour in automatic correlation with class difference, to quote only one example.[12] Similarly the trade union movement *is*, in many respects, 'backward' and chauvinistic.

So if the public field of meaning is indeed loaded against socialism, it can also be seen as issuing a quite legitimate reminder that in no sense is socialism somehow 'there' to be dug out of the crypts of history and stood on its feet in the present. If socialism ever does exist this will only be because an electorate recognises that it can be *made* in adequate relation not to the past, but to the complexities (historical indeed) of contemporary social life. In the face of these complexities, and as the Conservative press is only too willing to announce, no mystery cult, however talismanic its vocabulary or moving its stylistic appeals to history, is going to be adequate.

Socialism and the 'National Past'

I want now to turn from this rather dispiriting picture of a movement caught in the negative embrace of public meanings that exist only to discredit it, and to consider instead the resources through which a rather more hopeful relation to tradition and the 'national past' might be developed.

First, there is the clear record of socialist history to build on. This movement has worked consistently to contest the definitions of the 'past' which are dominant within the public field of meaning, and it will doubtless continue to be especially valuable as it works in close relation to current issues and problems. This sort of historiographical work is likely to be indispensable in opposing Tory arguments such as the one claiming that social and economic planning inevitably entails horrendous bureaucracy, inflation and the demolition of all personal choice, and that the surrender of social relations to the market is therefore 'natural' in some pseudo-anthropological sense. There is also, of course, the Labour Party and its crisis of petrification. It will only be historiographical work that answers the important question posed by Etienne Balibar in a talk on 'the crisis of the party' in London early in 1982: namely, what have been the historical relations between the Labour Party and the movement from which it derives – what has been drawn into the scope and discourse of the Party and what left outside and excluded?

Despite its positive engagement with issues and local communities or groups in the present, socialist history has faced difficulties maintaining its integrity as it is appropriated and taken up within the public field of meaning (which is, by and large, so hungry for a sense of cultural meaning that it can appropriate traditions independently of their original context). There is obviously no question that socialist history must enter this field, for it is only here that it can make its challenge, but it does so at the risk of transformation. To give an example, an assertion of working class history can be recontextualised to suggest that 'class' is just 'history' these days. Once this identification has been made the appropriation can move a stage further into a practice of exhibition and display: the extracted details of working class history can be staged in terms of ethnology so that they are comprehensible less in terms of political contradiction and more in relation to a quasi-anthropological stress on 'ways', 'structures' and 'forms' of everyday life.[13] This problem leaves no doubt, I think, that socialist history needs to be developed in deliberate and critical engagement with the 'national past'.

So with the 'national past' there is a second area in which historiography has a key part to play. Here the questions seem to flood in. How have initially aristocratic and bourgeois representations of past and landscape come to be both 'nationalised' and 'naturalised' over the last hundred or so years? How have publicly dominant versions of the past worked to marginalise and ridicule others? How and to what extent have the different agencies of public meaning co-operated in producing the 'national past'? What relations exist between public articulations of the past and private or privatised memories? To what extent do such articulations determine and control the ways in which they themselves can be interpreted? To what extent has British socialism, both in its historical development and its retrospective attempt to define a culture and style for itself, participated in reproducing the 'national past'? (The rural idyll, for example, was a moving force for radical social historians like the Hammonds as well as for William Morris, and there is also Tom Nairn's point about the 'Little Englandism' behind much Labour Party anti-Europeanism.) How does the 'nation' posited by the 'national past' work in relation to local cultures, and those other nations of Scotland, Wales and Ireland? To summarise, we need to know both *what* the 'national past' is and *how* it works. In the second area the question of consent is crucially in need of investigation. Obviously to consent to the 'national past' is not the same as identifying oneself consciously with it through belief, and there may well be some consolation to be found in the findings of a recent analysis of nationalism in Mussolini's Italy which suggests that the manipulative 'nationalisation' of public life and culture may lead only to a fairly sceptical, weak and therefore passing consent.[14] When we have gone some way towards answering these questions it will become more possible to work out which elements of the 'national past' might play a more positive part in a public sense of identity which is capable of pride and a sense of tradition, but which isn't so confused, unhappy and sick with reaction.

While these questions about history and the 'national past' can be addressed at a theoretical level there are also some messier practical contexts where they are already in play, and this introduces a third area in which work might be done. Perhaps the most relevant of these contexts, especially from the point of view of the presence of the past, is the preservation movement which has been growing steadily since the late nineteenth century.[15] In its cultural origins this concern with preservation is doubtless closely connected with the anti-industrialism of Romanticism and the Gothic Revival, with nineteenth century historicism, and with the consciousness of national past and tradition which was increasingly stressed within the educational system as it developed alongside the consolidation of the British nation-state. However, over the last three decades or so the preservation movement has been sharpened, on occasion more explicitly politicised, and its popularity greatly increased by extensive changes in both urban and rural life – changes which have drastically altered the face of both town and country. Over these more recent decades the preservation movement has gone on contributing to the concretisation of that sense of the past which is inscribed within the public field of meaning, but it has also played a most active part in expanding the definition of the 'national past'.

Throughout its century-long struggle to establish a legitimate public interest over market and private property relations the preservation movement has worked to develop means of registering and conserving sites of historical interest. In its endeavours to conserve old country houses and the like, parts of this movement have worked in apparent concordance with dominant interests, but much has also been done to secure rights of access as well, and these (as the mass trespasses of the thirties showed) are far from being simply convenient to any conceived status quo. Recent decades have seen a muting of the early radicalism of some of the older organisations like the Ramblers' Association or the National Trust. This muting is reflected in the career of the word *trustee* within the vocabulary of preservation. When in the 1870s William Morris applied the word to owners of significant buildings he intended to introduce limits into the notion of ownership – buildings were to be respected, looked after and handed on, but not demolished or 'improved'. When a man like Patrick Cormack uses it in the 1980s, the word serves far more to mystify and to defend the interest of ownership, against tax for example. The taming of preservation can also be seen in the legislation concerning monuments and the conservation of buildings and sites: throughout this century one strand of such legislation has concerned public rights of *access* to the heritage; in the softer terms of the National Heritage Act (1980), this question of access tends only to survive in the administrative terms of *exhibition*.

Preservation seeks to endow the past with an accomplished and secure reality; in doing so it can provide security for conservative values, but it also provides an unequivocal basis for debate and argument about the past and its political load. This basis exists in close connection with people's experience, and it is therefore not necessarily as externally structured by dominant public forms as that more abstract and 'mere' sense of history which was used to contain and ridicule Michael Foot on Remembrance Day 1981. There are, of course, problems of exclusion, of cultural pessimism and of an over-vague anti-industrialism, but recent years have also seen an expansion in the definition of National Heritage to include ordinary locales and even workplaces. Increasingly it is concerning itself with the local structures of everyday life. At times this expansion seems to be part of an all too understandable nostalgia for rooted social relations which can easily be articulated into Conservatism or worse, and at others it seems clearly to be part of a gentle process of domination which is finally bringing the 'nation' into the experience of ordinary people, so that they too may make their minor contribution to 'our' common heritage. Yet there can be no doubt that the expansion of National Heritage needs also to be recognised as an achieved change in public definition, won as part of a conscious resistance to the devastation of traditions and ways of life that has followed the Second World War. These developments have brought a preservationist attention to bear on the socio-historical texture of living memory itself, and in doing so they have also brought 'history' further out of the world of books, learning and culture, drawing it closer to the experiential and political arenas of everyday life. At this local level, contestations over history, preservation and the inheritance of traditions are going on in contexts which would seem to make their detachment as 'mere' history impossible.

Because contestations over preservation are increasingly close to the structures and processes of everyday life they are also increasingly close to being concerned not just with the local monument but with contemporary questions of housing, transport, the culture and use of the street, with the politics of local government, and with the relations between local government and centralised power. Preservation will doubtless continue to concern itself with buildings, sites and monuments, but it might also move to the limits of these (even expanded) definitions and broach the question of 'preserving' traditional ways of life or even essential social services. Developments of this sort are clearly already taking place, albeit mostly in rural areas where medical and postal services, for example, have been included in arguments about a community's rightful inheritance. Speaking sceptically, they may indicate yet another attempt to patch up the rural idyll for the benefit of those members of the middle class who have decided to move into it. However, they also indicate the possibility of a kind of contact with political reality which is direct enough to propel the movement through its original High-cultural pessimism and aestheticised anti-industrialism into a fuller engagement with the political issues determining its field of action. And as for those middle-class members of the preservation movement, even if they are motivated mainly by the urge to protect conservative values, why should they be held in contempt? Surely here at least one can agree with Rudolf Bahro and say that far from criticising such people for having bad or inadequate politics, the job is to offer them a somewhat better political home.[16]

The preservation movement draws questions of history and the past into a practical context; more specifically, the voluntary associations through which it has developed have been formed within *civil society*. This suggests some new lines for the socialist project within contemporary society. If socialism has for a long time been disabused of early illusions about the historical inevitability of its development, it has only recently lost its hopes for a fairly easy and direct identification with the working class. This has left it bereft and, according to its enemies, with nowhere to go except the museum. More urgent, therefore, than any question of developing a counter-rhetoric within the vocabulary of nationalism, our current crisis demands a reconsideration of the location or place that the socialist project would find for itself not in theory but in actual social development.

At present, civil society is dominated by the universalisation of the market, the exclusive character of private property and the growth of inequality.[17] But even within this reactionary and individualistic perspective there is established, albeit negatively, the concept of freedom. There is therefore a counter-logic of civil society which socialists can develop: Agnes Heller has defined it as 'the unfolding and enforcement of this freedom (of human rights), in the process of democratisation, equalisation, decentralisation of power.' Socialism is therefore in part 'a movement which promotes the second logic of civil society as opposed to the first.' In this struggle, the question of public meaning – around the 'national past' or forms of re-membrance and preservation, for example – is identified as a political one to start with. The public sphere, after all, was first developed within civil society as a critical agency which helped the bourgeoisie to establish the legitimacy of its claims over the absolutist state. Since then the public sphere has been occupied by private interests, fragmented and ideologically manipulated, and its field of meaning has therefore been similarly controlled. Only if it is realigned with the logic of democracy and freedom will the public sphere become genuinely open to domination-free discussion and debate. Such a refocussing of socialist work would certainly mean an end to the uncritical identification of 'socialism' with conformity to dogma or the existing institutions of labourism. As Agnes Heller has written, at this point History ceases to lie behind us at all. Instead, History becomes both utopia and *project* for a socialism which (in various ways and spheres of life) is seeking to *realise* a logic which it knows to be implicit in modern society.[18]

Notes

1. I am drawing from Jürgen Habermas here. See especially *Legitimation Crisis*, London, Heinemann Educational Books, 1976.
2. J. H. Plumb, *The Death of the Past*, London, Macmillan, 1969, p. 17.
3. 'The public field of meaning' is a phrase used extensively throughout this article. I cannot give a theoretical account of it here, but it is worth identifying the influence of Habermas's theory of the 'public sphere', a theory which has been developed by Negt and Kluge in Germany and, more recently, taken up in English by the American periodicals *Telos* and *New German Critique*. See especially Jean Cohen's essay 'Why More Political Theory?', *Telos* 40, Summer 1979, pp. 70–94. A very abbreviated outline of Habermas's and Negt and Kluge's work in this area is to be found in '"Charms of Residence"; the public and the past', an article by Michael Bommes and myself in Centre for Contemporary Cultural Studies, *Making Histories*, London, Hutchinson, 1982. A much fuller discussion of Habermas has recently appeared in J. B. Thompson and D. Held (eds), *Habermas: critical debates*, London, Macmillan, 1982. Oskar Negt's 'Mass Media: Tools of Domination or Instruments of Emancipation?' appears in K. Woodward (ed.), *The Myths of Information*, London, RKP, 1980.
4. In her *A Theory of History* (London, Routledge and Kegan Paul, 1982) Agnes Heller describes 'the sense of historical existence' as follows: 'We experience change in values and institutions, we experience our fate and the fate of others, even of remote peoples, as being interwoven. New events and experiences happen to us, and we participate in new undertakings or we suffer because established ones are shaken. We are the victims of world-catastrophes and we turn our faces towards the first glimmers of the dawn. We cherish hopes concerning the years to come and we despair when they betray our expectations. We ask: what is the sense of all this? We ask whether our children will live in a different world, in one better or worse than ours. We ask whether a better future is possible at all; and if the answer is in the affirmative, what we can do for it, if in the negative, when and how we "missed the bus".' (p. 218) A preliminary discussion of the interplay between representation of the past and lived experience is to be found in the CCCS Popular Memory Group's chapter of *Making Histories*.
5. Edward Shils, *Tradition*, London, Faber and Faber, 1981, p. 59.
6. Valerie Chancellor, *History for their Masters*, Bath, Adams and Dart, 1970.
7. Frances Fitzgerald, *America Revised: History Schoolbooks in the twentieth century*, New York, Vintage Books, 1980, p. 17.
8. Heller, *A Theory of History*, p. 67.
9. See Bommes and Wright, 'Charms of Residence' for a fuller description of these changes in the repertoire of National Heritage.
10. I follow Agnes Heller's critical definition of 'philosophy of history' here: 'All philosophies raise the question of the sense of human existence. Human existence over the last two hundred years is experienced as historical experience. Philosophies of history answer the questions about the *sense of historical existence* and so they satisfy the needs of our times. But they claim to answer another question as well, a question about the *sense of history*. In this claim resides the *ambiguity* of all philosophies of history: they equate the sense of historical existence with the "sense of history".' (*A Theory of History*, p. 218)
11. Patrick Cormack's *Heritage in Danger* (London, Quartet Books, 1978) is a minor classic in what is by now itself becoming a quite traditional genre.
12. I borrow the phrase 'vanished solidarities' from the editorial article in *History Workshop Journal*, no. 12, 1981.

13. Some very useful comments on this sort of 'Ethno-history' can be found in Philippe Hoyau's discussion of the French 'Heritage Year' launched under Giscard d'Estaing. See 'L'année du patrimoine ou la societé de conservation', *Les Révoltes Logiques*, no. 12, 1980, pp. 70–78.

14. See Victoria de Grazia, *The Culture of Consent: Mass organisation of leisure in Fascist Italy*, Cambridge University Press, 1981.

15. A useful advocatory discussion which shows something of the range of the preservation movement can be found in David Lowenthal and Marcus Binney (eds.), *Our Past Before Us: Why do we Save it?* London, Temple Smith, 1981. A more critical (and yet uncritically pro-'industrial') discussion of the emergence of the preservation movement is included in Martin J. Wiener's *English Culture and the Decline of the Industrial Spirit 1850–1980*, Cambridge University Press, 1981.

16. Rudolf Bahro, 'Ecology Crisis and Socialist Idea', in *Socialism and Survival*, London, Heretic Books, 1982, p. 35.

17. Heller, *A Theory of History*, p. 284.

18. See 'Introduction to a theory of history' which is Part IV of Heller's *A Theory of History*. Especially interesting are the chapters called 'History retrieved?' and 'The need for Utopia'.

Karen Knorr

GENTLEMEN

We
owe it
to the Free world
not to Allow Brutal Forces
to succeed. When the Rule of law Breaks
down, the World takes a further Step towards Chaos.

As he contemplated
the Long Arch of Centuries,
he was led to conclude
that it was Above all
the English character
which Enlightened
the Corridors of Time
flickering Now and then
but mostly
Pure and Clear.

Men are interested
in Power.
Women are more interested
in Service.

His Ideas began
to take form of Words,
to group themselves into Sentences.
The rhythm of his own Language
swayed him.
Something to Lift their Minds,
to Awake sentiment.
Instinctively, he Alliterated.

The Time has Come
for us to play the Trump card.
The more implacably we Play
our hand in the Falklands affair
the more likely we are
to have a hand to play.

Unwritten laws Bound him
as much as if They had been Printed
in black and white.
They came down to him
from Old Times.

The Recapture
of the Territory
is no more than an
Appetiser to
the big Match.

You may meet its Members
in London and Fiji,
in the Swamps and in the Desert,
in the Lands beyond the Mountains.
They are always the Same
for they are branded
with the Stamp
of the Breed.

It was an Idea
which Awakened
all that was Best in him,
reminding him of his own
Higher nature.
Chivalry, he believed,
should precede all subsequent
Decency in Relations
between Races.

What he had endured in silence:
She was uncouth, ignorant,
unpolished and unreliable,
he now expatiated Aloud:
She Could Not Be Allowed To Roam.
Nature must first be taken
in hand. Civilised.

Those who Fear
the Rule of Women
but Love the Monarchy
should reconsider their Prejudice;
to ensure the right
of his Firstborn to the Throne
will create a better Climate.

Whatever a Man's
Social origin,
once he has been elected
he is looked upon
as an Equal by his
Fellow-Members.

David Forgacs

NATIONAL-POPULAR: Genealogy of a Concept

1

The term 'national-popular' is a relatively new addition to the conceptual luggage of the British left and, of concepts originating in the work of Gramsci, it has been one of the slowest to arrive here. Its presence in the late '70s and '80s can be partly explained, I believe, by the toughening of the political climate which has taken place in this period and by the weakening of the grip of Althusserian Marxism upon certain sectors of the new left. In the mid-seventies, the Gramsci being discussed was mediated through the filter of Althusser, whose writings became widely known in English during the same period (the early '70s) and who had drawn on the Italian communist's work in several important respects. Yet the figure that emerged through this 'French connection' was one that was sanitized by Althusserian scientism. One paid this Gramsci due homage for having brought ideology from heaven to earth by incarnating it in material institutions and social practices and for having developed a non-economistic model for analysing conjunctures as asymmetrical relations of forces not reducible to a single all-englobing contradiction. But his 'absolute historicism', his collapsing together of philosophy, politics, religion and ideology, and his conception of Marxism as involving an intellectual and moral reformation were considered too embarrassingly primitive to be given serious attention by rigorous Marxist theoreticians. For as long as Althusserianism retained its cultural prestige as a kind of orthodoxy, the distinguishing wedge that Althusser and Poulantzas had driven between Gramsci's positive work of political analysis and his historicist Marxism remained operative and effectively served to suppress parts of his writings. The turn-about that is now taking place, by which these suppressed parts are coming to the fore, involves a reaction against the political impasse towards which Althusser's later formulations on ideology, science and the subject tend. For Althusser's radical anti-historicism and anti-humanism make problematical the moment of acquisition of mass revolutionary consciousness by implicitly polarizing on the one hand a mass of subjects-in-ideology and on the other the bearers of science, the intellectuals working in the van of the party. The moment of a liberatory mass action against oppression is thus radically deferred, taken off the agenda. Yet, at a time when the tough and flexible ideological resources of Thatcherism have proved capable of mobilizing a large popular base, the dangers of this kind of impasse become clear. Moreover, the last decade in Britain has seen a renewed spate of militancy among groups and social elements without a strict party or uniform class collocation – the women's movement, blacks, gays, unemployed youth, students, nuclear disarmament, community pressure groups and so on – which the traditional left has been uncertain of how to relate to itself or to channel, and which have tended to jostle together in a relatively loose and unco-ordinated way beneath or alongside the weakly articulated ideological umbrella of the Labour Party. It is these two things arrayed against one another – the new state formation and the heterogeneous oppositional forces – which produce the need for a concept like the national-popular.

2

In Italy, where published extracts of Gramsci's prison writings began circulating immediately after the end of the Second World War, the national-popular was treated largely as a *cultural* concept and associated with progressive realist forms in literature, cinema and the other arts, which the Italian Communist Party (PCI) began to back in the '40s and '50s. 'National-popular' became a sort of slogan for forms of art that were rooted both in the national tradition and in popular life, and as such it became identified with an artistic style or styles. In this form, the term was to become the symbolic target of stringent criticism in the '60s from the Italian new left, who interpreted it as the cornerstone of a 'typically idealist operation' by which Gramsci had allegedly cast the intellectuals and their collective incarnation, the PCI, in the role of inheritors of nineteenth century radical bourgeois culture.[1] 'Gramsci's national-popular', a critic wrote, 'ends up . . . being the cage within which all attempts at renewal turn out to be constrained by the iron laws of tradition and the Italian social "status quo".'[2] The concept was seen as involving a double terminological slide – *national* replaced *international* and *popular* replaced *proletarian*.[3] This in turn was symptomatic of a political elision of revolution into reformism, the parliamentary road and a form of political democracy based on broad class alliances: in short, the strategy of the PCI since the end of the war.

In Britain, the national-popular has been received and used as a *political* concept and identified with the notion of popular-democratic struggles without a specific class character which can be articulated in relation to the struggle of labour against capital. In this form, the concept has been involved in discussions of whether certain ideologies have a necessary class-belonging or whether an economistic perspective can be transcended and a broad ideological front theorized in its stead. It has also been involved in debate about how various forms of oppression are related to each other and to the class struggle, about whether the state in capitalist society is an instrument of bourgeois class rule or a site of class compromises with space for expansive democratization, and about how statist models of socialist struggle might be overcome by a broader theorization of struggle on several fronts in civil society and the state. As such, the concept underlay, in spirit at least, the 1978 edition of the Communist Party's *The British Road to Socialism*, which identified a number of forces for change in the working class, the intermediate social strata, the women's movement, black people, gays, youth, religious groups and pensioners, stressing that 'The need is to show that these struggles are linked to each other, and to unite the various sections in a broad democratic alliance.'[4]

These two applications or interpretations of the national-popular concept make curious bedfellows. Although in each case practices of class alliance are involved, there is a substantial difference of emphasis: the first is cultural, the second political. How did this come about? And how is it that, in its cultural form, it was accused of being a conservative notion, inhibiting cultural change? I suggest that Gramsci's concept is in fact an integral one, whose cultural and political faces overlap and fuse; that not to understand this is to make only a partial reading and therefore to lay oneself open to a misreading of it (as the early, culturalist, reading was); and that the only way to reappropriate the concept in full is to make an excursus through Gramsci's writings, to see how the term emerges and the meanings it assumes within them. The present article is intended to do no more than provide the spade-work of textual reconstruction that will make this reappropriation possible.

3

It was in response to the conjuncture of ascendant fascism in Italy and the ebb-tide of revolution in the West that Gramsci began to elaborate the concept of the national-popular. The period was between 1924 and 1926. Within these two years leading up to his arrest, he returned from Moscow and Vienna, took over the leadership of the PCI from Amadeo Bordiga, and imposed a new strategic line on the party. This involved an implicit self-criticism of his own earlier 'workerism', his concentration, in the period 1919–21, on the factory councils in northern industry as organs of workers' control and as political units of socialist democracy. It also involved an explicit critique of Bordiga's sectarianism, his vanguardist conception of the party expressed through a boycotting of parliament and elections and a refusal to apply the Comintern's formula of a united front with the socialists. Bordiga had been, back in 1920, one of the foreign socialists criticised by name in Lenin's *'Left Wing' Communism*, a text scored through by the economic and political compromises of the civil war and the period leading up to the New Economic Policy in the Soviet Union, by the defeats of revolution in the West and the need for tactical flexibility in recognition of the specific national conditions in which each foreign party was operating.

> 'As long as national and state differences exist among peoples and countries – and these differences will continue to exist for a very long time even after the dictatorship of the proletariat has been established on a world scale – the unity of international tactics of the Communist working-class movement of all countries demands, not the elimination of variety, not the abolition of national differences (that is a foolish dream at the present moment), but such an application of the *fundamental* principles of Communism (soviet power and the dictatorship of the proletariat) as will *correctly modify* these principles in certain *particulars*, correctly adapt and apply them to national and national-state differences. Investigate, study, seek, divine, grasp that which is peculiarly national in the *concrete manner* in which each country approaches the fulfilment of the *single* international task . . .'[5]

The features which Gramsci singled out in Italy were as follows: a highly advanced, but very small, industrial proletariat concentrated in the north-west of the peninsula; a large, but often ideologically backward peasantry, much of it located in the south and islands; a large stratum of petty-bourgeois intellectuals who exercised a degree of ideological control over the proletariat and peasantry and who, although themselves traditionally hegemonized by the bourgeoisie, tended to waver in the way they identified their class interest. By the time Gramsci launched his turn against Bordiga's leadership, fascism had installed itself in power by a class alliance between the northern industrial bourgeoisie and the large landowners with the crucial support of the petty bourgeoisie. Although it had not yet outlawed the PCI and other opposition parties, it had been conducting systematic repression of Communist activities and arresting Communist personnel. On Gramsci's reckoning, a political strategy based exclusively on the proletariat led by a vanguard party in isolation from other social forces was quite inadequate as a strategy to defeat fascism. It was necessary, rather, to construct a class alliance between three principal groups – the northern proletariat, the southern peasantry and the petty-bourgeois intelligentsia – under the hegemony of the proletariat, in order not only to provide a mass base for political action but also to prise open the interstices of the north-south industrial-landowner alliance.

In a report to the PCI central committee written in August 1926, three months before his arrest, Gramsci noted that the most salient feature of the conjuncture, in which support for Mussolini's party had been wavering since the murder by fascists of the Social-Democrat deputy Matteotti in the summer of 1924, was a tendency towards a 'disintegration of the old ideologies' among the middle strata of the working-class and petty-bourgeois intellectuals in the Socialist and other democratic parties – Republicans, Popular Party (Catholics), Sardinian Action Party. These intellectuals were tending towards forms of radical republicanism, and if the Communist Party and the working class were able to hegemonize them, win them away from bourgeois and petty-bourgeois influence and overturn their class values,[6] then it could construct a bloc powerful enough not only to topple fascism but also one which would already be organized for transition to dictatorship of the proletariat. It was precisely because an immediate transition from fascism to socialism was improbable, not least because 'the existing armed forces, given their composition, cannot at once be won over',[7] that an interlude was necessary in which the liberal-democratic political structures were restored to power. It is thus in a context of a disarticulation and ideological disintegration of consent for fascism, a context in which, nevertheless, direct seizure of power is ruled out because 'The state apparatus is far more resistant than is often possible to believe',[8] that Gramsci puts forward the concept of the national-popular in an embryonic, tactical form:

> 'For all the capitalist countries a fundamental problem is posed – the problem of the transition from the united front tactic, understood in a general sense, to a specific tactic which confronts the concrete problems of national life and operates on the basis of the popular forces as they are historically determined.'[9]

In the prison notebooks, written between 1929 and 1935, the national-popular concept is closely bound up with that of Jacobinism, which in Gramsci means a form of political domination based on the ability to overcome a narrow economic-corporate conception of a class or class-fraction and form *expansive, universalizing* alliances with other classes and class-fractions whose interests can be made to be seen as coinciding with those of the hegemonic class. Hegemony, in turn, differs from Lenin's conception of proletarian dictatorship because it involves ideological and not just political domination – in other words a coming to consciousness of a coincidence of interests. Only by breaking with an economistic correlation between ideology and class was Gramsci able to think this expansion of the concept of hegemony. Only one of the two fundamental classes – bourgeoisie and proletariat – can, however, be hegemonic. In the French Revolution, the radical bourgeoisie became hegemonic in the phase of Jacobin domination by universalizing and expanding its class interests to incorporate those of the urban artisans and the peasantry. The same process must be repeated in Italy, for Gramsci, by the proletariat in a socialist revolution. The class must secure hegemony over the peasants and the other intermediate social strata by making them conscious of a shared interest. Hegemony is thus a process of radiating out from the Communist Party and the working class a *collective will* which is national-popular:

> 'Any formation of a national-popular collective will is impossible, unless the great mass of peasant farmers bursts *simultaneously* into political life. That was Machiavelli's intention through the reform of the militia, and it was achieved by the Jacobins in the French Revolution. . . . All history from 1815 onwards shows the efforts of the traditional classes to prevent the formation of a collective will of this kind, and to maintain "economic-corporate" power in an international system of passive equilibrium.'[10]

In his notes on the Risorgimento, Gramsci observed how the democratic republican leaders around Mazzini and the Action Party failed to generalize their struggle beyond the radical bourgeoisie and win the support of the peasantry. They were thus subsumed and defeated by the Moderates under Cavour, who were able to construct a hegemonic alliance of the bourgeoisie with the southern landowners, an alliance whose continuation was secured in the state through transformism (*ad hoc* ministerial coalitions) and by the economic subjection of the South to the North in a colonial relationship offset for the big landowners by protectionist policies. This 'chapter of past history' bears on the concrete relations of force in the 1920s and '30s because of its historical parallel with the PCI at the time of the rise to power of fascism. This party too had failed to become hegemonic because of its inability to carry out the Jacobin task of linking countryside to city – peasantry to proletariat, south to north – to form a national-popular collective will. In its place, the Fascist Party had carried out a reform-revolution or passive revolution, based on the defensive, transformist alliance of the industrial bourgeoisie, big landowners and petty bourgeoisie, which involved no fundamental reorganization of the economic structure – only its technical modernization along rational 'Fordist' lines – coupled with an increase in state coercion and the securing of mass popular consent in civil society.

At a political level, then, there are four points to be noted about the national-popular concept. It was elaborated in response to fascism, a conservative social bloc made up of heterogeneous economic groups with a permanently mobilized mass base, possessing organizational reserves (military, ideological) which rule out a frontal attack (war of manoeuvre) and favour a construction of hegemony (war of position) as the correct strategy to defeat it. It was dependent on the relative numerical weakness of the Italian proletariat. It involved the formation of a collective will through the building of a mass party, where a number of social classes and class-fractions are successfully hegemonized by the party and the proletariat. It was conceived of as a transitional stage leading to the dictatorship of the proletariat, to socialist democracy (soviets) as opposed to bourgeois democracy (parliament). These concepts underwent no substantial modification at a political level, as a strategic perspective, between the period in which they were first formulated (1924–26) and the time of Gramsci's death in 1937. They were, however, qualitatively deepened by being developed in cultural and ideological terms.

4

The entry in the prison notebooks headed 'Concept of national-popular' has no overtly political content.[11] It discusses, instead, the problem of why Italian literature did not, with a few exceptions, have a wide popular readership in Italy and why Italian newspapers, which since the late nineteenth century had adopted the practice of serializing fiction to increase circulation, were publishing predominantly French and not Italian authors. Gramsci's answer is that in Italy

> '. . . neither a popular artistic literature nor a local production of "popular" literature exists because "writers" and "people" do not have the same conception of the world. In other words the feelings of the people are not lived by the writers as their own, nor do the writers have a "national educative" function: they have not and do not set themselves the problem of elaborating popular feelings after having relived them and made them their own.'[12]

Italian readers therefore turn to French writers, who had this national function, because in France there existed a 'close and dependent relationship between people-nation and intellectuals' which Italian readers feel.[13]

In several notes containing the phrase 'national-popular' (or 'popular-national', 'people-nation', 'nation-people') one finds this theme of the separation between intellectuals and the people in Italy (which is often, as here, contrasted with France). This separation was traditional[14] both in that it went back a long way into Italian history and in that it had been traditionally remarked upon, notably in the Risorgimento where it had become a leitmotif among democratic intellectuals (Mazzini, De Sanctis and so forth) who had seen the Renaissance as producing a cleavage between culture and the people, between knowledge and popular life. In fact, much of what Gramsci writes about the national-popular is a materialist recasting of these abstract and idealist formulations by a re-reading of Italian cultural history.

In a long discussion of the Renaissance in notebook 5, he traces the dualism back to a separation, occurring in the fourteenth and fifteenth centuries, of a literary and philosophical élite from the commercial, manu- facturing and financial bourgeoisie. The latter had acquired political domination in the period of the Communes (from the twelfth to the fourteenth century) but had been unable to consolidate it because it had failed to go beyond its economic-corporate limits and become hegemonic as a class. The return at a cultural level to classicism – humanism – was therefore a restoration which

> '. . . like every restoration, . . . assimilated and developed, better than the revolutionary class it had politically suffocated, the ideological principles of the defeated class, which had not been able to go beyond its corporate limits and create the superstructures of an integral society. Yet this development was "abstract", it remained the patri- mony of an intellectual caste and had no contact with the people- nation.'[15]

Humanism and the Renaissance in Italy were thus 'the phenomenon of an aristocracy removed from the people-nation'.[16] Whereas in the other Euro- pean countries the exported Renaissance produced a progressive scientific intelligentsia which played a crucial role in the formation of the modern national states, in Italy itself it led to the involutionary Counter-Reformation and the ideological triumph of the Catholic intellectual hierarchy. This outcome was itself linked to two factors to which Gramsci's analysis assigns great importance. The first was the fact that Italy had been the centre of the Roman Empire and then, by 'translation', of the Catholic Church, both of which exercised their power through cosmopolitan (international) intellec- tual castes. The second was the failure of a common national vernacular to develop in the peninsula, where instead two culturally prestigious written cosmopolitan languages (first Latin and then, after the sixteenth century, literary Tuscan) had dominated over a large number of less prestigious spoken dialects. The political disunity of Italy, of which Machiavelli com- plained in *The Prince*, was compounded by these factors. In the sixteenth century, the Papacy blocked the Protestant Reformation and with it the possibility of forming a modern national state. In the nineteenth century, it again constituted a major obstacle to national unification by its anti- liberalism and by jealously guarding its temporal power over central Italy. At the same time, the regional and cultural heterogeneity of the peninsula could be read off from the multiplicity of dialects, which acted as a practical obstacle to the diffusion of any national culture. The Italian nation had thus been more a rhetorical or legal entity than a felt cultural reality, existing at most for the intellectual and ruling élites but not for the masses. 'Nation' and 'people' did not coincide in Italian history:

'One should note that in many languages "national" and "popular" are either synonymous or nearly so (they are in Russian, in German, where *völkisch* has an even more intimate meaning of race, and in the Slavonic languages in general; in France the meaning of "national" already includes a more politically elaborated notion of "popular" because it is related to the concept of "sovereignty": national sovereignty and popular sovereignty have, or had, the same value). In Italy, the term "national" has an ideologically very restricted meaning, and does not in any case coincide with "popular" because in Italy the intellectuals are distant from the people, i.e. from the "nation". They are tied instead to a caste tradition that has never been broken by a strong popular or national political movement from below.'[17]

What is the aim of these meanderings through Italian history and culture, meanderings that make up a substantial proportion of the prison notes as a whole? The answer is that they flow into Gramsci's *political* project. They are readings of Italian cultural history undertaken in order to understand the structural reasons for the lack of any organic national-popular movement in the past and thus in order to work out the preconditions for such a movement in the present. 'Culture' in Gramsci is the sphere in which ideologies are diffused and organized, in which hegemony is constructed and can be broken and reconstructed. An essential part of the process by which the party builds the apparatuses of its social power is the molecular diffusion of a new humanism, an intellectual and moral reformation – in other words a new ideology, a new common sense based on historical materialism. A popular reformation of this kind is what has been lacking in Italian history, and Gramsci's notes on the national-popular reveal the extent to which the cosmopolitan traditions of the Italian intellectuals had impeded the molecular ideological activity by which such a reformation could be brought about:

'The lay forces have failed in their historical task as educators and elaborators of the intellect and the moral awareness of the people-nation. They have been incapable of satisfying the intellectual needs of the people precisely because they have failed to represent a lay culture, because they have not known how to elaborate a modern "humanism" able to reach right to the simplest and most uneducated classes, as was necessary from the national point of view, and because they have been tied to an antiquated world, narrow, abstract, too individualistic or caste-like.'[18]

When the prison notebooks were first published in Italy between 1948 and 1951, there was much talk on the left there about a 'national-popular culture' and the need for the intellectuals to contribute to the production of such a culture. As I have mentioned, this culture was identified with realism, and thus the national-popular slogan was neatly inserted into the discussions on socialist realism and progressive or critical bourgeois realism that were common currency among left literary circles around that period. Yet, though Gramsci's prison notes on literature certainly reveal that his own personal tastes ran to progressive realism, such as the nineteenth century Russian novel, and that he tended to see modernist writing as intellectualistic, coterie art, it was a fundamental misappropriation of the national-popular concept to identify it with a particular type of art in this way. When Gramsci wrote that the model of national-popular literature was constituted by the Greek tragedians, Shakespeare and the great Russian novelists,[19] he did not mean that an Italian national-popular literature would have to resemble those kinds of text. 'National-popular' designates not a cultural content but, as we have seen, the possibility of an alliance of interests and feelings between different social agents which varies according to the structure of each national society. A future Italian national-popular literature, which will result from a socialist transformation of society in which the working class creates its own organic intellectuals, cannot therefore resemble the national-popular literature that developed in the era of bourgeois revolutions elsewhere in Europe. It has clearly been one of the hardest points for Gramsci's interpreters to grasp that he cannot specify the content of a national-popular culture that has not yet formed, but only the social preconditions of its formation. It is, as he points out, an idealist error to think that a national-popular culture will resemble any hitherto existing cultural style, because those past styles have all been the product of social formations in which culture has been stratified into high and low and dominated by specialist intellectuals without organic links with the broad popular masses. 'Popular culture' has thus been constructed as the culture of the dominated classes in antithesis to 'artistic culture', a division that is perpetuated and reproduced daily by capitalist control of the organs of both high and popular culture. The theoretical break Gramsci made with his contemporaries in Marxist cultural theory was to think of a whole cultural formation or cultural space as a unity in which to intervene. As he points out, discussing the question of how to create a new literature:

> 'The most common prejudice is this: that the new literature should be identified with an artistic school of intellectual origin, as was the case with Futurism. The premiss of the new literature can only be historical-political, popular: it must work towards the elaboration of what already exists, whether polemically or in other ways does not matter. What matters is that it sink its roots in the subsoil of popular culture as it is, with its tastes, its tendencies etc., with its moral and intellectual world, albeit backward and conventional.'[20]

The formation of a national-popular culture in Italy would mean confronting and overcoming the same obstacles (dialects, folklore, local particularisms) as the formation of a national language. Because of this, what Gramsci says about language gives us the clearest example of how he conceptualized cultural change as a whole. In the prison notebooks, parallels are implicitly established between a series of dominant-subordinate couplings: language-dialects, philosophy-common sense (or folklore), high culture-popular culture, intellectuals-people, party-masses. The point in each case is not to impose the former on the latter but to construct an educative alliance between them ('Every relationship of "hegemony" is necessarily an educational relationship'[21]) so that one establishes an 'organic unity between theory and practice, between intellectual strata and popular masses, between rulers and ruled' which constitutes democratic centralism.[22] The spreading of a national language is the paradigm for all these other relationships:

> 'Since the process of formation, spread and development of a unified national language occurs through a whole complex of molecular processes, it helps to be aware of the entire process as a whole in order to be able to intervene actively in it with the best possible results. One need not consider this intervention as "decisive" and imagine that the ends proposed will all be reached in detail, i.e. that one will obtain a *specific* unified language. One will obtain *a unified language*, if it is a necessity, and the organized intervention will speed up the already existing processes. What this language will be, one cannot foresee or establish: in any case, if the intervention is "rational", it will be organically tied to tradition, and this is of no small importance in the economy of the culture.'[23]

As well as being a paradigm for the other hegemonic relationships, language is also their social medium. Thus what Gramsci is talking about here is a process of constructing ideological hegemony among a wide range of social strata. Just as, at present, 'the national-popular mass is excluded from learning the educated language, since the highest level of the ruling class, which traditionally speaks standard Italian, passes it on from generation to generation',[24] so the popular masses are excluded from high culture and '"official" conceptions of the world' and possess instead the unelaborated and unsystematic conceptions of folklore and common sense. Hence in order to be hegemonized, these strata must be addressed through a medium adapted to their different cultural positions. There will not, for instance, be a single party newspaper but a whole party press whose various organs can adapt their tone and content to different readerships.

'The unitary national elaboration of a homogeneous collective consciousness demands a wide range of conditions and initiatives. Diffusion from a homogeneous centre of a homogeneous way of thinking
and acting is the principal condition, but it must not and cannot be the
only one. A very common error is that of thinking that every social
stratum elaborates its consciousness and its culture in the same way,
with the same methods, namely the methods of the professional
intellectuals. . . . The ability of the professional intellectual adroitly to
combine induction and deduction . . . is not something given to
ordinary common sense. This is why the premiss of "organic diffusion
from a homogeneous centre of a homogeneous way of thinking and
acting" is not enough. When a ray of light passes through different
prisms, it is refracted differently: if you want the same refraction, you
need to make a whole series of rectifications of each prism.'[25]

In brief, then, there is no contradiction between the cultural aspects of
the national-popular concept and the political meaning it possesses. The
cultural and ideological terrains are merely sites on which the work of
political organization and change is carried out. In each case, what is at stake
in the national-popular concept is the construction of hegemony involving
the building of class alliances under the leadership of a unitary centre in
order to form a collective will which can disarticulate an existing hegemonic
bloc and establish a new social order in its place. In both cases, Gramsci's
analyses arise from an assessment of the bourgeoisie's failure to establish
itself in Italy as a 'national' class, in a Jacobin sense, and of the proletariat's
need to become a 'national' class instead. He had already voiced this
argument in an article of 1919 ('Historically the bourgeois class is already
dead . . . Today the "national" class is the proletariat.[26]) He repeated it in
the notebooks in terms of proletarian hegemony:

'The Italian people are the people with the greatest "national" interest
in a modern form of cosmopolitanism [i.e. socialist internationalism].
Not only the worker but also the peasant, especially the southern
peasant.'[27]

Nonetheless, the cultural ramifications of the national-popular concept
modify the way it looks as a whole. First, the fact that Gramsci elaborated the
concept in relation to a long-standing historical lack, a profound absence in
Italian culture as it had developed since the middle ages (the 'non-national-
popular') suggests that he saw it as more than a tactic for winning power
within the specific historical conditions of fascism. As he argues at one place
in the notebooks, distinguishing political from cultural change, 'cultural
transformations . . . are slow and gradual, because whereas passion [i.e.
politics] is impulsive, culture is the product of a complex elaboration.'[28] In

this sense, a real deepening of the concept takes place in the notebooks in relation to the way it appears in the political writings on class alliances in the two years before Gramsci's arrest, and this deepening can be seen as extending also to other concepts related to the national-popular, such as hegemony and war of position. A national-popular alliance, a war of position, are not merely a strategy against fascism in Italian conditions but are the only form possible of struggle in the West under normal conditions. Secondly, the way in which he conceives of the diffusion of a language (paradigmatic for and immanent in all hegemonic relations) as the diffusion from a centre of a unitary collective will, implies that the national-popular concept does not depart in Gramsci's hands from a centralist conception of the party. It is not, in other words, a concept identifiable with liberal-democratic pluralism, however much it involves a plurality of different class interests of an economic-corporate type. Thirdly, the concept is intimately bound up with ideology, with the erosion of existing ideologies and the construction of a broadly articulated ideological front adapted prismatically to a number of different social strata and groups. Gramsci's conception of Marxism as an elaborately articulated ideology which, at a popular level, can constitute a new and superior common sense able to eradicate and defeat the popular sedimentations of earlier ideologies (superstition, religious worship and so forth) is central to his own elaboration of the national-popular concept.

5

With these cultural dimensions, then, the national-popular concept clearly developed beyond the immediate conjunctural considerations from which it had originated in 1924–26, where it was linked to the Comintern tactic of the united front with the socialists (1921–26), and beyond the political expedient of inter-class and inter-party alliances as a temporary anti-fascist strategy – the Popular Front line of 1935, to which it has often been reductively and polemically assimilated. It became a *historical* strategy, dependent both on the historic absence in Italy of a revolution from below, on a specifically Italian economic and social structure with special disequilibria (combining advanced and third world characteristics, for example) and also on the development of capitalist societies in the West generally, as Gramsci witnessed them being transformed by American forms of social and economic management and elaborating extensive ideological resistances.

Nor is it hard to see why, at a general level, the concept retains its validity. It recognizes the specificity of national conditions and traditions. It valorizes civil society as a key site of struggle. It emphasises the role of ideological reorganization and struggle. It identifies struggles common to more than one social class, fraction or group which can be strategically linked together. It recognizes that different social elements can, and do, act in terms not only of economic or ideological self-interest but also in terms of shared interests. Yet it also leaves a number of problematical questions very much open. By what means does one initially win the consent of other forces and movements? How can what Gramsci called the economic-corporate interests of a class or social group then be transcended in a higher collective will? How can this will, once established, be secured and prevented from disintegrating back into competing sectoral interests? For Gramsci these problems were, after 1926, posed largely in theory, and they tended to be resolved in the notebooks within the formula of party centralism and the belief in the transitional nature of any form of interclassist alliance: in other words within a still essentially Leninist perspective of the single party and the replacement of parliament by soviets.

At a practical level, however, these problems were encountered by the PCI at the end of the war. When fascism broke up in the civil war of 1943–45, the PCI leadership, as is well known, adopted the line not of frontal assault but of a war of position, securing alliances with the other anti-fascist parties, including the Christian Democrats, first in the Committees of National Liberation and subsequently in the Constituent Assembly. Palmiro Togliatti, the architect of this strategy, was not only interpreting Moscow's directives but also realistically assessing the situation in an Italy semi-occupied by American forces and with a still numerically weak proletariat. In the summer of 1944, anticipating the insurrections in the major cities which brought the Resistance to its climax, Togliatti issued the directive: 'The insurrection we want must be not that of a party or only a part of the anti-fascist front, but of all the people, of all the nation.' He added that the Communists were to be 'a vanguard force in the preparation of the struggle and in its leadership.'[29] In reality, the PCI did not establish hegemony over its political and social allies. The alliance was unable to prevent, and very likely helped to bring about, the regrouping of bourgeois hegemony under the political leadership of the Christian Democrats. For the DC used the period of coalition government in the Constituent Assembly to extend its influence and organization among a wide range of social groups (peasant farmers, factory workers, housewives and working women) to such an extent that, by 1947–48, it could with American financial and propaganda aid split the trade union movement, shed the two left parties – the Communists and the Socialists (PSI) – and mobilize mass consent for a reconstruction of monopoly capitalism.

The crucial problem of the national-popular in this practical instance lies in this: that there is often a narrow distinction between class alliances that are effectively hegemonic for the working class, class alliances that are merely federative groupings around particular issues or at particular times (for instance elections), and class alliances that can be tipped the other way and reorganized under the hegemony of the bourgeosie. The PCI in the

1944–48 period not only conceded too much to its alliance partners in terms of the restoration of the old economic and political infrastructures and the maintenance of fascist personnel, notably in the police and militia. It also failed to radiate a collective will of a genuinely oppositional type into the rank and file at a time when the relations of forces were regrouping to the right, and it thus ended up excluded from the executive in 1947 and defeated at the polls in 1948.

That these practices were not simple realizations of Gramsci's theories but political choices overdetermined by all sorts of strategic choices need not be spelt out. Gramsci had not only stressed, as we saw, the essentially transitional nature of the constituent assembly under proletarian leadership but he had also emphasized that the assembly was to have been a site of struggle against 'all projects of peaceful reform, demonstrating to the Italian working class how the only possible solution in Italy resides in the proletarian revolution'.[30] Nevertheless, the questions of when a class alliance contains or does not contain a collective will and of when it lays itself open to reorganization under bourgeois hegemony were posed starkly by the Italian Communists' practical development of Gramsci's theories. And they remain of great actuality in the West today.

Notes

1. Alberto Asor Rosa, *Scrittori e popolo* (1965), Rome, Savelli, 1979, p. 222.
2. *Ibid.*, p. 221.
3. See Franco Fortini, 'Nazional-popolare, 1959' in *L'ospite ingrato*, Bari, De Donato, 1966, p. 68.
4. *The British Road to Socialism*, 5th edition, Communist Party of Great Britain, 1978, p. 17. Work in the area of the 'popular-democratic' includes the essays by Bob Jessop and Stuart Hall in Alan Hunt (ed.), *Marxism and Democracy*, London, Lawrence and Wishart, 1980; Roger Simon's chapter on 'National-popular' in *Gramsci's Political Thought*, London, Lawrence and Wishart, 1982; Ernesto Laclau, *Politics and Ideology in Marxist Theory*, London, NLB, 1977, chapters 3 and 4; John Urry, *The Anatomy of Capitalist Societies*, London, Macmillan, 1981, chapter 9.
5. V. I. Lenin, *'Left-Wing' Communism, An Infantile Disorder* (1920), Peking, Foreign Languages Press, 1975, pp. 95–96.
6. Antonio Gramsci, *Selections from Political Writings (1921–1926)*, translated and edited by Quintin Hoare, London, Lawrence and Wishart, 1978, p. 400.
7. *Ibid.*, p. 406.
8. *Ibid.*, p. 409.
9. *Ibid.*, p. 410.
10. Gramsci, *Selections from the Prison Notebooks*, edited and translated by Quintin Hoare and Geoffrey Nowell Smith, Lawrence and Wishart, London, 1971, p. 132.
11. Gramsci, *Quaderni del carcere*, ed. Valentino Gerratana, Turin, Einaudi, 1975, pp. 2113–20.
12. *Ibid.*, p. 2114.
13. *Ibid.*, p. 362.
14. *Ibid.*, p. 2110: 'the traditional literary dualism between people and nation'.
15. *Ibid.*, p. 652.
16. *Ibid.*, p. 648.
17. *Ibid.*, p. 2116.

18. *Ibid.*, pp. 2118–19.
19. *Ibid.*, pp. 1137 and 1934.
20. *Ibid.*, p. 1822.
21. *Prison Notebooks*, p. 350.
22. *Ibid.*, p. 190.
23. *Quaderni*, pp. 2345–46.
24. *Ibid.*, p. 2349.
25. *Ibid.*, pp. 2267–68.
26. Gramsci, *L'Ordine Nuovo (1919–1920)*, Turin, Einaudi, 1954, p. 278.
27. *Quaderni*, p. 1988.
28. *Ibid.*, p. 2269.
29. The text, dated 6 June 1944, is reproduced in Paolo Spriano, *Storia del Partio Comunista Italiano* Vol. V, *La Resistenza, Togliatti e il partito nuovo*, Turin, Einaudi, 1975, p. 366.
30. *Prison Notebooks*, p. xci: the statement is from Athos Lisa's report of his discussion with Gramsci in 1930.

Iain Chambers and Lidia Curti

A VOLATILE ALLIANCE:
Culture, Popular Culture and
the Italian Left

Fiat, Indesit, Olivetti, Zanussi, Pirelli, Lambretta: the international resonance of
these trade names speaks the confident tones of Italy's post-war 'economic
miracle'. In addition to the traditional exports of stylish clothes, luxury cars
and wine, they connote an image of Italianness in British popular culture. In
this article, we propose to step to the other side of that exchange, to examine
Italian popular culture since the war and, in particular, to follow the
changing political responses of the major party of the left, the Italian
Communist Party (PCI), to developments within popular culture. We can
perhaps best begin unravelling some of this particular history by turning
back to the immediate post-war period and the PCI's attitude to a new
journal, *Il Politecnico*.

The Affair of 'Il Politecnico'

During the summer of 1945, in a Milan of rubble and mud, Elio Vittorini and
some colleagues were preparing a weekly journal of cultural agitation which
would provide information and education for workers and anti-fascist
intellectuals. Although aware that Europe was 'no longer the heart of
history', *Il Politecnico* promised to import currents of contemporary culture
against which fascism had previously inoculated Italian society. The poetry
of Eluard, Eliot and Sanders, the prose of Babel, Hemingway and Gide, the
aesthetic ideas and works of the Bauhaus, the frescoes of Diego Rivera and
the existentialism of Sartre and Merleau-Ponty were supposed to release
blocked energies and stimulate a new start for national life. 'Culture must
participate in the regeneration of Italian society,' begins one of Vittorini's
notes about the planned publication. In the aftermath of fascism, the war
and the Resistance, *Il Politecnico* was committed to overthrowing the traditional version of the national culture and the image of the 'man of letters'
associated with it. According to its fourth issue, the journal was 'not an
organ of diffusion for a culture already formed but a working instrument for
a culture in the making.'

No doubt this radical impatience may have led the *Politecnico* group to
glide over certain political contradictions, but the heated polemic that arose

between them and the PCI – despite Vittorini and several of the others being party members – revealed something more momentous. In a disarmingly frank account of the affair written in 1953, Franco Fortini argued that the issue at the heart of the PCI's criticism was 'the relation between cultural activity (or authority) and political activity (or authority).'[1] Palmiro Togliatti, the leader of the party, accused *Il Politecnico* of an 'abstract search for the new, the diverse, the surprising', and it was made clear that a journal spreading uncertainty and bewilderment among the 'comrades of the base' would not be welcomed. The PCI's line during these years was clearly expressed in its own journal *La Rinascita*, which repeatedly advised writers and artists on appropriate themes and treatment and called for 'art which is precise and historically definable as popular and progressive.' But culture had to be seen within a wider field of priorities defined by the party – first there were the political and economic questions to be faced, and only later art and ideology. The PCI's irritation with *Il Politecnico* was provoked by the journal's 'irresponsible' reversal of these priorities. It also revealed the party's stubborn teleological faith that political and economic progress would lead directly to beneficial changes in the subordinate spheres of art and culture.

The PCI's claim to legislate for the writer and intellectual was incompatible with the experimental initiatives and novel forms of *Il Politecnico*. Vittorini's argument that the journal had to be autonomous of both major left-wing parties (the PCI and the Italian Socialist Party) was not tolerated, and *Il Politecnico* closed in 1947. Just as the PCI provided certitude for its cadres in the political sphere, so it considered itself in the front line in exerting ideological discipline on cultural questions. In politics, immediate considerations and the search for an 'Italian road to socialism' led to caution and the abandonment of blunt, polarising positions. In the arts, similarly, an unambiguous and progressive realism was expected, not the disorientating flak of the avant-garde. (The party's demands for discipline became more rigid with the break-up of the anti-fascist coalition government in 1947 and the onslaught of the Cold War.) Looking back on the short, tempestuous existence of *Il Politecnico*, Fortini perceived that it had brought to light a crucial issue: 'the problem of the position of modern marxism', which translated into practical language meant 'the relationship between cultural action and political parties, between a culture of "the left" and the Communist Party.'[2]

National culture, the two Italies and localism

Il Politecnico's ideas for a new cultural-political strategy predated the publication in Italy of Antonio Gramsci's writings – these appeared in six volumes between 1948 and 1951.[3] During his imprisonment by the fascists from 1926 until his death eleven years later, the Communist leader had written at length on the profound interchange between culture and politics in the modern state. Civil society, he argued, has tended to become the privileged site for the exercise and organisation of the state's political power by a particular historical bloc – a process he referred to as hegemony. Under normal circumstances the state acts more as a persuasive educator than as a coercive agent. Political society is diffused through the capillaries of the far more opaque body of civil society, through the pedagogic relations of family, school, religion, trade unions and political parties. Through these are formed the potent, apparently natural layers of common sense.

Central to Gramsci's picture of Italian culture as a complex material and political reality, understood in terms of the themes of civil society and hegemony, was his conceptualisation of the figure and role of the intellectual. He noted the absence of real cultural unity – a problem tied to the historical foundations of the Italian nation state and the late formation of national-popular unity – and he also perceived that in Italian culture the term 'national' operated with a restricted meaning that did not coincide with the idea of 'popular'. The 'national' had remained the prisoner of the 'bookish culture' of a caste of intellectuals who were not 'an articulation, with organic functions, of the people.' Popular reading habits – sentimental tales, detective stories, historical mysteries and so forth – were mainly catered for by foreign writers 'because the indigenous intellectual element is more foreign than the foreigners when confronted by the people-nation.'[4] The separation of Italian intellectuals from the daily life of the nation and their failure to develop a modern humanism testified to the persistence of a traditional philosophy at the expense of a democratic one. Cultural unity, Gramsci emphasised, was restricted to an extremely shallow stratum of the population – the popular masses had remained outside the narrow intellectual tradition, and would not have cared even if they had known of its existence. For him, as David Forgacs shows in his article, the 'national-popular culture' indicated more an absence than an existing reality. The concept prefigured a *future* political reality constructed through a new type of hegemony – that's why *Il Politecnico*'s cultural initiative in attempting 'to speak politically without being "political"' (Fortini) was so significant. And it is also why the PCI's reaction, confusing the possibilities of an organic cultural politics in the future with the party's more immediate concerns, was a miscalculation.

During the 1920s and '30s, fascism had sought to construct a new sense of 'popular culture' around the *Dopolavoro*. This was a national network of sports associations, clubs and leisure institutions (often incorporating the older workers' clubs) which backed up in a more insinuating way the spectacular manifestations of fascist culture – the national cinema, mass party rallies, air races and so on.[5] This dramatic illustration, along with

Gramsci's reflections, underlined the importance of rejecting the traditional liberal distinction between the state and the rest of social activity. To move beyond that narrow interpretation of politics meant confronting a wider range of social experiences and institutions. In particular, it meant engaging with the ubiquitous reality of Italian popular religion, with Catholicism.

Italian Catholicism has developed ideological links to civil society, firmly based in daily life, which have fostered harmony between the popular classes and the dominant social bloc. But Gramsci also pointed out its inability to develop fully an articulate popular culture able to occupy the vast area ignored by an élite lay culture. Nevertheless, he recognised its fundamental strength in the Italian way of life and referred to the local priest as an organic intellectual of the traditional kind. Naturally, the ideological hold of the Church is affected by other cultural divisions – it is generally weakest in the urban, industrial north and strongest among the peasantry of southern Italy. But even as a residual formation, its grip on education and the popular arts, on the family and the state, and on morality and cultural mores remains remarkably firm. Commonsense responses to everyday experiences are still largely woven out of a Catholic repertoire – village festivals in the agricultural calendar, urban street celebrations and saints' days, propaganda against abortion and divorce, the top-selling magazine *La Famiglia Cristiana*, even the media image of the present Pope. Catholicism remains particularly close to women. It offers their private and public lives, and the sexual division of social roles, a potent rationale that is echoed elsewhere in the public domain.[6]

In the political sphere, Catholicism has never represented a homogeneous bloc: its multiple institutional forms have been traversed by a series of civic currents. The experiences of fascism, the Resistance, the Committees for National Liberation and the anti-fascist coalition government had revealed the possibility of a national-popular alliance to forces on the left – they were careful to distinguish between the 'Catholic masses' and their leadership. These hopes were dashed by the 'betrayal' of anti-fascist unity. With the backing of the massive loans of the US Marshall Plan and the co-operation of the managers of Italy's capitalist reconstruction, the Christian Democrats were established as the dominant political force that would organise the post-war social settlement and shape the young Republic. Nevertheless, the Catholic question remained a major consideration for the secular bloc headed by the PCI. After the iron orthodoxies of the 1950s and Cold War isolation, the growth of the PCI's vote in the next two decades, complemented by a 'politics of tension' (bombings, rumours of impending coups), and the bloody lesson of the military destruction of the Allende government in Chile in 1973, provoked a new urgency in the search for a popular alliance with elements and groups in the Catholic area. This was the famous 'historical compromise'. It was to provoke major difficulties within the PCI as the leadership sought to convince its fiercely secular working class base of the necessity for such a strategy. Catholicism is still widely identified with Christian Democratic power and the undergrowth of government – corruption, patronage and financial scandals.

The possibility of forging a national-popular unity is complicated by other factors than the uneasy relationship between the powerful cultural blocs led by Christian Democracy and the secular left. The slow and late development of a national political and cultural formation (in comparison with France or Britain, for example), combined with the relative youth of the post-war republic, means that the state often intervenes directly in the cultural apparatuses – in the universities, in public broadcasting, in the press. Such elements, together with an uninterrupted thirty-five years of DC power and the consequent opposition it has generated, have produced a public culture generally far more politicised than elsewhere in western Europe. But the struggle over political and cultural powers is all the more acute due to the fragmentary realities that exist behind the facades of the major blocs. The apparently intractable divisions of geography, language, localism and uneven development, persistently interrogate any project for a national-popular culture.

Even today, the contrast between the world of the agricultural south (the *Mezzogiorno*) and the industrialised rhythms of the urban north remains stark. The south is still economically, politically and culturally so subordinated to the north that, according to Umberto Cerroni, national unity seems more a 'diplomatic collage' than an 'organic operation'. Since the war there have been half-hearted attempts to bring the *Mezzogiorno* more closely into the national orbit by introducing industrial plant and organisation. Even when northern capital has overcome its aversion to moving south, the scheme has had little success. Its promoters – with the left led by the PCI prominent among them – have tended to assume that progressive consequences would follow industrialisation and the expansion of an industrial proletariat, no matter what the actual local conditions.[7] Agriculture has remained largely untouched by new capital; local commerce and small industry receive little official recognition. Instead, 'cathedrals in the desert' modelled on Fiat's Mirafiori plant at Turin have dominated the imagination of planners and politicians – the Italsider steel works in Naples and Taranto (now threatened with closure), the Alfa-Sud car plant just outside Naples, major chemical plants in Sicily and Sardinia. Despite this investment, the position has not altered substantially since 1953, when Milan was the richest province in Italy and the poorest was Agrigento, at the opposite geographical extreme in Sicily. Throughout these thirty years the south's major product remained labour – during the 1950s there was a massive haemorrhage of male workers migrating to the European industrial belt of northern Italy, Switzerland and Germany.

Beneath this dramatic north/south split, other fragmenting strands of regionalism and localism interweave within Italian popular culture. One of the most striking is the persistence of dialect. This has been helped by the geographical barriers of a mountainous environment, but results primarily from the prolonged existence of different economies, administrative rhythms and cultural patterns long after the territorial unification of 1870. In 1955 the habitual use of standard Italian rather than a local dialect was restricted to around eighteen per cent of the population. Twenty years on, after the impact of television, the spread of compulsory schooling (especially in the south) and the increasing urbanisation of social life, Italian was no longer a minority language. But such dialects as Neapolitan, Sardo, Venetian and Milanese remain both a part of everyday linguistic competence and the historical repositories of local cultures. They represent a double-edged inheritence, embodying conservatism and myopic barriers as well as survival and resistance. The relation of a national language to subordinate dialects is not, as Gramsci pointed out, merely a linguistic question. Examined in the light of existing economic and cultural conditions, Gramsci concluded that particular linguistic dominations and the problem of the national language was best studied in relation to the formation of the intellectuals and the hegemonic culture they represent.[8] In a similar vein, the historian Carlo Ginzburg has recently argued that the slow but irrefutable victory of a written culture over an oral one 'has been above all a victory of abstraction over the empirical. In the possibility of freedom from particular situations there lies the root of the connections that have always inextricably linked writing and power'.[9] Writing, power, the dialect, the peculiarities of the traditional intellectuals' culture, the oscillating tensions between national and local popular cultures: these are the turbulent co-ordinates to be considered in any understanding of Italian literate culture.

There are more than seventy daily newspapers in Italy today. Most are local or regional, and only the *Corriere della Sera* sells more than half a million copies. In 1978 total sales of daily papers were less than five million copies. That represents one for every eleven inhabitants, the same ratio as in 1920 when illiteracy was far higher and the population substantially smaller.[10] In Italy's politicised popular culture, many of the national dailies are vehicles for the major political parties – *L'Unità* for the PCI, *L'Avanti* for the Socialist Party and *Il Popolo* for the Christian Democrats. Many politicians are therefore also journalists, regularly writing articles, editorials and comments for the press.

Although papers like *Il Mattino* in Naples and *Il Resto del Carlino* in Bologna are well established and command a large local readership, a substantial reading public for books and periodicals has only been formed in the post-war period. By the 1950s the rate of illiteracy among adults was down to less than ten per cent, and corner newsagents stocked 'serious' books as well as magazines, comics, photo-romances and thrillers. In April 1965 the publishers Mondadori began to issue their immensely successful Oscar series. These retailed at 350 Lire a volume, and included titles by Sartre, Borges, Nietzsche, Neruda and Eco. By the end of the decade more than seventy per cent of them were being sold by newsagents. Meanwhile, though, it seemed to escape the notice of the intellectuals that the revival of Italian publishing, led by Einaudi, Mondadori and Feltrinelli, and the spread of the reading habit, were also part of the cultural industry and mass media boom they so much lamented. The attention of the intellectuals was now focussed fearfully on another contemporary drama: the advent of television.

Popular television

Lascia o raddoppia? – 'Leave it or double it?' – was a quiz programme which in 1955 turned Italy into a nation of television viewers overnight. In small towns and villages every Thursday night, people crowded into bars owning a television, into the few houses blessed with a set, and into the local cinemas which interrupted the evening's film for an hour – and inevitably attracted the largest audience of the week. The programme imported the American formula of *The 64,000 Dollar Question* and was presented by the Italo-American Mike Bongiorno. In 1961 Umberto Eco wrote a rather apocalyptic article analysing the Bongiorno phenomenon as the stereotype of the national *average* man, the affirmation of mediocrity and the reduction of superman to everyman. 'The spectator sees glorified and officially conferred with national authority the portrait of his own limits.'[11] Mike was happily ignorant and anti-intellectual, he had a petty-bourgeois sense of money and social convention, he spoke a very basic Italian full of linguistic and cultural errors, he was clumsy and oblivious of irony, ambiguity and the tragic dimension of life. In the provincial Italy of the '50s, gasping for breath as it caught up with a newly discovered consumerism, *Lascia o raddoppia*'s five million Lire prizes offered a magical resolution of the real antagonisms in Italian society. Mike Bongiorno promised to transport the contestants – and, vicariously, the viewers – out of a narrow past and towards an imagined but almost tangible prosperity.

Italian television began in 1954 with 88,000 subscribers. Within a decade this number had increased to five million and by 1978 to over twelve million, covering over seventy per cent of families evenly across the country. (The true figures are almost certainly higher: paying the television licence is not a popular habit.) The history of Italian state broadcasting is studded with abrupt changes and dramatic transformations. In its early years, management of the RAI was firmly and unashamedly in the hands of the Christian Democrats – F. Guala, director between 1954 and 1956, referred directly to the Vatican for moral guidance on what to broadcast. (After leaving, he became a Trappist monk.) Such absolute control by a single political-Catholic organisation contrasts strongly with the situation today. The struggle to break the Christian Democrats' monopoly of the RAI and to establish more democratic and secular control came to a head in the mid-1970s after years of pressure from the opposition parties and the unions. First, in 1975, a reform law established a more open constitution for broadcasting. But then within a year this was followed by an unexpected turn of events, when a remarkable ruling by the Constitutional Court in practice allowed a free hand to private initiatives in the field of public broadcasting. So by the end of the decade there were not only three state channels and an elaborate political system for partitioning positions within the RAI (with the PCI represented on many of its official bodies, particularly in the locally orientated third channel introduced in 1979.) There were also 180 private networks, often pumping out pornographic films and strip-tease. This explosion of private broadcasting helped to break the strangle-hold of the Christian Democrats, but it has also caused headaches for the left. They have frequently found themselves caught between the ambiguous rhetoric of a locally based populism and pressing commercial imperatives – for all Italian broadcasting, including the RAI, is a primary medium for advertising.

Italian television is relied upon for information far more than any other medium and to a greater extent than in other European countries. While only a fifth of the adult population regularly reads a newspaper, at least twenty five million viewers watch three quarters of an hour's news every evening. It has thus became 'the most powerful form of consensus organisa-tion in Italy.'[12] The *telegiornale* of the RAI's two channels was also affected by the reforms of the mid-seventies. Under the direction of Andrea Barbato, for example, there was a major renovation of *Rete 2*'s current affairs and news programmes. Its main bulletin *TG2 – Spazio Aperto* introduced a more informal, flexible and analytical presentation of the news, incorporating live studio debates and coverage of cultural topics like music, art and cinema. In contrast to the twenty million viewers for the first channel's news, *TG2* attracted figures of about five million – an audience characterised by a 1979 survey as left-wing and more interested in interpretation than 'facts'. Even so, the experiment lasted only a few years. Barbato was dismissed for excessive independence and the latitude of those journalists who did not resign in protest was dramatically curtailed. The political climate had changed. A Communist-Catholic alliance seemed ever less probable and Bettino Craxi's Socialist Party was making a ruthless drive for the political centre. The dwindling of the distinction between the first and second channels was further accentuated as the RAI then closed ranks against the acute compe-tition of the private networks.

The 1976 liberalisation of broadcasting had opened up the possibility of television (and radio) stations acting as vivid channels for local cultures and political currents and extending direct public involvement at regional, city and urban district levels. A private station like *Canale 21* in Naples was soon able to build up an audience of five million viewers with its brand of Neapolitan populism. The predictable schedule of Hollywood movies and American telefilms was punctuated with its own productions featuring local sport, music and theatre (the Neapolitan *sceneggiata*), quizzes and phone-in programmes, political commentary (often ill-disguised attacks on the Communist town administration) and an attempt at a local news desk. In 1979 its popular support was so strong that it was able to contest the cultural policy of the local PCI and the *Festa dell'Unità* organised each summer in the town park. Under the provocative slogan 'For a Naples that is ours', *Canale 21* organised its own street festival. This brought the city to a halt as thousands of families flooded into the streets to witness the spectacle. Today, however, *Canale 21* is threatened with closure. It is in deep financial crisis as it struggles to hang onto the remnants of this popular audience in the face of competition from three northern based networks. Each of these has bought local stations in all areas of the country and linked them together to compete directly with the RAI network. This has tended to further squeeze local currents out of the frame, leaving only the RAI's third channel to take timid steps towards localism. A strategy of centralised financing and programmed cultural uniformity has largely glossed over local differences and segmented tastes. It is *Dallas* and *Colombo*, not the tough knots of localism, that command screen time.

Left Intellectuals and 'Cultura di Massa'

For the Italian left – and, as Eco's response to Mike Bongiorno suggests, for left intellectuals in particular – the reconstruction of popular leisure by television and the 'culture industry' was profoundly disquieting. Behind the denunciations of their capitalist forms, it is possible to detect deeper motives connected with the wider cultural formation of the Italian intellectual and what this implies for an 'organic' relation to contemporary popular culture. To understand these, however, it is necessary first to consider the transformation of the figure of the left intellectual during the socio-political upheavals of the 1960s.

In this period, the factory became for Italians not only a model for industrial and civil progress, but also the focus of much left-wing intellectual activity. After more than a decade of quiescence, major industrial working-class struggles organised around the point of production broke out in 1962. These intensified throughout the decade and led to demands and tactics which outstripped the organization and imagination of the unions and the

PCI – factory occupations, the blocking of roads and railways, interventions in the local area and involvement in non-factory issues such as housing and prices. This offensive culminated in the wave of militancy and strikes known as the 'hot autumn' of 1969. At the same time, the influential inquiries into the contemporary labour process pioneered by Raniero Panzieri, the expulsion from the PCI of the critical intellectuals around the journal *il Manifesto* and the explosion of the student movement in the universities in 1968 combined to produce an Italian New Left. Young intellectuals like Panzieri, Mario Tronti, Alberto Asor Rosa and Adriano Sofri congregated around journals like *Quaderni Rossi*. They perceived in the factory a symbol and the promise of a direct link to the (male) working class.[13] Proposing a return to the concrete realities of working-class politics via a 'return to Marx' (Rossana Rossanda), the proponents of this principled Leninism wanted to construct a militant line in opposition to the 'soft reformism' of the PCI and the trade union federation. The first fruits of this movement were the extra-parliamentary groups – *Potere Operaio, il Manifesto, Lotta Continua, Avanguardia Operaio* – and a startling new sense of intellectual commitment to political culture.

Connected to this movement, the hierarchical structures of academic power within the universities were also heavily contested. But the hermetic world of letters and high culture emerged remarkably unscathed from the fray. New, politically informed directions were taken within it, but its right to dominate the concerns of the academy were rarely challenged. If an alternative culture was proposed, it was almost invariably the world of supposedly genuine popular expression – an archaic rural Italy with its folk customs, the surviving dialects or country and town festivals. Left-wing intellectuals remained impervious to the realities of 'mass culture'. Those who dirtied their hands with it did so the better to criticise it. It was not considered an area of society to be occupied: the 'culture industry' was simply denounced as part of the capitalist plan. This left the northern working class, recently swollen by migration from the rural south, precariously balanced between the lost authenticity of an earlier folk culture and the contemporary poison of urban mass culture. The overwhelmingly negative connotations surrounding the label *cultura di massa* signalled a real weakness in the response of left intellectuals to the important novelties of post-war Italian popular culture. American sociologism and Frankfurt-school cultural pessimism were crossed with Leninism to produce a notion of 'the masses' as the political subjects of the party needing redemption from the contaminating pleasures of capitalism. It was, of course, an extremely patronising idea of how people actually participated in this culture and made some of its substantial aspects their own.

In a round table discussion at a *Festa dell'Unità* in Milan in 1974, the poet, writer and film director Pier Paolo Pasolini provocatively linked the advance of mass culture to the explosive theme of genocide.[14] A completely new and more dangerous form of fascism had appeared, he argued. The mass media had successfully secularised the masses of the centre-south, 'delivering them to the power of the mass media, and through it to the real ideology of power, to the hedonism of consumer power.' A subtle and complex violence was unremittingly extinguishing a subaltern world, colonising it with a false model of conduct and values. This 'occult persuasion' was achieved by the mass media: its victims, in Pasolini's opinion, were less the working class than those on the margins of Italian society: those who had previously lived outside the 'history of bourgeois domination and the bourgeois revolution.' Between the media's promised visions and this reality lay the gap of brutal frustration. A local linguistic and cultural vitality was blocked by a new language, sometimes leading almost to clinical aphasia and a crippling acculturation.

Pasolini's language may have been extreme, even hysterical, and his defence of urban marginals and 'the diverse' found little support, certainly not within the PCI. (Pasolini's openly acknowledged homosexuality would also have been an intolerable scandal for the organised left at the time.) Nevertheless, his fierce attack on the powers of the mass media struck a chord with many intellectuals. So too did his location of a potentially healthy popular culture in the archaic peasant world: an image repeated in Italian cinema right down to the present day.

Such a concern with the south and with marginal groups did however pinpoint a critical blindness in more typical attitudes on the left. Apart from dutiful references to Gramsci's writings on the 'southern question', the realities of life in the *Mezzogiorno* remained generally unexplored: important anthropological and folkloric studies were seldom followed up. The growing lumpen-proletariat on the margins of city life was dismissed as being politically unstable and having pronounced right-wing tendencies. Neither experience could be accommodated by a national politics committed to a 'productivist' perspective on industrial development and proletarian advance, a politics in which the 'progress' of a national culture was assumed to march one step behind. Finding their opposition to the new opium of the people largely ineffectual, left intellectuals were hardly in a frame of mind to tackle the question of how to live *within* the mass culture. That required further dramatic transformations within the political culture of the left itself.

The volume dedicated to post-war Italian culture in *La Storia dell'Italia*, published by Einaudi in 1975, is a striking testimony. Written by Alberto Asor Rosa (no longer associated with the 'workers' autonomy' journals *Quaderni Rossi* and *Classe Operaia*, but now a leading PCI intellectual), it tends to reduce a complex history to a series of limited intellectual debates, largely around the function of literature, and a rather laboured defence of the PCI's cultural policy since 1945. Remarkably, the book fails to mention either the coming of television, the existence of radio, the characteristics of popular film (remember those muscle-bound epics set in antiquity and their baroque successors, the spaghetti westerns), popular reading and fiction, sport, popular music or any of the other daily details of contemporary Italian culture. Here, two aspects clearly emerge: the conservative élitism, right across the political board, in most discussions of 'culture' and, secondly, the contemporary power exercised by Italian intellectuals in constructing social definitions of public life. Politicians, journalists and television programme makers, for example, all consider themselves intellectuals in a way inconceivable within the more pragmatic divisions of Anglo-American societies.

The concept of culture remains firmly bound by the horizons of the classical, humanist education still dominant in Italy.[15] Compulsory schooling ends at the age of fourteen. After that, in both the classical and scientific *liceo*, the study of Latin remains an obligatory part of the syllabus. So, in the classical *liceo*, are Greek, philosophy and the history of Italian letters – the formation of the intellectual is still as a person of letters. This training perhaps helps to explain the tendency to favour systems building and speculative models at the expense of informed description or empirical research into historical contingencies. It certainly contributes to a bias we have already noted: a sense of culture that incorporates both Art and folklore as authentic, but which remains deaf and blind to the insistent complexities of contemporary taste, popularity and cultural consumption.

The paradoxical formation of intellectuals through such a formidably classical education and within a mass-democratic and centralist party like the PCI has meant that Gramsci's desire for a new type of organic intellectual has not been fulfilled. The question that is too seldom asked is whether such 'organic' qualities might have to be developed outside the existing constraints of party organization and intellectual categories of culture. In 1981, at a conference in Florence to launch a volume on culture and power in *La Storia d'Italia*, some leading PCI intellectuals did suggest that the time had come to put aside the concept of the organic intellectual. The political party, they argued, can no longer be considered the source of truth, the 'collective intellectual' in which absolute certainties are deposited. But however persuasive the self-criticism, the suspicion remains that it fails to tackle the fundamental problems – the rather traditional paradigms of intellectual concerns, practices and conduct that still dominate on the left, and the intellectuals' direct participation in an existing consensus, rather than a future one. The problem, no matter what name it eventually carries, has by no means disappeared. On the contrary, the advent of what in Italy is called 'mass culture' (though more usually 'popular culture' in Britain') has merely given it a new intensity.

Pop, Rock, Folk: Searching for the 'Popular'

Sunlit terraces, the sea and a baritone voice – this is the persuasive image of Italian popular song. But in Italy the term *musica popolare* refers exclusively to traditional folk music. A relatively weak commercial infrastructure for the national distribution of records and organisation of popular music tastes helps to explain folk music's survival. However, it has had virtually no effect on commercial popular song. The latter is publicly celebrated each year at the San Remo Festival. The songs – lyrical, sentimental and floridly dramatic – are strictly Tin Pan Alley. While probably no longer attracting the sort of television audience that it did in 1966, when twenty one million (virtually the whole of Italy's adult population) watched it, San Remo remains a major media event. The annual album of Festival entries consistently leaps to the top of the charts.

The impact of the folk tradition has been less musical and commercial than ideological and political. It has been taken up and developed by singers and writers looking for a national authenticity opposed to the contaminations of pop.[16] The tradition of work songs and protest songs was revived in the 1960s by groups like Cantacronache, with whom intellectuals like Fortini and Calvino collaborated, and Nuovo Canzoniere Italiano, who opened up an important space for women's songs. Towards the end of the decade, fanned by broader social confrontations, the tradition was supplemented by the introduction of contemporary political songs composed by writers like Ivan Della Mea, Giovanna Marini and Paolo Pietrangeli. Behind them, and their patronage by the left, were the more vaguely 'committed' singers like Luigi Tenco, Sergio Endrigo and Fabrizio De André who leaned towards the musical and poetic style of the French *chanteurs* (Brel, Ferré, Brassens).

This suggests a paradox in Italian popular music. Although the traditional pop song has superficially assimilated certain international mannerisms – a touch of disco synthesisers, a pinch of funk – it has remained suprisingly immune from the influence of Anglo-American pop. The political tradition, on the other hand, despite its strong national folk roots, has imported a number of foreign influences. The most notable in the 1960s were white American folk and protest music, and especially the songs of Bob Dylan (or at least the pre-1965, pre-electric Dylan.) This impact spawned a generation of singer-songwriters in the early 1970s: Francesco Guccini, Francesco De Gregori and Edoardo Bennato. The striking insularity of Italian pop in the '60s meant that Anglo-American rock could actually be appropriated as a form of cultural opposition – and so the Rolling Stones, Jefferson Airplane and the Doors provided the soundtrack for a 'politics of liberation'. Pietro Ingrao, a leading radical voice in the PCI, has claimed with hindsight:

> 'A music for young people emerged, for young people confronting the problem of sexuality by themselves, who were emancipating them-

selves from the family. We [the PCI] did not regard that phenomenon with aversion, we accepted rock'n'roll.'[17]

This version of the PCI's response to rock music, and to the youth culture of the '60s in general, should be treated with some scepticism – it was far more troubled than Ingrao suggests here. Nevertheless, at the close of the decade, the underground paper *Re Nudo* unhesitatingly hailed the Rolling Stones as revolutionaries and John Lennon as virtually a Marxist-Leninist.

Such eulogies became more rare when American rock shed its political hues in favour of artistic pretensions and the Italian extra-parliamentary left adopted a more ascetic style. The militant critique of everyday capitalism by the Students Movement of 1968 denounced libertarian confusion on cultural questions. Frivolous importations like rock music were incompatible with proletarian values: it was the musical expression of cultural imperialism. Only suitably politicised native groups – Banco del Mutuo Soccorso, Stormy Six – were able to escape these harsh strictures. What was demanded was not rock but a popular style adapted to militant songs and demonstrations. One extra-parliamentary group, Lotta Continua, launched its own record label to promote these contemporary political ballads.

In the early 1970s singers and groups whose political line was suspect were directly challenged. The commodity form of rock was attacked. Under the slogan 'TAKE OVER THE MUSIC' young males from the extra-parliamentary groups stormed stadiums and halls, dismissing tickets or payment. A concert, they argued, is youth property. The music is performed because you go to it, not the other way around. You are a protagonist, not a spectator. Having to pay to be there and meet your comrades is therefore absurd. The police charges and tear gas, the cancelled concerts and tours which ensued removed the presence of the cultural imperialists, even if not commodity alienation. After Lou Reed's concert in Rome was invaded and destroyed in 1975, no major Anglo-American singer or band appeared in Italy for four years. It was a blunt challenge and it raised questions about the nature of the pop concert, and especially about the hierarchical distribution of powers between performer and public. It also began to break down the earlier public/private division between political songs for the demonstration and rock for leisure time.

The last development, the confusion over the boundary between political and leisure space, was directly tied to a realignment in left political culture occurring after 1977. The 'political song' lost its status as it became evident that no one musical genre is intrinsically political. The break-up of far left certainties destroyed the ideological labelling of musical tastes. The result has been a proliferation of support for the most diverse musics: from US country music and blues through jazz to punk, disco and funk. In 1976, the popular singer-songwriter Francesco De Gregori was publicly put 'on trial' during a Milan concert by the political grouping known as the *autonomi*. They demanded to know why De Gregori was not contributing his concert earnings to the Innocenti workers then in struggle. Three years later, in the Stalingrad discotheque in the same city, someone had written on the wall in English: 'REBELS WITHOUT A CAUSE'.

'Women Cannot Be a Consequence of the Revolution' (Carla Lonzi)

When organised feminism began in Italy in the early 1970s, it was a small movement based mainly in Milan and Rome.[18] By the end of the decade, even when its impact was denied, it had transformed the existing political culture of the left. On the surface, this showed in the switch away from the stern, purposeful style of political marches in the 1960s and the introduction of festive colour to these public occasions. More important has been the invasion of the empire of the political by the private and fantasy. An internal and external feminist critique had questioned the significance of the militancy and party discipline of the male left. Refusing a politics that privileged industrial production in every twist and turn of its strategy, feminism produced a critical alternative to the base/superstructure model. As Lea Melandri put it, 'the moment in which the survival of emotions and the materiality of sexual conflicts will enter the expectancies of communism, even the analysis of economic exploitation will be deeply modified.'[18]

Some male comrades, particularly in the extra-parliamentary left, felt wounded by this critique and were further disillusioned by the failure in the 1976 general elections of the far left ticket, Democrazia Proletaria. They tended to become 'loose dogs', dispersing themselves in the amorphousness of the 'Movement', or else dropping completely out of sight into armed struggle. Others in the Movement consciously appropriated much of the repertoire of feminist public spectacle and the style of personal politics when they experienced the full force of metropolitan marginality. Feminists' attempts to produce new politico-cultural languages also brought to light tensions and contradictions with the existing organization of the 'historical left' – principally the PCI. The traditional parties continually tried to subordinate feminism's radical energies by appealing to the wider 'reason of the party' and reminding feminists of their responsibility to civil society in general.

The effects of feminism have by no means been restricted to the narrow world of institutional politics. Feminism has also influenced the institutional practices of the mass media, for example. In the press, a fairly wide range of feminist journals, magazines and papers enjoy a reasonably secure existence – they suffer momentary collapses and financial crises, it is true, but on the whole less than other sectors of the independent press in Italy. *DWF*,

Memoria and *Effe* represent various positions within the historical spectrum of feminism. *Quotidiano Donna* and *Orsaminore* move between feminism and other political areas of the left. Mass circulation journals like the Unione delle Donne Italiane's long-standing *Noi Donne* or the modernist *Grattacielo* address women on news, politics, society fashion and so on. For a while, even the established commercial women's magazines like *Amica* and *Annabella* were refurbished with a feminist veneer.

Although women have done some extremely important work in public broadcasting, the amount has always been small and its existence precarious. *Si dice donna*, a fortnightly television programme administered solely by women, established an audience of six million on the RAI's second channel. The producers themselves criticised the programme for what they saw as its theoreticism, and in 1979 the second series attempted a more popular format in an attempt to draw in a wider female public. Then it disappeared. Meanwhile, the morning radio programme *Noi, voi, loro donne* moves cautiously between coverage of women's civil rights and a critical presentation of feminist positions. It has survived for many years as an important minority voice alongside the more typical morning programmes aimed at housewives. But the fragility of women's position in the media has been most dramatically illustrated by the recent relations between a group of women film makers and the RAI.

In April 1979, this group produced *Processo per Stupro*, an hour-long documentary about a famous rape trial held in Latina. It described the institutional violence embodied in the mechanisms of the law and at the same time showed the complex cultural forces that lay behind it. Alongside the defence lawyers were seen lumpen-proletarian women, relatives of the accused men, whose violent outbursts in court were directed against the rape victim and her feminist supporters. In the words of one of the women who made the film, 'the montage was organised by contradictory, dialectical statements . . . a way to open problems rather than closing them.'[20] Broadcast twice by the RAI, the film created enormous interest and received international recognition with the award of the Prix Italia. It seemed an irreversible step forward for women.

A year later, the same group made a second documentary, again exploring aspects of Italian male sexual conduct. Using a 'candid camera' technique, but avoiding 'offensive' images, *A.A.A. Offresi* documented the relation between a prostitute and her unidentifiable clients. This time there was a widespread outcry and even men on the left publicly expressed their disquiet at the possibility of such a programme being shown. It never was. The film was impounded and the women film makers were subject to public prosecution for intending to corrupt public morals.

Feminist cultural activity is always liable in such ways to the reimposition of existing institutional norms. Nevertheless, moving through the dense fabric of daily life, negotiating Catholicism, the patriarchal family and a cultural resistance that sometimes slips into ugly reaction, it has produced novel and sometimes unexpected effects. One example is the recent history of the Unione delle Donne Italiane, which was founded in 1945 as an autonomous women's organization under the protective wing of the PCI. It championed women's rights in campaigns around divorce and abortion, but at the same time continued to reject the trenchant feminist discourse on sexuality and separatism – which had often been constructed in open polemic against Leninism and what Lea Melandri has called 'red asceticism'. In the late spring of 1982, however, in the wake of major cultural and political upheavals, the UDI finally broke with the PCI. Using their membership cards for the last time, delegates to the XI National Conference in Rome voted to dissolve the organization. Although the Conference's talk of autonomy and separation may already have seemed slightly outdated, it remains an important event. It indicates a will to move beyond the crisis of politics and to experiment with new political practices. Margherita Repetto has expressed this mood: 'Let us try and keep the road open: our history has only just begun.'[21]

The Spectacle of the Contemporary Metropolis

What has been the response of the Italian left to the 'geological anxiety' created by its ideological crisis since the mid-1970s? The climate then was dominated by student unrest, the political organization of the growing ranks of the unemployed and the virulent opposition of these groups to a PCI entertaining the illusion of entering a national government in the near future. In this tense climate, Asor Rosa launched his famous 'two societies' thesis. Abstracting from his earlier 'workerist' positions, he argued that Italian society could be divided between the 'producers' and the 'emarginated' (the unemployed, students, precarious labourers, and others). His model is fundamentally a pathological one. Signs of disorder in the social body are diagnosed according to a monodimensional vision.

This type of analysis has recently been contested by another PCI intellectual, Massimo Cacciari. He has introduced the term 'catastrophic antagonism' to highlight a sense of incompatibility and of break.

> 'Let us call the *left* the on-going criticism of every type of organic teleological dogmatism, of all the forms of mechanical-linear imposition used in representing political and cultural antagonisms. Let us call the *left* that *part* which internally organises itself on the basis of recognising the catastrophic nature of antagonism. But in all this there is the absence of a secure episteme? a lack of any type of anchorage to the philosophy of history or to dualistic sociologies? an absence of the

myth (the Class and the Promise which it embodies)? Negatively, one would be tempted to say that the acute sense of this loss is the left. The left is a *part* of the Benjaminian time of poverty. In this tempo we witness the setting of the Great Politics? It could be – certainly the possibility of a Great Opportunism does not set: a particular attention to the catastrophic, an adaptable programme, a "plastic" capacity.'[22]

Here the 'catastrophic' should not be confused with disaster or with anarchic explosion. It registers Cacciari's recognition in the historical 'long wave' of the dimension of discontinuity, the irruption of abrupt change, the loss of particular ideological anchors, the unstable equations of crisis.

The responses of Asor Rosa and Cacciari to the 'crisis of marxism' are not just distinct. They are actually incompatible and discontinuous. But to what extent does this difference indicate a radical change within the Italian left? The subtleties of Italian politics – including the PCI – and the orthodoxy of much of the left mean that change tends to be sluggish, perspectives slow to adapt. Equally, though, the organised left has had to respond to the accelerating tempo of contemporary uncertainties. An increased involvement in local government after 1975 brought the PCI to control the administrations of significant major towns like Rome and Naples, cities far removed from its traditional 'red belt' base in Emilia Romagna. The progressive shedding of existing 'socialist models' during the 1970s culminated, after the

An absence of myths: 'Even Marx has been repudiated.'
'Nothing is sacred any more.' (*La Repubblica*, 2 March 1983)

military repression of *Solidarnosc* in Poland in 1981, with the PCI leader Enrico Berlinguer declaring that the revolutionary and innovative energies of the 1917 October Revolution had now been exhausted. Western Europe now needed to look to itself to elaborate a new phase of democratic struggle. The attacks by the Movement of 1977 had taken different forms, ranging from the situationist Metropolitan Indians through the disciplined militancy of the *autonomi* to the descent into armed struggle. All these developments left their mark on the party. The impact of feminism has also been profound. And in the broader cultural sphere, the reform of the RAI and the liberalisation of public broadcasting in 1976 have helped to develop an awareness of the need to struggle for the spaces within mass culture, and not just to denounce it. At the same time, a fresh group of intellectuals has emerged within the PCI. Drawing on foreign philosophers like Nietzsche, Benjamin and Husserl, they speak for a marxism that tries to comprehend a new sense of rationality – one founded on a loss of organicity, on fragmentation and the confused drives and desires of metropolitan society.

In this context we can at least begin to talk of a new cultural strategy in the making.[23] It is profoundly urban in tone. What Gramsci called the directive function of the city in a national culture has been spectacularly reasserted, particularly each summer in such PCI administrations as Rome, Naples, Milan and Bologna. Earlier distinctions are reshuffled to produce a collage of local, national and international cultures. So the Clash play a free

Eurocommunism: Enrico Berlinguer discarding Marx in favour of Proust. *(La Repubblica,* 2 March 1983)

concert in Bologna's historic main square, Lindsay Kemp performs beneath the night sky in a Neapolitan castle, giant screens in public gardens and in the Coliseum project Hollywood films through the night. Renato Nicolini, Rome's councillor for culture, provocatively justifies this strategy:

> 'In cultural habits and custom today there no longer exists the possibility of organic interpretations of society or values. On the contrary, there is a confused, contradictory, uneven plurality of wills, cultural expressions, values ... and we must consider it a positive phenomenon.'[23]

Stretching over the summer months (when many cinemas, theatres and restaurants normally close down in Italian cities), these mammoth cultural festivals are all organized and financed by the town administration. (When in the summer of 1982 the Rolling Stones played in Turin and Naples, the price of a ticket, around £6, included access to free camping, free public transport in the city and reduced prices in restaurants and hotels.) The barriers between Culture and mass culture have been breached, at least temporarily. Free or low-priced tickets encourage unexpected meetings between a diversified urban public and a mixture of traditional arts, the avant-garde and popular culture.

The PCI's promotion of these initiatives has, of course, provoked some critical distrust and dismay. The defence of the autonomy of Art or high culture, the fear that it would be contaminated by 'garbage cinema' and

Welcoming the contradictions

'garbage arts' and horror at historic monuments being invaded by a mass public were predictable responses. But within the left there has also been another debate, about what is referred to as the 'ephemeral', in comparison with the production of more stable cultural forms. Often this debate thinly disguises an older, moralistic social commitment in which pleasure was considered something to be indulged privately, once public duties were completed. Even here, however, the terms have been shifted by the acknowledgement of what Berlinguer calls the 'increasing entwinement of structural and superstructural phenomena'. So when Umberto Cerroni attacks the indiscriminate acceptance of the ephemeral and asserts the need for 'a prince against the barbarism of mass society', he is careful to propose a mediation between the directional function of political society, the Gramscian prince-party, and the recovery of individual expression and existence: '. . . a Prince who has a project not with a capital P (after illuministic values) but a project filtered through the actual articulations of society.' To which the urbane Nicolini, emphasising a sense of democracy that abandons instrumentalist approaches and has to be expressed outside totalising structures, replies: 'The Prince is obliged to become a vassal, a subject himself, a Prince without a crown who does not think of being a figure outside history.'[24]

This apparent willingness to embrace the chaotic, fragmentary and contradictory possibilities of contemporary metropolitan culture marks a distinctive change in the perspectives of the Italian left. But the desire for a popular articulation of diverse cultural forces, which could help to make a 'national-popular culture' a real possibility, owes as much to the development of forces outside (and often opposed to) the PCI as to internal shifts. As the exchange between Cerroni and Nicolini over the modern Prince illustrates, the new perspective continues to interrogate deeply the nature of the relation between party and culture. This becomes particularly apparent when the attempt to elaborate a more mature sense of civil hegemony genuinely abandons an instrumentalist approach.

These problems are by no means resolved. But the vitality of recent developments and the changes within the context in which they are debated suggest, if not actual transformation, at least a critical shift in a *part* of political culture and a fuller comprehension of the potentialities of a contemporary Italian popular culture. The significance of such a project had been foreshadowed by Franco Fortini when, discussing the relationship between *Il Politecnico* and the PCI and especially between Vittorini and Togliatti, he had written:

'And then it seems impossible that Vittorini in some of the most passionate parts of *Letters to Togliatti* (when he discusses the revolution that has as its purpose the individual, when he speaks of his hope for an extraordinary revolution, or refuses to play the piper's tune for the revolution or to define the tasks of the revolutionary writer) did not realise that, even in the apparent confusion of his counsel, he was asking not only for a change in the cultural politics of the PC, but also for a new political theory, a new philosophy.'[25]

We would like to thank Catherine Hall, Stuart Hall and Marina Vitale for their criticisms and suggestions.

Notes

1. Franco Fortini, 'Che cosa è stato *Il Politecnico*?' in *Dieci Inverni*, Bari, De Donato, 1973, p. 70. Fortini arrived in Milan in 1945 after his involvement in the short-lived partisan republic of Valdossola. After working with Vittorini on *Il Politecnico*, he contributed to the major cultural journals of the Italian left throughout the next three decades, examining in particular the relation of intellectual 'service' to the problem of ideology and the social organisation of culture. His most significant essays are collected in *Dieci Inverni* op. cit.; *Verifica dei Poteri*, Milan, Il Saggiatore, 1974; and *Questioni di frontiera*, Turin, Einaudi, 1977. Fortini is also a noted poet. The critical essay/autobiography *I cani del Sinai*, prompted by the Six Days War, was transformed into a film by Danièle Huillet and Jean Marie Straub. His essay 'The Writer's Mandate and the end of anti-fascism' (from *Verifica dei Poteri*) was published in *Screen* vol. 15, no. 1, Spring 1974.
2. *Dieci Inverni* p. 69.
3. The critical edition of Gramsci's complete prison writings, fully cross-referenced and indexed, finally appeared as a four volume set in 1975: *Quaderni del carcere*, Turin, Einaudi.
4. *Quaderni* p. 2117.
5. For a detailed account of *Dopolavoro*, see Victoria de Grazia, *Culture of Consent*, Cambridge University Press, 1981.
6. Equally, the image of the mother and the wife, invested with a sacred aura and the authority of the Church, has become a national symbol. On its imposition through fascist ideology and legislation, see Maria Antonietta Macciocchi *La donna 'nera'*, Milan, Feltrinelli, 1976. On its iconography across the spectrum of post-war political discourse, see Adriana Sartogo's book on the female image in Italian political posters, *Le donne al muro*, Rome, Savelli, 1977.
7. In the gap between this frustrated political project and the social margins it attempted to incoporate and supersede, alarming symptoms of a fractured civil society have flourished – above all, the institutionalised criminality of the Sicilian *mafia*, the Neapolitan *camorra* and the Calabrian *'ndragheta*.
8. See *Quaderni* pp. 738–9, p. 1377 and p. 2350.
9. Carlo Ginzburg, *Il formaggio e i vermi*, Torino, Einaudi, 1976, pp. 69–70. (Translated as *The Cheese and the Worms*, London, RKP, 1980.)
10. These statistics are taken from Enzo Golino *La distanza culturale*, Bologna, Capelli, 1980 p. 49 and p. 14.
11. Umberto Eco 'Fenomenologia di Mike Bongiorno' in *Diario Minimo*, Milan, Mondadori, p. 32.
12. A Calabrese and U Volli *Come si vede il telegiornale*, Bari, Laterza, 1980, p. v. Much of the information on television news is taken from this source.
13. One emphasis of this focus was to marginalise yet further the non-industrialised countryside and *Mezzogiorno*.
14. Pasolini's contribution was published in *La Rinascita*, 7 September 1974.
15. This point is made by Enzo Golino in *La distanza culturale*, op. cit.
16. See F. Fabbri 'What kind of music?', in *Popular Music 2*, Cambridge University Press, 1983.

17. Quoted in A. Carrera, *Musica e pubblico giovanile*, Milan, Feltrinalli, 1980, p. 43.
18. There have been women's organisations in existence since 1945 both within the political parties and outside them. Some have been tied to Catholic associations, but more to working-class politics. In the late 1960s, the extreme left groups contained a substantial proportion of women, though the division of roles and the subordination of women's issues to 'politics' and workerism were no less acute here than in the historical parties of the left. Contemporary feminism began in close proximity to some of these extra-parliamentary groups, and sometimes from splits within them.
19. Lea Melandri, *L'infamia originaria*, Milan, L'erba voglio, 1977, p. 82.
20. Quoted in *Effe*, May 1979, p. 52.
21. Margherita Repetto '. . . la nostra storia è appena cominciata. Note sul saggio di S. Rowbotham', in *DWF*, no. 14, Rome, 1980, p. 86.
22. Massimo Cacciari, 'Sinisteritas', in Cacciari et al, *Il concetto di sinistra*, Milan, Bompiani, 1982, p. 19.
23. In Enrico Berlinguer at al, *Il PCI e la cultura di massa*, Rome, Savelli, 1982, p. 55.
24. *ibid* p. 118, p. 126, and p. 122.
25. *Dieci Inverni*, p. 72.

Fernando Ferrara

THE FESTE DE L'UNITÀ

During the years of Fascist rule in the late thirties, many Italian Communist intellectuals became expatriates in the Paris of the Popular Front. There they experienced at first hand the festival organised by *L'Humanité*, the French Communist daily; one of its stands was dedicated to *L'Unità*, the paper of the then clandestine Italian Communist Party (PCI).

On 4 September 1945 some Communist militants, who still remembered the success of that original enterprise and the feats of partisan warfare, assembled in a wood near Mariano Cremonese – not far from Milan – and there organised the first Festival of *L'Unità* (FdU). This was a roughly ritualised, exclusive meeting of devotees whose only aims were to join together in solidarity and celebration and to collect funds for the Communist press. This type of recreational meeting spread rapidly throughout Italy between 1945 and 1948. In *L'albero in piazza* (1975), a brief collection of memories of the origin and development of the FdU, Claudio Bernieri has described these early festivals:

> 'They were not so strongly political as today's FdU's; they were based on going out in the country, sitting on the grass, and eating large amounts of food and drinking huge quantities of wine. Wine-drinking was the most common feature . . . at the end there was a *Comizio* (a political speech).'

The spirit of the *Resistenza* and of class struggle were at the heart of these meetings. Their main aim was to strengthen the ties within the PCI through the unifying ceremonies of eating and drinking together and the final ideological ritual of the *Comizio*. Very soon, however, despite the scepticism of most PCI leaders, the FdU's dropped their somewhat furtive character and grew into an effective instrument of political propaganda. Again according to Bernieri:

> 'That was it, the Festival was simply a *Comizio*, then the password spread: make the Festivals somewhat like the religious festivals of the Holy Patron. The only difference was this: on one side the Procession, on the other the *Comizio*.'

Both the analogy and the opposition are still evident today in rural FdU's, although these features have been obliterated in the larger provincial or national festivals. Originally the FdU's grew out of the ruins of popular religious festivals, as their lay counterpart celebrating the coming of a new rational gospel of equality and social justice. From this point of view, they provided an effective answer to Catholic propaganda, which was diffused through the parish churches. In a similar way, the PCI set about using its network of branches to develop these new ritual practices.

The year 1948 marked a turning point in the political struggle of the Communist Party in Italy. Palmiro Togliatti, then its General Secretary, was shot by a fanatic and for some time his life was in danger. The menace of civil war hovered over the country. Numberless Communist militants congregated from all parts of Italy for the FdU held in Rome, and on this occasion added a new political rite to the *Comizio*. This was the *Corteo*, an orderly but menacing, almost military parade with placards, flags and banners. It started out from the festival site and wound its way through the city, demonstrating the strength and discipline of the Party's organisation. Throughout the fifties, the resolute attitude of the PCI and its militant hostility to the reactionary administrations led by the Christian Democrats often led to violent demonstrations and clashes with the police. This opposition was reflected in the sober political and cultural rites of the FdU's.

In Italy, as in many other countries, the sixties saw important changes in the social and cultural fields. The conservative powers responded with a moderate policy, trying to avoid direct clashes. Their attitude towards the PCI became more and more moderate and, in some local administrations, even co-operative. Meanwhile the strength of the Communists gradually increased as innovatory movements changed the face of Italian society.

During these ten years the FdU's were opened up to youth groups and the middle classes. Many of the signs which had formerly distinguished them as festivals for the working class were played down or excluded. All shows of physical force and intolerance were dismissed in favour of mediating, if not ingratiating, attitudes and a subtler negotiation with the evolving fashions and manners of a mixed, inter-class public. An informal group of Marxist intellectuals, 'the friends of *L'Unità*', took over the task of organising the visual, artistic and spectacular features of the festivals. *Italia canta, Ltd* (Singing voices of Italy, Ltd) brought in folk singers and musical groups. The FdU was changing radically. From a secluded meeting of comrades, it was turning into a variegated, spectacular celebration punctuated by broadly progressive political and ideological rituals. Two opposed outlooks clashed during this decade: the traditional folk-singing-plus-politically-engaged-film-or-play trend versus the modernistic-pop-music-plus-entertainment attitude which opened the way to stars from the San Remo festival and radio and television personalities. The *Corteo* was abolished and a new ritual event substituted: the *Dibattito*, or round table debate, which signalled a new pluralism and the acceptance of democratic rules. By 1970, the year of an important electoral victory in which the PCI won a majority in several local administrative districts, the FdU's had developed an acute sensitivity to local problems and proposed solutions along the lines of the 'red districts', which were well known for the efficiency and honesty of their administrations. The FdU's adhered more closely than ever to the strategies and tactics of PCI policy and had to shift continually in response to rapidly evolving political realities.

The PCI's substantial electoral victories during the seventies reached an apex in 1976, when the Communists were on the point of becoming the largest single party in parliament. This success started a new political line which eventually led to the 'historical compromise', the proposed union with the Catholic masses, and to Eurocommunism which finally caused the breach with Moscow. The PCI, no longer an opposition party, made a bid for power by styling itself a progressive governing party and even by seeking some form of sanction from the USA. The FdU's reflected these new trends. Multi-coloured pluralist symbols stood side by side with the red flag. Lenin's portraits – though not Gramsci's – were noticeably absent. Party leaders addressed their audiences as *amici e compagni* ('friends and comrades'). In the round table debates, progressive churchmen and liberals sat next to the neophyte Marxist intellectuals who had enrolled *en masse* after the first brilliant electoral victories of the PCI. The output of this communication system was complex and ambiguous, at times contradictory or apologetic. On the stages of the FdU's the Inti Illimani, a group of expatriate Chilean folk singers adopted by the PCI, met rock stars or jazz artists imported by ARCI (the Agency for the Diffusion of Popular Arts and Sports, sponsored by the PCI.) Old comedians repeated their slapstick farces or popular Neapolitan *sceneggiate* alongside the once fiercely satirical cabaret entertainers from the years of resistance and struggle. On the screens of the FdU's Westerns and Pasolini films alternated schizophrenically. Television was everywhere.

The national FdU's became one of the largest cultural phenomena of the seventies, showing 'all the best that is available from all over the world'. A new type of vacation was born: people would spend a month going from one FdU to the next. Press teams covered them and well known semiologists and anthropologists wrote articles about them. These FdU's are the evidence of a Marxist cultural hegemony which was unchallenged in the seventies.

The Structures of the FdU

What is the average FdU actually like? The big national festivals extend over several square miles and usually last three weeks, including hundreds of events. They are organised by large cities and visited by several million people. The smallest local festivals in rural centres may last only an afternoon and evening. The average festival, between these extremes, is a three day celebration featuring six or seven events. The area of the festival coincides with the communal park or soccer field, and the town which organises it has a population of five to ten thousand people. Each FdU is announced by two definitive signs. The *plan* denotes its spatial organisation; the *programme* denotes its temporal organisation. All the features included under these two meta-signs are regulated by an official publication from the PCI Central Office for Press and Propaganda, the *National Seminar on the Festivals of L'Unità* (1974), which contains a set of rules for the spatial morphology and temporal syntax of the festival.

The *plan* of the FdU is criss-crossed by a network of *routes*. These form an ordered itinerary which leads step by step from the 'system of accesses, or entries' to the various areas subdivided into 'exchange and sale areas, refreshment areas, and areas for cultural manifestations.' This well-defined enclave is quite different from the spatial arrangement of traditional religious festivals. Whereas in the FdU's space is limited by a boundary, in the religious festivals there are no boundaries and the space coincides with the whole territory of the celebrating community. The events and happenings transform everyday space into festive space every time they traverse it. The 'exchange and sale areas' have two invariable features: a stand of local handicrafts and a stand of books, magazines and papers from left-wing publishers. Its ideological output is therefore represented, on the one hand, by popular tradition and, on the other, by lay left-wing culture. These are closely tied to the intended political meaning of the festival, although in country areas the exhibition of handmade sacred objects can interfere with this. Sadly missing in the FdU's orderliness are the characteristic confusion and profusion of the *Fiera*, the special market that always goes with the religious festival, whose connotations of abundance and squandering are strictly connected with the idea of the feast. The 'refreshment areas' in the FdU's are devoted to food and drink. Despite various efforts, they have not developed a close association with any particular foods and drinks. The original proposal was to adopt the popular food and wines of Romagna, the most prominent 'red district', but central and southern Italy hung onto their regional tastes. So the fare is now indiscriminate, and eating places range from the snack stand to the quality restaurant – reproducing a social division hardly in keeping with the FdU. This also contrasts with the special associations of food in the traditional religious festivals. This may be biscuits or a certain type of bread, special dishes or sweets, or even fruits of the season. But always there is some food you *must* eat if you are participating. The lack of a special food, representing the communion of all the participants, deprives the FdU of a powerful message of solidarity that the red flags and banners bristling round each eating place cannot replace.

The 'areas of cultural manifestations' include a platform with microphones and loudspeakers for *Comizi* or round table debates, and a screen for showing films. Here too plays or concerts can be performed. It is mainly in this area that the events of the *programme* take place. Often the people gathered around the platform listen to the first part of a concert by a well known rock band, then a political speech by an authoritative PCI leader from Rome, and finally to the second part of the concert. The *Comizio* is often sandwiched like this to make sure that the audience stays to hear it! The juxtaposition of entertainment and political rhetoric on the same FdU platform again contrasts with religious festivals, in which a much clearer division operates. The ideological, sacred message comes from the church, whereas the mundane, festive messages (often connected to sexual life and licence) come from the scaffold erected in the piazza or from the celebrating crowd. The two moments of sin and expiation are connected but not fused in a single utterance. Within the religious symbolism of the festival, this dialectical distribution functions to incorporate both experiences at the same time as discerning between good and evil. The same cannot be said of the FdU, where both profane (evasionist) and sacred (ideological) messages alternate on the platform in a confusing mixture.

The Semiotics of the FdU's

Two complex and varied sets of signs together constitute the overall message of the FdU. The first set is made up of the ideological messages required by the political matrix of the festival. These are embodied in its physical structures and are communicated through visual signs (icons, symbols, slogans and so on) and auditory signs (music, songs, announcements and so on.) They are also conveyed through the individual events, rituals and ceremonies in the festival's programme. Together, this set of messages constitutes the 'hegemonising message' which tries to impose ideological coherence on everything going on in the festival – eating and drinking, shows and entertainment, sports, the social interaction of groups and individuals. This second set of inchoate practices forms the 'hegemonised message' of the festival. The final impact of the FdU depends on the blend and interplay between these two sets of messages. If the hegemonising message is too overbearing, the festival becomes like a public or political institutional ceremony. If the hegemonised message predominates, the festival can lose all ideological meaning.

The relationship between the two can vary considerably, of course. The simplest and least effective form is *juxtaposition* – a thick row of red flags near the entrance to a high-class restaurant may not drive all doubts about social privilege from the participant's mind. *Superimposition* can sometimes be effective, but only if the various connotations are properly judged in performance. A diminutive red flag above the platform for a rock concert can look ridiculous if the lighting effects turn it into a pock-marked purple rag. If the flag is big enough, though, if the wind is in the right direction, and if the band makes reference to it in their performance (by introducing snatches of communist anthems, for example), then it may be decoded as an effective symbol of the predominance of communist ideals over modern cultural forms. By far the most effective relationship is *interpenetration*. This can only be achieved by drawing on the powerful, extra-rational symbolic connotations of ritual practices, which have their roots in rhythm and myth. Seen as a whole, a well made FdU is an effective ritualistic practice to the extent that it stands for and prefigures the myth of Communist utopia – the full attainment of every person's potential in an harmonious context of equality, social justice, peace and brotherhood (and to a lesser though increasing extent, as Iain Chambers and Lidia Curti show in their article, sisterhood.)

'Putting on your badge' is the rite of entry into the FdU. As soon as the visitor comes through the entrance, he or she is welcomed by a PCI militant offering the badge bearing the symbols of the Party and of *L'Unità* and asking for a contribution for the Communist press in exchange. Only by displaying the badge will the visitor avoid more requests for a donation. Clearly, the display also indicates adherence to the group, and the payment of a toll decided by the visitor may be related more to liberatory and penitential practices than to the modern idea of buying entrance tickets. This little rite transforms the vistor into an initiate who is also the bearer of signs expressing the fundamental meaning of the festival – which is why no enemy of communism would enter and why indifferent visitors may experience something of a crisis. In the early festivals of the late forties, the badges were hand made by members of the party branch organising the FdU. This made the preparation more laborious, but perhaps also heightened the significance of the celebration. The industrial production of stickers and badges may have reduced the intrinsic value of these signs but, on the other hand, it has extended their use to the large festivals where people come in their hundreds of thousands.

Shows and games make up the bulk of the festive side of the FdU. Those who took part in the festivals of the fifties and early sixties nostalgically recall musical shows built around folk ballads and political songs, which would end with communal singing that underlined the political commitment of the festival and produced that feeling of sharing a common creed and a special code of values and beliefs which have a ritual of their own, wholly disconnected from (and often hostile to) political beliefs. There is not a wide variety of games in the FdU's – the organisers have resisted any temptation to imitate Disneyland. One which remains universally popular deserves special mention. This is *il porcellino*, The Little Pig, a betting game derived from rural communities. The piglet is kept under an upturned crate at the centre of a circular space, surrounded by numbered boxes with their openings facing the centre of the circle. The visitors place bets on the boxes and, when all the bets are made, the pig is released. Frightened by the cheering crowd, it rushes frantically around and finally seeks refuge in one of the boxes. That is the winning box. This has the true flavour of the popular game, with laughter, shouting, bawdy, spontaneous reactions of hope and despair – and perhaps a degree of cruelty. Of course there are red flags and other PCI paraphernalia, but they do not really matter. The game is 'naturally' egalitarian. Like all popular rituals it has its own brand of communistic symbolism, derived in this case from the myth of Fortune and Nature dispensing their favours not according to rank or degree but as prizes awarded to virtue or need.

The most significant political rites of the FdU – the *Corteo*, the *Comizio* and the *Dibattito* – have already been mentioned. The *Corteo* was once the most striking moment of the festival, symbolising its capacity for militant struggle, for penetrating society and for spreading Communist ideals beyond the PCI. It has now been superseded because the PCI has abandoned its original commitment to physical force. The *Comizio* represents the prophetic voice of Marxism. The PCI leader who delivers the speech ritually embodies not authority but the inspired quality of the Communist 'word'. The responses of the crowd during and after it are part of a well known liturgy. The participants can give vent to their feelings in standardised but effective utterances through which both their approval and disapproval are revealed and where their solidarity is tested and manifested. The *Comizio* is a political ritual hinting at the myth of the unity of the working classes. It is not a glorification of the speaker: it is the epiphany of Marx's exhortation to unite, addressed to the working people of the world. The *Dibattito* has now taken the place of the *Comizio* and is a ritual of democratic pluralism. In spite of its open symbolism, founded on the free access for all opinions to public utterance, it effectively cuts off from participation those who are not familiar with the devices of public address. It plainly favours professional and would-be politicians and reveals more of an engagement with the old enemy of 'bourgeois democracy' than a commitment to the 'unique truth' of Communism.

Aftermath

In the closing years of the seventies, the craze for political festivals suddenly seized all the Italian political parties. After attempts by extra-parliamentary groups to organise polemical counter-festivals, both the Socialists and Christian Democrats realised that the challenge of the PCI could not go unanswered. Political festivals dedicated to *L'Avanti* (the newspaper of the Italian Socialist Party), to Friendship, to Justice, to Liberty and so forth clamorously multiplied all over the country. They were less accomplished and neatly organised than the FdU's but, for an outsider, hardly distinguishable. This second wave has been followed by a tide which started in 1979 and is still in flood: local administrations and communal authorities are organising cultural festivals and celebrations of all kinds. They last the whole summer, with circus shows, poetry readings, plays, films and all kinds of music. Among all these happenings the FdU has lost the distinction of being the only lay popular festival in opposition to the traditional religious celebrations. The press, which formerly gave the FdU's extensive coverage, hardly mentions them nowadays. Their popularity is rapidly dwindling. On the other hand, no new features have been added to the FdU's and the sheer number of reproductions has blunted their originality. Their messages, confused among too many similar voices, do not carry through and are hardly discernible in the general noise.

A new form of cultural communication, if it is really genuine and alive, is characterised by features so integral and unique that it will withstand any attempt at imitation. Its form takes shape gradually through a slow process of trial and error. It retains everything that is essential and irreplaceable and discards anything superfluous. Such is the case in the origin of a new literary genre – the novel, for instance. For a couple of centuries this new form retained the basic element of prose fiction, while trying on occasional additions like oratorical or rhetorical insertions, verse passages and so on. Eventually all those extraneous elements – suggested by fashions and temporary vogues – were expunged and the unmistakable features of the novel remained. Imitations in the same line (verse tales, for example) were attempted but they too disappeared and were soon forgotten.

Any popular form can only grow organically if it contains a core of immutable principles which all new accessions have to confront in order to be kept or discarded. These provide its essential structure, the relatively unchanging matrix around which the form evolves. Perhaps inevitably, this has not been the case with the FdU's. Their deeper structure was originally the basic creed of communism as expressed in Marx's *Manifesto*. But as time went on and the political conjuncture changed, this fundamental commitment was tempered by the tactical shifts of a restless PCI policy. These continual changes hindered the sedimentation of the festival's outer structures. The switches from the rite of the *Comizio* to the *Corteo* and then to the *Dibattito*, for example, were responses to changes in the deeper structures from a conception of defence to one of struggle and finally one of pluralism – or deeper still, from the fundamental idea of a party of the working classes to a conquering party extending its power beyond the working classes, to an inter-class party for the whole of society.

Moreover, the rapid growth of the FdU's and the inconsistent attitudes of the PCI leaders did not favour the organic, gradual growth of this cultural practice. Its links with the culture industry bound it to the ever-changing whims of fashion and to the processes of homogenisation characteristic of industrial production. And homogenisation means infinite reproducibility and, as a consequence, a dramatic drop in significant communication. Considered as a contribution to the culture of festivals and popular celebration, the FdU's have clearly paved the way to a new phase of the civilization of communal living in Italy, anticipating the present-day situation by thirty or forty years and accelerating the shift from religious to lay festivity. From the standpoint of their specific political impact, however, the FdU's have ceased to be influential and seem doomed to extinction.

Lucy Bland and Frank Mort

LOOK OUT FOR THE 'GOOD TIME' GIRL:
Dangerous Sexualities as a Threat to National Health

When she was the castaway on *Desert Island Discs*, Pamela Stephenson chose as one of her eight records 'the most tasteless song' she had ever heard – 'The Goodtime Girl' by the Andrews Sisters.[1] Roy Plomley played it, though he was anxious to point out that we weren't hearing the Andrews Sisters original but the version from *Over Here*, a 1974 Broadway musical about World War II. Part of the song goes like this:

> 'So, she may look clean
> Like a loving movie queen,
> Look out for the "good time" girl.
>
> No, she talks real sweet,
> When she's walking down the street,
> Look out for the "good time" girl.
>
> And during the dance,
> You may think you've found romance,
> 'Cos she cuddles and your eyebrows curl.
>
> She'll communicate a sore
> Like you've never seen before,
> Look out for the "good time" girl.'

This article looks at the way such sexual 'good times' – and especially the sexuality of women – have at various historical moments been perceived as a dangerous threat to the health of the nation. This has taken different and often lurid forms – the threat of urban poverty in the nineteenth century, the concern for a healthy imperial race, fears about the effects of prostitution and venereal disease on the family, right through to contemporary concerns about sex education and the consequences of 'permissiveness' and 'prom-iscuity'. These concerns have been tackled by a variety of agents, as the medical profession has formed shifting coalitions with social reformers and moral purists both 'inside' and 'outside' the state. Two axioms have re-mained constant throughout – that the 'health' of the nation is intimately bound up with the correct forms of sexuality, and consequently that individual and national health can only be understood and treated in both physical *and* moral terms.

Moral Environmentalism

In the early nineteenth century, representations of health and disease stood as the signifiers for a number of the preoccupations of the first generation of state administrators intent on addressing the 'social' consequences of Britain's shift into industrial capitalism.[2] The binary metaphors of health and disease were used as vivid illustration of the social and political choices confronting the new industrial state: public order *or* the threat of political sedition, familial and civil government *or* immorality, national progress *or* the threat of foreign invasion. But the emphasis on national health was not only a metaphorical evocation. In the 1830s and '40s, medics were instrumental in promoting the wide-ranging concerns of the health and disease debate in key state institutions.

Early preventive medicine insisted on the intimate relation between physical-moral concerns and both individual and collective health, stamina and strength. In the debates over the origins of disease which were precipitated in the wake of the cholera epidemics of 1832 and 1848, Chadwick, Kay-Shuttleworth, Southwood Smith and other medics argued for a national system of health administration to promote a broad based programme of physical and moral reform directed at the working classes. Chadwick, in the famous Health of Towns Report, 1842, insisted that the health of individuals, promoted by a national scheme of sanitary engineering, was the key to the development and survival of an industrial nation. He compared Britain's position unfavourably with the state-backed health programmes of France and Prussia.[3] Similar arguments, put forward by the Statistical Societies in the 1830s and '40s, stressed the commercial and industrial benefits of a healthy population – a healthy labour force would reduce capital's costs and increase the efficiency of labour power.

Receptivity to disease depended on the individual's physical and moral condition, together with the state of the urban environment. Immoral and disorganized habits of life, particularly among the urban poor, were an invitation to disease. Equally, physical disease was often seen to *stimulate* moral depravity. Mind and body were intimately related in early medical theory. Disease was also characteristically represented as an invasion *from without*; cholera was a foreign pestilence, often associated with the Irish, which demoralized the fundamentally healthy condition of the national social body. In the evangelical language of the 1830s, clerics saw disease as the divine punishment for national immorality, the turning away from religion and the disruption to the national community caused by rapid industrialization.

Hence the early strategies for environmental reform combined a concern for moral as well as physical disciplining, directed towards the improvement of national prosperity and the 'promotion of happiness.'[4] Sanitary legislation, street clearance and housing schemes, the work of the local medical officers, and philanthropic and rescue agencies were all concerned with this dual improvement. The population – its health and longevity, its norms and regularities of fertility, production capacity, its rates of death and disease – was identified as the target for this national programme. The family, and the position of women within it, was seen as the main agency for the transmission of the expansive principles of health and morality from the state to the individual. As Robert Peel put it in 1836, in the debate over civil population registration, the family was the first principle of national government, and on it was founded national health, happiness and morality.[5] The measures advocated in the early reports of the factory inspectors stressed that women's position in the family was the key to the reform of working class health and morality.

The creation of the short-lived General Board of Health in 1848 was the realization of Chadwick's scheme for a centrally directed system of national health supervision organized on Benthamite principles. Slightly later John Simon, as Chief Medical Officer to the Privy Council, also highlighted the national importance of health regulation, but from an ethical and humanitarian position. The improvement of the physical and moral health of individuals was one of the main duties of a civilized and christian nation; the level of health reflected the degree of civilization attained by the national population.[6]

Prostitution: Medical Regulation and Feminist Response

Sexual immorality was one of the key domains specified in medico-moral programmes throughout the nineteenth century. Sexuality was consistently defined as *im*morality in conjunction with the significations of dirt, disease, squalor and the cultural threat of the urban poor. Dangerous sexualities, particularly incest within the working class family and promiscuity and prostitution among working women, were identified as a physical and moral threat both to the respectable working class and to the population as a whole. In the Report of the Factory Commissioners (1842), female depravity was cited as one of the main causes of the general demoralization among the working class.[7] Medics, clerics and philanthropists often saw illicit sexuality at the heart of environmental and moral squalor. Both Kay in his *Manchester* pamphlet (1832), and much later Charles Booth in his *Life and Labour of the People of London* (1897), constructed their inquiries as nightmare journeys to the centre of corruption, moving from cholera and other forms of contagion, through to sexual immorality and debauchery, and, allied with these, forms

of criminality and political resistance. As Kay confessed at the time of the
first cholera outbreak:

> 'He whose duty it is to follow in the steps of this messenger of death
> must descend to the abodes of poverty, must frequent the close alleys,
> the crowded courts . . . and behold with alarm, in the hot bed of
> pestilence, ills that fester in secret at the very heart of society.'[8]

The unrespectable poor, or residuum, condensed and focused middle class
fears about the national threat *from within* – submerged, but ever ready to
break out and overflow the confines of the ghetto, bringing both pestilence
and immorality in their wake. These anxieties were intensified by the
geography of the metropolis and many of the early industrial towns, where
upper and middle class residential areas were often close to the centres of
urban poverty.[9]

In the debates and struggles surrounding the Contagious Diseases
Acts in the 1860s and '70s, these fears crystallized around the figure of the
female prostitute. In a series of official inquiries into the health of the army
and navy in the 1850s and early '60s,[10] military chiefs drew on the expansive
medical discourse to articulate their fears about venereal disease. In the
report of 1867, for example, Sir William Fanshaw Marshall saw it 'not only
sapping the health of our seamen and troops, but . . . spreading wide its evil
consequences over the population.'[11] The Contagious Diseases Acts of 1864,
1866 and 1868 were justified by the medico-military establishment in terms
of the national sanitary strategy of the public health movement. *The Lancet*
commented in 1871 that the state intervened to regulate diseased women 'on
the same ground and by the same right that it interferes with the typhus
fever or the small pox patients.'[12]

The jurisdiction of the Acts applied to a number of naval ports and
army garrison towns in England and Ireland. A woman suspected of being a
common prostitute could be taken to a certified hospital for medical inspection. If she was found to be suffering from venereal infection she could be
detained for up to three months. The regulations and the medical discourse
surrounding the Acts thus identified active female sexuality as both a moral
danger and a physical threat to the nation's health. Prostitutes were to be
subjected to forcible inspection and detention, with the resulting loss of
personal rights, precisely because they disrupted the norms of this health
consensus.

Together with the more coercive system of legal regulation went a
reformulated medical discourse around male and female sexuality which
was used in a campaign launched by the pro-regulationists to separate out
'fallen women' from urban working-class culture.[13] Central to these medical
reformulations was the greater polarization of definitions of women in terms
of moral or immoral sexual behaviour. Prominent medics like William Acton

and W. R. Greg, for example, reworked theories of prostitution put forward by medics and evangelical clerics such as Michael Ryan, William Tait and Ralph Wardlaw in the 1830s and '40s.[14] Acton stressed the absolute separation of sexually immoral and licentious women from the norms of female purity and asexuality.[15] The earlier studies had seen sexual union within marriage as an important part of the duties of the married couple – Ryan, for example, had insisted that human love within marriage was not asexual.[16] The representations dominant in the campaign over the Contagious Diseases Acts marked the increasing polarization of female sexuality in terms of asexual purity/depraved sexuality. These definitions were promoted both by the regulationists and by some of those involved in the Repeal Campaign. The strenuous moral régimes in the Lock Hospitals (hospitals for v.d. treatment) and in the Rescue Homes for fallen women run by repealers stressed that prostitutes needed to atone for their sins through moral and religious instruction and hard labour. While this was advocated in the interests of reclaiming the women, its practical effect was to reinforce the moral/immoral definitions of female behaviour.

Middle-class women who fought the campaign for the repeal of the Acts, including feminists like Josephine Butler, found themselves awkwardly placed in relation to these double formulations around national purity/immorality and national health/disease. At one level they fought an effective propaganda campaign, arguing that far from contributing to national health and morality, the Acts were a source of continuing immorality in the country by reinforcing the double standard, and that they did nothing to promote the health of the nation.[17] Butler, arguing from a radical liberal position, maintained that the state's involvement in regulating sexuality could only be coercive and oppressive, particularly towards women and the poor. She stressed that a more effective strategy for improving the nation's morals needed to acknowledge feminist demands for the reform of the double standard and insisted that private and voluntary efforts could do far more for moral reform than statist initiatives. Middle-class women mobilized around the national issue of health and morality as a means of advancing feminist demands – moral discourses provided them with their means of entry and representation into the world of public political debate. The difficulty was that the intimate connection between middle-class feminism and notions of moral purity and national regeneration reinforced definitions of women as pure and asexual and as watchdogs of the nation's morals. This contradiction was highly visible in the social purity movements in the late nineteenth and early twentieth century, where middle-class women continued to advance feminist demands through a wide range of programmes concerned with moral disciplining and the promotion of national health.

Bodily and Racial Health

Though moral environmentalism continued to be central to preventive medicine, the turn of the century saw a reformulated notion of national health. There was an increased and intensified medical scrutiny of the individual him/herself – a new focus on the body and its physical and mental characteristics and capacities. As Sir George Newman, Chief Medical Officer to the newly created Ministry of Health, pointed out in 1924, nineteenth century preventive medicine had been chiefly concerned with the environment, with the individual's relation to the environment conceived of as direct and unproblematic. But, he insisted, contemporary medicine was increasingly person-focused – concerned with the *whole man*: 'his life history, his heredity, his family, his domestic life, his personal habits and customs, his rest and his occupation.'[18] Developments internal to preventive medicine had provided the main theoretical conditions for this shift. The development of germ theory, after Pasteur's and Koch's work on viruses and vaccines in the 1870s and '80s, had resulted in the rapid isolation of the bacilli of all the major infectious diseases between 1870 and 1910.[19] This knowledge had produced a new conception of disease and a new notion of pathological processes which was focused much more on the internal bio-chemistry of the individual rather than on the older and simpler individual/environment relation. Disease was a process that was now conceived of as beginning in the cell. The maintenance of laws of health depended on 'the orderly sequence of a series of processes and functions. If they cease or become impaired or irregular, there is disease, imperfect correspondence, absence of rhythm.'[20] Pathological processes of disease occurred when *the laws* governing human physiology had become disrupted or perverted. But the rules of health were understood both biologically *and* morally, for though disease was now defined increasingly in terms of the internal malfunctioning of the body, its causes included the whole of the moral and the biological history of the individual and the nation.

> 'Medicine is human in application as well as technical; it is social in purpose as well as scientific in method; it is moral in claim as well as intellectual. Only a people clean in mind and body, within and without, can withstand "the pestilence which walketh in darkness"; and thus the social and moral standard of a people, its national character, bears relation to its health.'[21]

While the medical profession was increasingly concerned with questions of morality, moralists were beginning to draw on medicine and science generally as a backing for moral 'laws'. As the Rev. James Marchant, a notable eugenist and social purist, expressed it: 'It is now being fully recognized that all moral reforms or regeneration of mankind must be brought about by the combination of religion and science.'[22] A number of feminists, erstwhile opponents of the medical profession in the struggle over the Contagious Diseases Acts, now saw medicine and medics as their potential allies. For example, in 1913 the feminist journal *The Shield*, in reference to control of venereal disease, declared: 'We and our former antagonists can work cordially together.'[23] This new medico-moral coalition operated not simply at the level of the interlinking of concepts and beliefs, but also institutionally in the formation of public bodies concerned with physical, moral and racial health. The National Council for Public Morals, set up in 1910 and concerned with the 'promotion of moral and physical regeneration of the race', had members ranging from moralists and clerics, through a few social purity feminists to medics, eugenists, Fabians and new liberals such as Hobson. A similar pattern could be observed in the membership of the National Council for Combatting Venereal Disease in 1914 (in 1925 renamed the British Social Hygiene Council) and in the People's League of Health in 1917. These organizations cannot be discounted as marginal; their membership included many prominent intellectual and political figures of the period, whose expertise was drawn on regularly by numerous contemporary government commissions and committees.

This coalition of forces was dependent not only on factors relating to the relative status of scientific discourses, but also on wider political and international concerns. Natural scientists and medics had capitalized on the gains won in the debate over Darwinism and evolutionism to promote the more general hegemony of scientific explanations of human affairs and human progress. The older moral and religious causalities were challenged by a broad scientific offensive which forged a new relation between science and morality. Clerics and other moralists, including certain feminists, were forced to negotiate this changed situation in the period of profound political and international upheaval before the First War. Anxieties over the Boer War (including the ill-health of recruits) and the economic, political and military threat to the central prominence of the British Empire from other burgeoning nations (in particular Germany and to a lesser extent the USA and Japan) represented a rallying point for a wide spectrum of political forces. The demand was for a campaign to regenerate Britain's national health – physically, morally, racially, economically and militarily. 'Science', used both as a metaphor and in its practical application to a range of specific problems, occupied a prominent place in the debates over national regeneration.

The emphasis on the *racial* component in health maintenance marked a significant new development. From the 1870's post-Darwinist debates over racial progress, efficiency and evolution had transformed the way in which physical and moral processes were understood. These issues exerted an important influence on preventive medicine. Social Darwinists such as

Spencer claimed that evolutionary theory demonstrated scientifically what earlier social scientists had only understood in moral terms – namely, that the individual was to be seen as part of the evolutionary development of the race, through processes which obeyed observable and predictable laws. Both the individual and the nation were conceived in racial terms. There was a growing focus on the hereditary transmission of characteristics for individual and racial progress which implied a sustained critique of environmentalism. Environmental improvement was at best a mere palliative; what was needed was a strategy for gaining control over the conditions under which the race was reproduced.[24] Eugenics or, as Francis Galton put it, the science of selective breeding, applied itself to that problem – the qualitative and quantitative improvement of the population through the regulation of procreation.

Eugenics never gained the overall hegemonic position that its advocates hoped for, but it did inform national concerns around motherhood, birth-control, debates over criminality, psychology, and the problem of poverty. The reformulation of the principles of preventive medicine also revealed the impact of racial and evolutionary thinking, and a number of prominent medics such as C. W. Saleeby, Alfred Tredgold and Thomas Hyslop were also eugenists. As Newman pointed out, in assessing the capacity for health 'the racial character of the individual must be considered . . . the area of parentage and ancestry cannot be ignored.'[25] The influence of racial theories focused a greater medical scrutiny of the conditions of procreation. The sex instinct became redefined as the *racial* instinct. Havelock Ellis maintained that health and hygiene must not merely be concerned with 'the conditions under which life is lived', but must push back the process to birth and beyond.[26] A number of diseases – alcoholism, feeblemindedness, venereal disease – were seen as racial poisons, as threats to national health. Similarly, contemporary explanations of prostitution and other so-called sexual perversions drew on the evolutionary notions of atavism – the biological throwback to an earlier stage of human development. The active sexuality of primitive women studied by early anthropologists was presented as proof of such atavism in the female prostitute.

The resulting strategy for national health was an expanded and deepened environmentalism – now physical, moral and racial. As the People's League (whose slogan was 'a nation's health is a nation's wealth') put it in 1922: 'we have to emphasize . . . that heredity and environment are the two determining factors in our lives.'[27] Education for health consisted in the inculcation of the norms of physical and moral cleanliness through a broadly based programme to combat ignorance and eliminate unhealthy habits which stressed individual responsibility and scientific demonstration of the laws of health. The stress in the early health education programmes in elementary schools in the '20s was both physical and moral. The emphasis on physical exercise, fresh air, sunlight and personal cleanliness carried a strong set of moral imperatives.[28] Health maintenance was also promoted as one of the duties and responsibilities of citizenship.[29]

The Great Scourge and the 'Amateur'

Venereal diseases stood as the prime case of the drastic effects of transgressing physical and moral norms of health. On the one hand, they were contagious diseases with recognizable symptoms and accessible to diagnosis and treatment by the medical profession; on the other, they were diseases perceived as 'immoral' because they were usually seen to be transmitted through prostitution or 'promiscuous' sex. In this latter sense their control could legitimately be seen as the concern of moralists. This twin aetiology – the conditions under which a person was susceptible to catching and transmitting these diseases ('irregular sexual encounters') and the causative agents (the bacteria responsible for the disease) – were two sides of the same coin. One laid oneself open to the risks through immoral sex, one caught the disease through the presence of a physical agency – the bacillus. This twin aetiology seemed logically to call for a twin strategy, moral and medical, working in the interests of both the individual and the nation.

Such a medico-moral coalition was evident during the panic over the spread of venereal diseases in the years immediately before and during the First World War. Again, these anxieties signified a host of national and racial concerns: national efficiency, the physical, mental and moral degeneracy of civilians and troops, the falling birth rate (venereal disease was believed to contribute substantially to the level of sterility and infant mortality) and infant morbidity (to which venereal disease, especially gonorrhea, was also believed to contribute.) The v.d. rate also seemed to provide an index of the nation's sexual immorality. Moreover, many feminists believed that this rate not only indicated the extent of prostitution, but also the extent to which numerous women were the unsuspecting victims of venereal disease imposed by their profligate husbands. But if certain bacilli were now medically identifiable as the bacteria responsible for the spread of venereal diseases, at the height of the moral panic particular *human* agents were identified as the guilty transmitters of these diseases. It was above all at the amateur prostitute that the finger of blame was pointed as the 'real centre of infection'.[30]

If in the nineteenth century the prostitute from the residuum was seen as a central threat to the nation's health and welfare, by the First World War the fear of the 'submerged tenth' remained, but the threat of the prostitute was replaced by the threat of the 'amateur'. She was seen above all as a *health* threat. An anonymous letter to *The Times* in 1917 referred to such women as 'sexual freelances' who 'stalked through the land, vampires upon the nation's health, distributing and perpetuating among our young manhood diseases which institute a national calamity'.[31] The term 'amateur prostitute' or simply 'amateur' appeared as if overnight.[32] To many, its meaning was unclear, but there was general agreement that the term applied to a young woman engaging in promiscuous sex for 'free'. That she was referred to as an amateur *prostitute* indicated the continuing equation of active female sexuality with prostitution, yet it was her distinction *from* the professional prostitute which was of most concern. Not only did she seek and give gratuitous sex, not only was she believed to be drawn from all classes, unlike the working-class professional, and to be younger than most professionals, but she was also thought to take no precautions against venereal disease – hence the danger.[33] According to Macpherson of the War Office, about seventy-five per cent of veneral disease came from the amateur prostitute,[34] while in 1920 the Medical Women's Federation put it as high as eighty per cent.[35]

Not surprisingly, given the contemporary ideas of women's sexuality, commentators had difficulty understanding the amateur's motives. To many, the explanation lay in the transition of such women from the 'pure' pole of female sexuality (women as innocent and sexually passive) to the 'impure' pole (woman as corrupted and fallen), thereby rendering them *corrupting* and sexualized. For Corbett-Smith, for example, 'the amateur prostitute takes her first step through ignorance and frequently for love, and thereby becomes an entirely different woman, her maiden reserve torn from her.'[36] The feminist doctor Helen Wilson claimed that 'many of the unscrupulous "harpies" of today were merely irresponsible flappers a year ago – and the transformation wouldn't have been effected without the help of evil men.'[37]

The debate within official circles and various state institutions as to the most effective means of regulating the amateur, revealed the felt concern over her supposed threat to health. Towards the end of World War I the 'amateur' as well as the professional prostitute was subjected to the regulatory powers of the Defence of the Realm Act (Dora 40d): 'no woman who is suffering from venereal disease . . . shall have sexual intercourse with any member of HM forces, or solicit/invite any member to have sexual intercourse with her.' A woman so charged would be required 'to be remanded for not less than a week for medical examination.'[38] Faced with widespread protest, spearheaded by feminist organizations, and the rescinding of 'Dora' at the end of the war, 40d was revoked in November 1918. The same year also saw concerted feminist opposition to two clauses concerning venereal disease, within a reintroduced Criminal Law Amendment Bill and a Sexual Offences Bill. These were concerned with criminalizing venereal disease's transmission.

Although both Bills failed to become law, the debate around the two clauses highlighted the wider question of how best to deal with promiscuous sexual relations and with what was seen as their concomitant health threat. Many feminists, following a basic tenet of the medico-moral definition of the venereal disease problem, held that infection through promiscuous inter-course (as distinct from venereal disease as grounds for divorce for the 'innocent' party), belonged to the sphere of Public Health, rather than private or criminal injury. To many social purity feminists and moralists, promiscuous intercourse was by definition unhealthy and could never be otherwise;[39] they wanted the state to act in its public health capacity as a *moralizing* agency – to discourage promiscuity and encourage responsible sexual relations through moral education.[40]

One crucial difference between feminists of the early twentieth century and those campaigning earlier against the Contagious Diseases Acts lay in their attitude towards the state: the former's desire to see active state involvement in national health issues, the latter's ambivalence towards any such involvement. This shift must be seen as in part related to the statist strategy of the medico-moral coalition in this period and to the more general contemporary stress on the importance of centralized state initiatives. But it also points to the involvement of certain middle-class feminist groupings in official strategies of social disciplining around the norms of health. Groups such as the National Council of Women Workers – technically outside the state in the narrow sense but in constant dialogue with government – advanced feminist demands through their commitment to a range of pro-grammes concerned with physical and moral regulation.[41]

Yet the question of the scope and limits of state intervention in this area remained a contentious issue. The two government apparatuses most directly concerned with health regulation and moral education – the Minis-try of Health and the Board of Education – acted only tentatively throughout the inter-war period over the treatment of venereal disease and the wider issue of sex education. Despite the promotion of general health education programmes by both government departments in the '20s, when it came to tackling sexuality successive administrations preferred to delegate responsi-bility to the various public voluntary bodies. The National Council for Combatting Venereal Disease, and later the British Social Hygiene Council, received central government grants and ministerial support for its work on venereal disease and sex education in the 1920s and 1930s. This ambivalence reflects a more general unease about the relation of sexuality to male-dominated political discourse. Parliamentary debates over legislation addressing sexuality were often prefaced by remarks insisting that the domain of sexuality was not a fit subject for political discussion; it was seen as either innately immoral or to be confined solely to the private sphere of the family and domesticity. In the debate over birth control in 1935, for example, Nancy Astor felt the need to apologize for introducing sexuality into parliamentary discussion.

Nevertheless, positive definitions of sexuality were incorporated into the development of the programme for citizenship in the interwar period, where sexual health was defined in terms of sexual responsibility and education for family life. But the achievement of this norm was thought to necessitate the continuing scrutiny and regulation of the amateur – now defined against the healthy, sexually responsible citizen. Attempts were made to locate (and thus 'explain') the promiscuous young woman as a member of the 'social problem group' – a term coined in this period, which represented the medicalization of the nineteenth-century 'residuum'. The term sprang from the eugenical marriage of two concerns: the attempt to identify 'feeble-mindedness' and to locate the grouping most prone to social problems such as unemployment or maternal inefficiency.[42] Eugenists and new liberals were united in their efforts to define the status of citizenship for this residuum. New liberalism redefined citizenship not simply as a political right but as a moral responsibility. As Greta Jones points out, 'This concept of citizenship implied not only an extension of opportunities to the citizen, but a reciprocal set of duties on the part of the citizen of the state.' Those who failed to reciprocate, the undeserving 'social problem group', represented 'a group whose moral character and social life did not live up to these ideals of citizenship.'[43] This group was thereby defined as not qualifying for national citizenship and its freedoms, as well as its duties and responsibilities. Attempts to label the amateur or promiscuous young woman a member of such a group were largely unsuccessful;[44] the real difficulty was her very *lack* of distinguishing characteristics – other, that is, than her promiscuous sexual behaviour. It was her virtual invisibility 'within our midst' that caused such grave concern. (After all, 'she may look clean, like a loving movie queen.') Nevertheless, during the Second World War, an attempt was made to remove the full citizenship rights of the amateur through the introduction of a measure similar to 40d (Dora 33b). The justification was spelt out clearly by the Ministry of Health in November 1942:

> 'The new regulation leaves the voluntary basis unchanged, but pro-
> vides for compulsion, where necessary, to bring under treatment the
> group of persons who are *impervious to methods of education and persua-*
> *sion* and who refuse to attend voluntarily for treatment although
> known to be infected and to be spreading infection.'[45]

Popular Representations

In the inter-war years, the popular press – especially Sunday papers like *Reynolds News*, *The News of the World* and *The People* – developed a lurid style

Second World War propaganda poster by Reginald Mount, 1943.

of investigative journalism which crystallized issues of sexual morality and their impact on national life. Corruption and decadence in the heart of the metropolis were presented as a threat to the quality of English life. Central to these debates were the polarized representations of female sexuality –

women either as an immoral source of national corruption and disease *or* as the pure, passive victims of sexually depraved foreign men.

In the '20s, *The People* ran a series 'Unmasking the Underworld', which 'exposed' the depravity beneath the surface of London's fashionable society. It was clearly influenced by the debate over amateur prostitution. Female sexuality, defined against the norms of marriage and the family, was represented as both corrupt and corrupting, yet highly erotic. In one article (4 February 1924), London was described as:

> '. . . a subterranean sink of iniquity – a short cut to Hell – frequented by the Mayfair harpies, by women separated from their husbands, by the mistresses of big game in the commercial or financial world. A few of them are comparatively innocent as yet . . . But . . . they are quickly settling down to a career of professional vice . . . it makes one's heart bleed to realize that this . . . is going on unchecked, in the capital of the most civilized country in the world.'

Physical glamour and sexual attraction were seen to hide a moral and physical unhealthiness: 'they are the last word in physical beauty. But . . . Dainty Daphne's exquisitely moulded figure will ere long be a living putrefaction, despised and shunned.' Men were frequently referred to as the victims of female vice. This active and corrupt female sexuality was also associated with continental vice, with the threat of immorality from without. Women were part of a world of 'mellifluous and complimentary phrases . . . salacious innuendos, French and Spanish exclamation', where jazz, 'a foreign importation not unlike tom-tom of the West African savage, finds an echo in the primitive passions of human nature.' Female immorality was seen to have developed in conjunction with the vicious influence of particular national and racial groups.

The immoral traffic in English girls to the Continent – the so-called white slave trade – was another favourite topic in the popular press. But here women were represented as the passive victims of male sexual lust, which was both animal and foreign. As *The People* warned in another exposé (6 January 1935):

> 'White slaves in African harems. Traffic they cannot control. Reports shortly to be issued . . . will show an alarming increase in a new form of slavery in the African colonies of France. These reports concern the traffic in white girls for the harems of coloured potentates.'

The Home Secretary, William Joynson Hicks, considered the effects of such representations in films and magazines to be a matter of terrible and far reaching importance. Films shown in India and the East depicting white women as objects of degradation were seen as possible incitements to immorality among native populations and as challenging the symbolic imperial power of white womanhood.[46]

At times the sexual threat was pinpointed *within* the national community. The Chinese living in the metropolis, for example, were seen as a potential source of national corruption and a danger to white women: 'Twenty-Five Years of Chinatown Secrets . . . Riddle of Hidden Dens . . . White girls mix freely with Easterners' (*The People*, 25 August 1935). This linking of national identities with representations of sexuality had its parallels in eugenic concerns over national fitness, miscegenation and degeneracy. But within popular representations this sexual racism produced a set of sexualized or erotic meanings. The image of women as passive, white, civilized victims worked to intensify notions of its opposite – primitive, animal masculinity, seen as non-white, non-European and non-civilized.

If foreign men were not actually luring innocent women abroad, they were thought to be luring them into prostitution in this country through their role as pimps. In the 1950s this racist imagery resurfaced in the imputed connection between the 'problem of prostitution' and the 'problem of immigration'. In post-war London many of the pimps were held to be Maltese, Italian and West Indian, living off the bodies of white women; a chorus of MPs called for their deportation.[47] Whether or not many pimps were in fact Maltese, Italian or West Indian is not the issue here; the important point is that the media fuelled the panic over prostitution in terms of racial imagery. But should this imply that the female prostitute was seen solely as *victim* of the evil foreigner, it must be noted that in the same breath the professional prostitute was condemned as a challenge to the family and the contemporary ideal of pleasurable *marital* sex, and her 'amateur' sister as a greater venereal threat.[48] For example, to Eustace Chesser, the well-known author of numerous sex and marriage manuals, 'there is more danger of infection from "amateurs" than from professional prostitutes today, since the latter take stringent hygienic measures for their own protection.'[49] And the number of 'amateurs' was still believed to be multiplying.[50]

Sex Education and Promiscuous Sex

What implications do these strategies regulating sexuality in the nineteenth and early twentieth century have for current debates and struggles? The link between sexual health and concepts of the nation has undergone a number of important transformations in the post-Second World War period, but medical discourses around health and disease are still being used to isolate sexually 'deviant' populations from the 'normal', healthy majority. Women, in particular, are frequently defined as sexually normal or deviant according to whether they are inside or outside the medical health consensus. This is the legacy of the earlier definitions of national health. Sex education and the recent renewed concern over sexual diseases are the main sites where these strategies are formulated and reproduced.

Fighting the v.d. threat has been central to the development of sex education, which, from its inception in the purity and hygiene movements in the early years of this century, has always been concerned with dangerous sexualities. Education programmes have consistently specified norms of sexual conduct supposedly consonant with individual and national health, and designed to combat the threat of deviance. The expansion of sex education for both sexes in primary and secondary schools since the early '70s has taken place in the context of an integrated programme of *health* education.[51] This is in line with the earlier conceptions of national health, but the older discourse has been partially transformed. Health education, like social hygiene before it, draws together several strategies – preventive medicine, liberal pedagogies of education, and the community-based stress of much contemporary social work. Moreover, it is presented as a 'progressive' solution to social problems ranging from venereal diseases, 'irresponsible' sexuality and teenage pregnancies, through to alcoholism, drug addiction and problems of modern chronic diseases.[52]

The concept of health in play involves a stress on individual and *community*, rather than on national responsibility. The Department of Education in its 1977 guidelines for health education in schools cites the World Health Organization's definition of health: 'a state of complete physical, mental and social well being. This implies that there are few . . . aspects of life or education which can be excluded from . . . health education.'[53] Given the increasing medical emphasis on health maintenance (rather than disease cure), the primary objective becomes the socialization of the individual into certain norms and procedures. 'Freedom to choose' is essentially freedom to make the correct choices based on personal responsibility to oneself and to the community.[54] Health education should encourage the child to develop into a 'productive and useful citizen.' Within this programme for health, sex education outlines a gradualist progression to mature heterosexuality emphasizing the avoidance of disease, promiscuity and sexual deviations – all seen as cul-de-sacs in normal development rather than evils to be condemned. Personal and social responsibility for one's sexuality is also related to the importance of human love as a mutual exchange of pleasures between caring individuals.

If sex education represents education for mature and healthy sexuality, debates since the '60s over promiscuity return to the concern over dangerous and diseased sex. The 1959 Annual Report of the Chief Medical Officer at the Ministry of Health, which drew attention to the rise in the incidence of venereal diseases, insisted on the familiar relation between physical health and moral standards. It noted that: 'Though our society may seem physically strong and healthy, it is a matter for consideration whether its roots in family life may not be suffering from decay.'[55] The 1964 Report by a Committee of the British Medical Association on venereal disease reiterated that the problem was not simply medical, but involved all who were concerned with the physical, mental and spiritual welfare of young people. Great concern was expressed that the increase in adolescent venereal disease was far greater among girls than boys. In fact, the number of men with venereal disease still greatly exceeded that of women (for syphilis a ratio of about 2:1, while for gonorrhea usually 3–4:1) and the Chief Medical Officer of the Ministry of Health noted in his Annual Report for 1965 that most cases of venereal disease occurred in people aged twenty-five and over.[56] Nevertheless, it was the promiscuity of girls and young women which was highlighted as the main venereal disease problem: 'As a prime cause it [prostitution] is . . . outstripped . . . by the advent of the promiscuous or "good time" girl.'[57]

The past couple of years has witnessed a renewed panic over the incidence and treatment of venereal disease. As a *Man Alive* programme put it in 1981: 'Sexually transmitted diseases are making a come-back; the war is on again.'[58] 'Permissiveness' is often blamed: 'that old scourge of the sexually promiscuous – VD – is hitting back at the permissive society with a vengeance.'[59] The Department of Health has noted that in 1981 the number attending NHS v.d. clinics had, for the first time, exceeded half a million – five times more than in the '50s.[60] Recent medical debates over the prevention and treatment of sexually transmitted diseases (a term coined to avoid the stigma attached to venereal disease) have involved the identification of so-called high risk or target groups.[61] Male homosexuals, international businessmen, foreign tourists and above all, young single women are defined as potential health hazards; while their life style, psychology and habits (in other words, their promiscuity) are seen to be the main causes of the spread of infection. Failure to make lasting or long-term relationships is frequently cited as the underlying reason for the sexual promiscuity of young women and gay men and for the consequent spread of disease. According to Dr R. R. Wilcox of St Mary's Hospital, London, sexually transmitted dieases among men 'frequently result from . . . mating with high risk females', women who do not accept 'the responsibilities of marriage' and who suffer 'from a sense of inadequacy, loneliness or rejection with an anxiety to please, or an antagonism to parents or society.'[62]

To the Department of Health, the most worrying development is the increase in the number of patients with sexual diseases resistant to antibiotics – the virus diseases, especially herpes.[63] Concern over herpes is predominantly due to the lack of any known cure, the disease's recurrence and its disturbing consequences for women – the probable association with cervical cancer and the dangers during pregnancy of infection of the foetus and the newborn child. In the absence of an effective cure, 'remedies' often take the form of a lecture condemning the sufferer's 'promiscuity' and recommending sexual abstinence.[64] A *Cosmopolitan* article approvingly quotes an American herpes sufferer as saying, 'This promiscuity thing is just too unhealthy – both physically and emotionally.'[65] According to Archway Women's Health Group, 'many women who sent in accounts talk of doctors who were dismissive of their physical discomfort and were not only insensitive to their anxiety but actually contributed to it. They do this by taking a moralistic stance and do not give women adequate information about the infection and its possible consequences.'[66] The 'Special Clinic' or 'Clinic 13', whatever the euphemism, is often staffed by medics who are at best uninterested and at worst downright moralistic about sexuality. Women have recorded experiences where they have been condemned as promiscuous or treated as potential prostitutes. The entanglement of moral and physical 'cleanliness' is still very much with us; the 'good time' had by the 'good time girl' always takes its toll.

However, gay men have also recently been subjected to extremely moralistic warnings about sexual promiscuity and the threat of disease. In May 1982 a leading article appeared in *The Lancet* entitled 'Risk Factors for Karposi's Sarcoma in Homosexual Men.'[67] The article described how an American study of twenty gay men with this particularly rare form of skin cancer showed up connections between the spread of the disease, the use of a number of 'recreational' drugs (particularly 'poppers' or amyl nitrate) and the exposure to sexually transmitted viruses associated with promiscuity. The piece drew attention to the alarming difference between the sex life of the infected gay men and a control group of non-infected heterosexuals. It concluded that the sexual lifestyle of gay men was an important factor in the spread of the disease. Similar articles by medical research teams in the *New England Journal of Medicine* claimed to have identified a new form of 'acquired cellular immunodeficiency syndrome' ('Aids') which is developing rapidly among gay men.[68] This is a virus which attacks the natural capacity of the blood cells to defend themselves against disease. Medics have continually stressed that, given the high promiscuity rates of gay men, some form of sexually transmitted virus or exposure to a 'common lifestyle' has a critical role in establishing the immunodeficient state. The argument is that promiscuity could increase the chances of viral infection, so that eventually the body's defences are massively overwhelmed.

In September '82 the Communicable Diseases Centre at Colindale, part of the public health administration, announced that it was to investigate the incidence of Aids in Britain. By that time the British gay press was reporting that the disease had claimed nearly two hundred victims in the US. Responses by gay men to the Aids panic have tended either to confirm the medical link between promiscuity and disease or have only developed a very partial critique of medical definitions of sexuality. The first response has been stressed in a number of recent articles and discussions within the gay community. The headline in a recent article in *Capital Gay* ran 'Cupids Help the Carriers.'[69] The call is for gay men to re-assess their sexuality as a result of the disease threat. This is not merely a reflection of medical panics: it also expresses real ambiguities felt by many gay men about an identity and lifestyle increasingly centred on sex. On the other hand, groups of gay medics, both here and in the US, have put forward a critique of the inadequacies of the statistics used to prove the connection between gay promiscuity and Aids.[70] Their useful educational work has been organized around efforts to correct 'wrong' information and to monitor research, but the problem is that it can very easily remain wholly inside the medical debate. These campaigns over medical misrepresentation may criticize inadequate treatment facilities and information, or the lack of research into s.t.d's, but they do not ultimately challenge medical knowledge or the profession's right to pronounce on sexuality. An improved, accessible treatment service is indeed a crucial demand. But its organization must be freed from moralisms and from medical hegemony over knowledge. As the panic over Aids has shown, moral fears take root where treatment facilities are inadequate *and* still carry a moral stigma.

There are signs that the medical lines of demarcation between those who are sexually healthy (and by implication part of the respectable community) and the diseased, promiscuous and unrespectable could intensify in a period of economic, political and cultural crisis. This is not to suggest that official definitions of sexuality are directly linked to the political shift to the right, but it is increasingly clear that Thatcherism does have a distinctive moral component and this may begin to exert a forcible impact on the experts and the knowledge they produce. The disclosures early in 1983 of the Cabinet's Central Policy Review Staff, with their grandiose schemes for social engineering and their attack on the power of the experts, may mark a more sustained offensive by the right to transform social and moral behaviour.[71] In this climate, there could well be an intensification of the definitions which have re-emerged in the current panics over promiscuous sex and disease. These representations are part of the continuing legacy of medical discourse which linked moral health to national concerns. They continue to regulate by establishing powerful norms around sex and health and by reaffirming the social and cultural divisions between the respectable and the unrespectable, the normal and the deviant, defined in medico-moral terms.

Acknowledgments

Many thanks to Cora Kaplan, Nancy Wood, Martin Durham, Nicholas Green and Richard Johnson for their helpful comments.

Notes

1. Desert Island Discs, Radio 4, 17 July 1982.
2. Prominent among these intellectuals were: Edwin Chadwick, in the field of Poor Law administration and sanitary reform, the medics James Kay and Thomas Southwood-Smith and William Farr at the General Register Office.
3. *Report from the Poor Law Commissioners into the Sanitary Condition of the Labouring Population of Great Britain*; H. L. Papers, 1842, XXVI.
4. For a discussion of the relation of physical and moral elements within early environmentalism see Frank Mort, *The Domain of the Sexual*, University of Birmingham Doctoral Thesis, forthcoming.
5. Sir Robert Peel, 'Debate on the Marriage Bill', June 14, 1836; *Hansard*, 3rd series, Vol. XXXIV, col. 493.
6. *Thirteenth Report of the Medical Officer of the Privy Council*, 1870; GBPP, 1871, XXXI, p. 763.
7. *First Report of the Commissioners for Enquiry into the Condition of Children in Mines and Manufactories*, 1842; GBPP, 1842, vol. XV.
8. James Kay, *The Moral and Physical Condition of the Working Classes Employed in the Cotton Manufacture in Manchester*, 1832, p. 8.
9. See for example, Charles Girdlestone, *Letters on the Unhealthy Condition of the Lower Classes of Dwellings especially in large towns*, 1845.
10. *Report of the Royal Commission on the Health of the Army*; GBPP, 1857, XVIII and *Report of the Committee to Inquire into the Prevalence of Venereal Disease in the Army and Navy*, PRO War Office Papers, WO 33/12, 1862.
11. *Venereal Disease, Army and Navy, Committee Report with Minutes of Evidence*, 1867–68.
12. *The Lancet*, 29 July 1879, vol. 2, p. 166.
13. See Judith Walkowitz, *Prostitution and Victorian Society, Women, Class and the State*, Cambridge University Press, 1980.
14. Ralph Wardlaw, *On the Nature and Extent of Prostitution*, 1842; William Tait, *Magdelenism – An Inquiry into the Extent Causes and Consequences of Prostitution in Edinburgh*, 1840; Michael Ryan, *Prostitution in London*, 1839.
15. William Acton, *Prostitution considered in its moral, social and sanitary aspects*, 1857.
16. Ryan, *Lectures on Population*, 1831, p. 3.
17. For a sustained critique of the medical involvement in the Acts, see Mrs Hume-Rothery, *A Letter Adressed to the Rt Hon. W. E. Gladstone, MP*, 1870.
18. Newman, *An Outline of the Practice of Preventive Medecine*; GBPP, 1919, XXXIX, p. 683.
19. *ibid*.
20. *ibid*., p. 693.
21. Newman, *The Place of Public Opinion in Preventive Medicine*, 1920, pp. 11–12.
22. James Marchant, *The Master Problem*, 1917, p. 128.
23. *The Shield*, October 1913.
24. See Havelock Ellis, *The Problem of Race-Regeneration*, 1911.
25. Newman, *An Outline*, p. 722.
26. Ellis, op. cit., p. 722.
27. *Second Report of the People's League of Health for the Years 1922–1925*, p. 13.
28. See, for example, Board of Education, *Syllabus of Physical Training for Schools*, 1919.
29. See Edward S. Woods (ed.), *The Citizen of Tomorrow*, 1929 and Newman, *Citizenship and the Survival of Civilization*, 1928.
30. Alison Neilans, 'Disorderly women', *The Shield*, February 1915.
31. *The Times*, December 1917.
32. Although the term had been around for many years: see *The Shield*, December 1899.
33. See 'Sources of infection', *The Shield*, December 1917.
34. *Joint Select Committee of Both Houses on Criminal Law Amendment Bill 1918 and Sexual Offences Bill 1918*: GBPP, 1917–18, vol. III.
35. *Joint Select Committee of Both Houses on Criminal Law Amendment Bill . . . 1920*; GBPP, 1921, vol. VI.
36. A. Corbett-Smith, *The Problem of the Nations*, 1914.

37. Helen Wilson, *The Times*, 19 February 1917.
38. Statutory Rules and Orders, 1918, pp. 331–2.
39. See Dr Helen Wilson's evidence *Joint Select Committee*, 1918, and the evidence of Johnson and Neilans, *Joint Select Committee*, 1920.
40. See Wilson, *ibid*.
41. For a discussion of middle class feminist involvement in the disciplining of 'the social' see Nancy Wood, 'Prostitution and Feminism in Nineteenth Century Britain,' *m/f*, no. 7, 1982.
42. Greta Jones, 'Eugenics and Social Policy between the Wars,' in *The Historical Journal*, vol. 25, no. 3, 1982.
43. Jones, *ibid*.
44. See F. Neville-Rolfe, 'Biological Aspects of Prostitution,' in C. P. Blacker (ed.) *The Social Problem Group?*, 1937.
45. Quoted in Sydney Laird, *V.D. in Britain*, Penguin, 1943, p. 49; our emphasis.
46. See Rt Hon. Viscount Brentford (W. Joynson Hicks) *Do We Need a Censor*, 1929, p. 21.
47. See Carol Smart, 'Law and the Controlling of Women's Sexuality,' in Hutter and Williams (ed.) *Controlling Women*, Croom Helm, 1981.
48. See Lucy Bland, Trisha McCabe and Frank Mort, 'Sexuality and Reproduction: Three Official Instances,' in Michèle Barrett, et al. (ed.) *Ideology and Cultural Production*, Croom Helm, 1979.
49. Eustace Chesser, *Live and Let Live*, 1958.
50. See Church of England Moral Welfare Council, *Sexual Offenders and Social Punishment*, 1956.
51. In Michael Schofield's study conducted in 1964 an estimated 47% of boys and 86% of girls had received some sort of sex education at school. The figures for Christine Farrell's research from 1974–75 were 87% of boys and 97% of girls. See Michael Schofield, *The Sexual Behaviour of Young People*, Penguin, 1965 and Christine Farrell, *My Mother Said . . . The Way Young People learned about Sex and Birth Control*, 1978.
52. See for example National Council of One Parent Families, *Pregnant at School*, 1979; Department of Education and Science, *Drug Misuse among Children of School Age*, 1977; Department of Health and Social Security Advisory Committee on Alcoholism, *Report on Prevention*, 1977.
53. Department of Education and Science, *Health Education in Schools*, 1977, p. 1.
57. See 'Counting the Dead is not Enough,' *The Lancet*, July 18, 1982, vol. 2, p. 131.
55. *Annual Report of the Chief Medical Officer of Health of the Ministry of Health*, 1959, part II, 'The State of the Public Health.'
56. See R. S. Morton, *Venereal Diseases*, Corgi 1966, p. 114 and Schofield, *op. cit.*
57. Morton, *ibid.*, p. 12.
58. 'Some of the nicest people I know have had V.D.,' *Man Alive*, BBC 2, 9 April 1981.
59. 'Revenge on the Swinging Sixties,' *Sunday Times*, 5 December 1982.
60. *Daily Telegraph*, 10 December 1982.
61. R. R. Willcox, 'Society and High Risk Groups,' in R. D. Catterall and C. S. Nicol (ed.) *Sexually Transmitted Diseases*, 1976.
62. Willcox, *ibid*.
63. *Daily Telegraph, op. cit.*
64. See *Sunday Times, op. cit.*
65. 'The Sex Epidemic', *Cosmopolitan*, July 1982.
66. 'Herpes,' *Spare Rib*, September 1978. The article also presents some suggestions for 'self-help.'
67. *The Lancet*, 15 May 1982, p. 1083.
68. *The New England Journal of Medicine*, 10 December 1981, vol. 305, no. 24, pp. 1425–1443.
69. *Capital Gay*, 29 May 1982.
70. See, for example, the *Gay Men's Health Crisis Newsletter* in New York, similar groups have been formed in San Francisco, Los Angeles and Houston.
71. See the disclosures first published in *The Guardian*, 17 February 1983.

Caroline Rowan

FOR THE DURATION ONLY:
Motherhood and Nation in the
First World War

The position of women in the First World War was determined by two –
potentially contradictory – factors. On the one hand, they entered the
industrial labour force and for the first time played an active role in the war
effort while, on the other hand, there was a new emphasis on the importance of their domestic role and the ideology of motherhood. The latter was
partly a continuation of pre-war child-welfare policies but it was intensified
and received a particular inflection as part of a specific ideological mobiliza-
tion aimed at boosting civilian morale and strengthening national unity.
Motherhood – the bearing and rearing of the race – became the symbol of a
future for the nation and a guarantor of peace and prosperity at the end of
the War. At the same time, though, this traditional ideology of motherhood,
locating women's work only in the home, was threatened by the inescapable
need to have women active in the general labour force. What were the
ideological negotiations and re-alignments which enabled these two contradictory positions to be held, for a time, in a state of uneasy coexistence? In
this article, I shall concentrate on welfare work, for women and children,
both at home and in the factory, arguing that it was mainly through
discourses on public health that the state and its various agencies were able
to construct a specifically national ideology of motherhood. I shall also
examine the relationship between the explicit ideologies elaborated principally by the Ministry of Munitions, the Local Government Board (later the
Ministry of Health) and the press, and women's actual experience of war –
its effect on their mental and physical health, their self-confidence and their
political awareness.

The concern with child welfare in the period preceding the First World
War had itself been a product of an imperialist crisis.[1] The public outcry over
the shortage of fit recruits to fight in the Boer War caused the problem of ill
health in the working classes to be redefined as a problem of national
importance and concern: the Interdepartmental Committee on Physical
Deterioration (1904) was forced to acknowledge publicly the full extent of
working-class poverty. This was a problem which could no longer be
relegated to the category of pauperism, at the margins of society. The health
of the working class as a whole now became a legitimate object of state

concern and regulation. And since the preferred solution seemed to be not the abolition of poverty, overcrowding and insanitary conditions, but the 'education' of working-class mothers in the areas of domestic hygiene and infant management, a new 'subject' would have to be constructed. This was the ignorant but well-meaning working-class mother who would now be addressed directly by state agencies and not, as before, indirectly via the male head of the family. A range of facilities and services was established, including infant consultations, baby-weighing sessions and schools where mothers could go for medical advice, the early detection (but not treatment) of infant diseases and more general advice on infant feeding, domestic cleanliness and making children's clothes. The lucky ones also got a cheap meal and powdered milk for the child, but this was not in accordance with the principles of the centres. Local authorities employed a large number of health visitors who were to ensure that advice given at the centres was followed up at home. Another of their functions was to chase up those recalcitrants who failed to attend the centres.

The administration of child-welfare schemes by local authorities allowed some room for manoeuvre – some socialist councils, such as Woolwich and Bradford, were able to apply the schemes more in favour of the working class. The general aim of the reformers, however, tended to be the imposition of middle-class norms of childrearing and a stable, home-centred family which would involve a distinctive challenge to the more gregarious forms of working-class culture. This was, of course, a subordinate culture, with its social centre in the pub, the street or the tenement court precisely because home conditions were so uncomfortable. Children often assumed distinctive and sometimes adult responsibilities such as the care of younger children or errand-running at an early age from economic necessity. It was a culture, though, which to an extent could define its own terms and conditions. Despite some aspirations to middle-class living standards and values, there was also resentment of any middle-class interference, particularly when it was not accompanied by material assistance. This is how the socialist Ada Nield Chew described one woman's attitude:

> 'Miss Seaton, who came hindering yesterday, asked if she knew that milk contained all the necessary elements to sustain life; and hoped she gave her children a good milk-pudding every day. Of course she said "Yes, 'm' "; it was easiest to get rid of her that way, especially when you wanted to be getting on with your work; but she (Mrs Turpin) would like to know where a quart of milk per day (and a quart wouldn't make a pudding big enough to feed her five – leaving out herself and the baby) was to come from.'[2]

A culture where children learned and played in the streets and where moonlighting was an accepted solution to the problem of rent arrears was also out of line with pressures from another direction. A developing system of factory production with new and sophisticated production techniques which were accelerating rapidly in the war years and the twenties demanded a more stable and reliable labour force. As Anna Davin states, 'the development of a new kind of family, with head and household and pride in possessions, bound to one place and one job by a new level of emotional and financial investment in an increasingly substantial home' clearly had an important role to play here.[3] Such long-term social and economic trends form the backdrop to wartime developments.

In practice, though, little progress on welfare initiatives was made before 1914. Central government, with responsibilities for health divided between the Medical Departments of the Board of Education and the Local Government Board (LGB), provided moral support but very little else. Legislation on School Meals (1906), School Medical Inspection (1907) and Notification of Births (1907) was never binding on local authorities. It facilitated the work of those who were already committed but left the others untouched. By 1914, therefore, the picture was one of vast areas of inactivity, a few philanthropic initiatives and some more developed municipal schemes usually organised by the local Medical Officers of Health. These schemes, which included Manchester, Liverpool, Bradford, Birmingham, Sheffield and Glasgow, offered more coordinated assistance programmes and provided examples which other urban authorities were encouraged to follow in child welfare work during the war.

The Future of the Race

A falling birth-rate among the middle classes and a generally high infant mortality rate had led to fears about population decline. These were exacerbated by the influential doctrine of Eugenics which focused concern upon the more qualitative fear of racial degeneration. Supporters of this doctrine advocated drastic solutions such as the sterilization of the unfit, as well as more rational ones like family allowances. The latter were conceived as an incentive to the thrifty to have more children. These various concerns were, of course, magnified with the outbreak of the First World War and they form the ideological hinterland to the generalised concern with motherhood at this time. With a high death-rate abroad and a low birth-rate at home, combating infant mortality assumed new significance. In October 1918, *Woman Worker* carried an advertisement for *Allenbury's Baby Foods*: 'Now more than ever the welfare of Baby is important to Country and Empire. While nine soldiers died in every hour in 1915, twelve babies died at home.' The size of the population became relatively more important after 1914 and Eugenic discourses of selective breeding were subordinated to the need to improve the health of the whole nation. But only by making public health a national concern could the still persistent demand for quality as well as quantity be met. Discourses around the issue of motherhood were therefore almost invariably located in the context of child health.

One consequence of the population scare was the inclusion of unmarried mothers as recipients of state welfare services. Attitudes did not change overnight – the dominant tone was still patronising – but there were now many who believed that the unmarried mother might 'regain her self-respect'. The Welfare Officer of the National Amatol Factory at Aintree described with pride one unmarried mother who worked at the factory until the eighth month of her pregnancy while provision was made for her confinement and for nursery care for her baby after her return to work: 'She was protected from the comments of her companions by the evident interest of the Welfare Department, and is regaining her self-respect.'[4] After the 'War Baby Scandal' swept the press in 1916 (a year which actually had an exceptionally low illegitimate birth-rate), the number of children born out of wedlock did in fact rise during the war to a level thirty per cent above that of the pre-war years. The new tolerance towards unmarried mothers was a complex phenomenom, not unconnected with the idea of 'giving the boys a good time', as the *Manchester Guardian* put it in September 1918. There was also a related belief that the children of British Servicemen, whether born in or out of wedlock, should be a source of national pride. However the press saw it, though, the fact remained that the infant mortality rate for children of unmarried mothers was double that for those born in wedlock. Concern about this was expressed in the 1917–18 Report of the Chief Medical Officer at the LGB, and the National Council for the Unmarried Mother and her Child, founded in 1918, skilfully articulated its appeal to Nursing Associations to attend unmarried mothers on confinement in populationist terms: 'In view of the fact that the nation can ill afford this great drain on its infant population . . . their attention was drawn to the urgent need for the skilled care of every woman in childbirth.'[5] The War Emergency: Workers' National Committee, a labour movement organization mainly concerned with welfare, also consistently lobbied the government for separation allowances to be granted to unmarried mothers in cases where the father was serving in the forces.

The Ideology of Motherhood

Faced with both an external threat and internal hardships, a pressing problem for the government was to develop policies which could foster civilian morale and national unity. The idea that class differences were narrowed through social policy as the whole population became involved in the war effort may be true for the Second World War,[6] but it does not seem to apply here. Although the number of people involved was high – whether through losing men at the front or through munitions work and shortages of essential supplies at home – social policy was not directed towards a level-ling-up of material standards for the poor. Class differences remained as sharp as ever. Industrial unrest and the growth of the Shop Stewards Movement caused the government grave concern. In munitions factories all over Britain there was conflict at another level between middle-class women motivated by patriotism and women who worked because they needed the money. In child welfare, class differences were so acute that separate creches were established for the rich and the poor. The Basil Blackwood Day Nursery and Hostel were founded by Lady Plunket for 'the children of the professional and educated classes.' Its sponsors justified its necessity like this: 'Excellent creches for the babies of the slums are now provided by municipalities, etc., backed by Government grants – in the poorest areas of London', but these were not suitable for 'mothers reared and educated under refined conditions who have suddenly found themselves in straitened circumstances.'[7]

In spite of such differences, official sources attempted to present a classless image of motherhood; they succeeded to the extent that the idealization of motherhood became a powerful unifying factor during the war. The concept of motherhood conveyed a strong sense of the future since the protection of the mother and the projection of this image as the bearer of future generations quelled fears of population decline and conveyed a potential sense of peace and a better civilization long before it became possible to speak of reconstruction in any explicit sense. Arthur News-holme, Chief Medical Officer at the LGB described the mother as 'the Maker of the Home, the link between past and future, the transmitter of life and civilisation.' The Final Report of the Health of Munition Workers Commit-tee, published in 1918, introduced its discussion of the employment of women with these words:

'Upon the womanhood of the country most largely rests the privilege first of creating and maintaining a wholesome family life, and, sec-ondly, of developing the higher influences of social life – both mat-ters of primary and vital importance to the future of the nation.'

Such rhetoric was not confined to government circles. In July 1918 the journal *Home Notes* introduced a competition to describe Britain's ideal baby with equally high-sounding phrases: 'For the babies are our biggest national asset and our greatest responsibility in these critical times – in their tiny hands the whole future welfare of our nation will rest.' And the editor of *Child Welfare Annual* wrote,

'For long, we have been accustomed to speak of children as the most valuable of Imperial assets . . . The child of today . . . will be the citizen of the coming years, and must take up and bear the duties of state-manship, defence from foes, the conduct of labour, the direction of progress, the maintenance of a high level of thought and conduct and all other necessities for the perpetuation of an imperial race.'

Maternity and adequate child care seemed to promise a physically fitter generation of children. And by extension the mother, as the custodian of family life, also became the guardian of the 'higher influences of social life.' In this way the themes of racial superiority and the future welfare and unity of the nation become fused around a single image during the First World War. It was clear, though, that the construction of a 'national' image of motherhood could not be based solely on its middle-class variant. The new ideology of motherhood as the spiritual and physical bearer of future civilization meant that working-class mothers – the majority of the female population – could no longer be portrayed in official documents as ignorant. Thus, though many reformers still secretly held onto the pre-war ideology of educating working-class mothers, there was a subtle shift in emphasis from education to welfare in ministerial statements and reports. Moreover, this new concern for women's welfare could only be effective if it bore at least some tenuous relationship to the material conditions of the majority of Britain's mothers and babies. Since it was now widely known that this majority lived in poverty and ill-health, an intensification of maternity and child-welfare work was clearly called for.

I have already noted that central government activity in this field before the war was minimal. However, as wartime conditions made state intervention generally more acceptable, the scope for its involvement in child-welfare gradually widened. In 1914, the LGB drew up a scheme of maternity and child-welfare services for which local authorities would receive a fifty per cent grant from the board. This, together with legislation the following year to help provision in rural areas, led to a dramatic increase in the number of maternity and child-welfare centres and salaried health visitors during the war. Generally, these were organised along the lines of the more efficient existing schemes, although there were some important changes. There was an increase in provision consistent with the shift of emphasis from education to welfare. Dinners for expectant and nursing mothers, powdered milk, vitamins, Virol and Glaxo were provided at most centres. These were now called infant *welfare* – not consultation – centres. As food shortages increased and prices rose, the LGB was finally forced, under the 1918 Milk Order, to provide grants for local authorities to supply milk to mothers and children on the same terms as other infant welfare facilities. At the same time, more attention was paid to the confinement itself, to the provision and training of midwives, and to the need – voiced by both the medical profession and women's organizations such as the Women's Co-operative Guild – for more hospital accommodation for maternity and pre-maternity cases. This was a double-edged weapon. Practising midwives began to achieve some of the status and economic security which they deserved, and there is little doubt that their improved training reduced the suffering of many women in pregnancy and childbirth. It became much harder, though, for working-class midwives to practice since they lacked the academic skills for the qualifying examination: this disruption of working-class traditions of assistance in childbirth caused considerable hardship. For example the outlawing of the handywoman, who ostensibly helped the midwife but frequently delivered the baby herself, left a gap in provision since the handywoman had traditionally been prepared to look after the family and household duties during the mother's confinement. Consequently, much harm was done by mothers having to get up too soon to attend to the household duties.

The stress on clinical expertise and the desirability of hospital births was eventually to displace control of the birth process from the mother and midwife to the predominantly male medical profession. At this time, however, given the deplorable living conditions of most working-class women and the shortage of doctors away at the front, combined with their lack of interest in obstetrics, the new focus on clinical skill was probably an advantage to mothers and midwives alike. Some of its dangers can be seen in the development of ante-natal care during this period: this made it possible to begin the supervision of the mother in her home even earlier. The most negative feature of this treatment was its preoccupation with the eradication of VD, believed to be the cause of a large number of stillbirths and miscarriages. Treatment was through arsenic and diagnosis, difficult in itself, was often made on social rather than medical grounds. Previous stillbirths and miscarriages were sometimes taken into account in the diagnosis and, since these were often caused by malnutrition and heavy labour (domestic or paid), it was the poorest sections of the population which were most penalized. Newsholme, in his LGB Annual Report for 1917–18, suggested that ante-natal, and especially anti-syphilitic, treatment might reduce the exceptionally high infant mortality rate among workhouse births. Typically, he did not suggest that aseptic conditions in these notoriously unhygienic institutions might have a similar effect.

There was, therefore, a price to be paid for improved maternity care and child welfare. The development of clinical expertise cannot be separated from a general trend in this period to develop a corps of state experts – psychologists, teachers, probation officers, health visitors and midwives – all concerned with the more efficient supervision of the working-class family.[8] This fed an ideology of expertise which disrupted existing working-class traditions. Occasionally it was successfully resisted – the payment of National Insurance maternity benefit direct to mothers was implemented in 1913 after a determined fight by the Women's Co-operative Guild and the 1918 Maternity and Child Welfare Act met the demand that two working-class women should be included on local authority Maternity and Child Welfare Committees. But these remained exceptions to the general pattern.

The impact of maternity and infant-welfare policies on the health of mother and children is hard to assess. Although there is some evidence that their health improved, this was by no means universal. 1916 saw the lowest infant mortality rate ever and the *Working Classes: Cost of Living Committee* (1918) noted an improvement in the health of children. But this improvement was of a short-term nature. Immediately after the war, women's claims for sickness benefit, which had declined in number since 1915, increased, and widespread ill-health among women and children, including a high maternal mortality rate, continued into the 1930s.[9] Nor can the whole improvement in working-class health be attributed to the maternity services. It is probable that improved midwifery and infant welfare provided a useful service to only a limited number of women. The centres were well spoken of by women like the socialist and suffragist Hannah Mitchell and in the WCG's *Maternity: Letters from Working Women*, but they related to only a small section of the population. Other factors, such as the payment of separation allowances to servicemen's wives, were important in improving the living standard of the low-paid – although, according to the Reports of the North Kensington Baby Clinic (1915–17), this was short lived. With the exception of the 'poorest class of irregular workers' all others found that the effect of rising prices and the scarcity of food and fuel outweighed the benefit of separation allowances within six months of the outbreak of war. Where there was an improvement in the health of mothers and children, the most important single factor was undoubtedly the opportunity for women to earn decent wages in industry as part of the war effort.

Mothers in the Factories

Munitions work was no soft option for working-class women, particularly when it was added to a burden of domestic work already increased by hours of queuing and food and fuel shortages. It often meant working with toxic materials and long hours of work and travelling, including night shifts which, as the Health of Munitions Workers Committee noted in 1918, was particularly unsuitable for women: 'In a working-class home, the difficulty of obtaining rest by day is great; quiet cannot easily be secured; and the mother of children cannot sleep, while the claims of children and home are pressing on her.' Employers could obtain exemptions from factory legislation limiting the number of hours worked, and this was severely abused in the first years of the war – some women worked ninety five to a hundred hours a week. From 1916, the Ministry of Munitions tightened up on exemption orders and, while there were doubtless still abuses and the night-shift continued throughout the war, Sunday working was abolished. Although the twelve-hour shift was the norm, the Ministry had some success in convincing employers of the importance of meal and rest breaks, and generally from 1916, conditions began to improve. Janet Campbell's memorandum to the Health of Munitions Workers Committee included a survey of 1,183 workers, of whom only eight and a half per cent showed marked fatigue and thirty four per cent 'slight fatigue'. While she stressed the seriousness of 'slight fatigue' and its possible long-term effects, including on the worker's potential maternity, this was nonetheless a marked improvement in the situation compared to the Committee's 1915 Report which revealed widespread ill-health and extreme fatigue among munitions workers.

More important were the countervailing influences: regular employment with good wages leading to more nourishing food, better clothing and improved living conditions. One observer noted that 'many well paid women gave up the supposedly feminine habit of living on bread and tea for more substantial meals of meat and vegetables' and one former munitions worker, Jessie Arrowsmith, remembers the war as a 'flush' time characterised by a joint of sirloin for Sunday dinner.[10] The improved health of munitions workers gives the lie to assumptions about their ignorance of budgeting and their preference for jewellery and luxuries over the necessities of life. A great number of these war workers had been recruited initially from the low-paid, predominantly sweated trades in which women had found work before the war: '. . . the additional women workers were mainly the wives of working-men's families, most of the married women having worked before marriage. Soldiers' wives often found their separation allowances insufficient.' Speculating further on the women's motives, the same commentator continues, 'In general both patriotic motives and the rising cost of living undoubtedly played a part, and finally, a small number of women of a higher social class entered the factories from patriotic motives.'[11]

The large-scale employment of women in industry cut across the idealization of motherhood. The connection between employment outside the home and bad motherhood had been assumed since the first enquiries into infant mortality in the mid-nineteenth century. It had been difficult to prove, since the industrial employment of women had always been accompanied by other negative aspects of urban life such as overcrowding and bad sanitation. The counter-argument was that the benefits of women's wages, leading to better nutrition in pregnancy and healthier infants, outweighed the evils of employment itself. Surveys supporting both sides of the argument such as Newsholme's study *Infant Mortality in Lancashire* in 1914 and Dr Jessie Duncan's comparison of two poor wards in Birmingham, in one of which women were industrially employed, failed to produce any conclusive evidence. In spite of the absence of proof, prejudice remained strong and the government stressed that women's employment was an emergency measure only. The Health of Munition Workers Committee was explicit about women's role as an industrial reserve army and about motherhood as a national asset:

> 'Clearly, everything should be done to reconcile the woman's conflict of interests between her home and her work in the factory. Wherever other labour is available, the employment of mothers with infants is to be deprecated, as is also that of the mother of any young family . . . The Committee takes the view that to use up or damage its women by overstrain in factory work is one of the most serious and far-reaching forms of human waste that a nation can practise or permit.'

Like the government, the labour movement was also anxious to limit women's employment to the duration of the war. The Amalgamated Society of Engineers (ASE), the most powerful union of skilled workers, insisted on the restoration of pre-war practices – in effect, the withdrawal of women from industry – as soon as peace was declared; they signed a Treasury Agreement with the government to this effect in March 1915. The unions feared dilution by unskilled labour and post-war unemployment but their arguments too were sometimes reinforced by a concern for motherhood and the future of the race. One member of the Ship Constructors' and Ship-wrights' Association objected that the presence of women in the dockyards was 'detrimental to the mothers of our future generations and cannot conduce to the raising of a strong and virile race for the maintenance of our country.' An article in *The Call*, quoted in the *ASE Monthly Journal* sums up the balance of concern to protect jobs and protect the race, felt by many trade unionists:

> 'Under all these circumstances [i.e. dilution] the feminisation of industry carries with it grave perils to the race, to the workers as a class and to the women and girls themselves. The employers eagerly seize on female labour, because it is cheap, unorganized and easily depressed into absolute subservience. They have no conscience in the matter. For the sake of profits they would ruin the future of the race.'

Thus, women's industrial employment was seen, by employers and labour movement leaders alike, as being for the duration of the war only, and, moreover, as requiring special arrangements for their welfare. Improvements in the munitions factories – such as better canteen facilities, longer breaks and shorter hours – were justified in terms of preventing fatigue among women so that the family would not suffer. This was particularly important, given the additional problems faced by working-class women: 'Where home conditions are bad, as they are frequently, where a long working-day is aggravated by long hours of travelling, and where, in addition, housing accommodation is inadequate, family life is defaced beyond recognition.'[12]

The improvement of factory conditions was undertaken by the Welfare Department of the Ministry of Munitions, who unfortunately entrusted the task to factory welfare workers. These were generally middle-class women responsible, unlike the factory inspectors, to the employer rather than to the Ministry. Since relatively few employers shared the Ministry's view that a healthy workforce was conducive to improved production, welfare workers devoted their attention to disciplining the dress, manners and even social life of the employees rather than concerning themselves with the provision of canteens, restrooms, and first-aid or other medical facilities. Although some progress was made, the Ministry's schemes were never fully implemented.

Pregnancy presented specific problems in munitions factories. The arguments against women's employment during pregnancy were gradually being undermined by their evident good health. While it was acknowledged that certain forms of work such as heavy lifting or standing or sitting in one position for long periods, were harmful, it was now being argued less and less that work itself was detrimental to pregnancy. Janet Campbell, who was later to become head of the Maternity and Child Welfare Department at the Ministry of Health, argued that 'In whatever class of society, a sedentary unoccupied life is not healthy for the expectant mother. The working woman in her own home is busily occupied and often undertakes heavy work (e.g. washing) not well-suited to her condition.' In the factory, light work and regular meals were possible and the question of diet was paramount: it was better to work and have a reasonable diet than to be malnourished at home through poverty. Although no solution is offered to the heavy domestic work left undone and the dirty washing piling up at home, this change of attitude towards the employment of pregnant women was nonetheless important, not least because with so many women now the family's main wage-earner, their dismissal early in pregnancy would have caused severe financial hardship. The corollary of Janet Campbell's recognition of the financial needs of pregnant women was her demand for compensatory measures which would allow them to continue working without harm to themselves or their children. In her Memorandum to the Health of Munitions Workers Committee, Dr Campbell suggested that, rather than dismissing pregnant women, as was the usual practice, they should be transferred to light work from the fourth to the eighth month. They should work only a shortened day-shift and be provided with extra food and milk, if necessary, through the works canteen. In many districts, creches and even night-creches were required to allow mothers to return to work. Early notification of pregnancy was essential since both miscarriages and attempt-

ed abortions occurred in the early months and women generally tried to
conceal their condition for fear of dismissal. In addition, Campbell advocated a comprehensive maternity scheme for the confinement, ante-natal
and post-natal care of pregnant women and their children and also financial
assistance until they were fit to return to work. Both in this Memorandum
and in that to the War Cabinet Committee on Women in Industry, she
argued strongly against further restrictions on mothers' employment unless
accompanied by financial aid:

> 'A breast-fed infant is more likely to thrive than one which is brought-
> up by hand, but an ill-nourished mother is either unable to nurse her
> baby or continues to do so only at undue cost to herself. Until the State
> is prepared to recognise the claim of nursing mothers to assistance and
> financial aid, the lesser of the two evils might be for the mother to go
> back to work as soon as she is physically fit to do so, provided she can
> ensure the care of her baby during her absence.'

Campbell's scheme was implemented in two factories – the National Amatol
Factory at Aintree and the National Ordnance Factories in Leeds. The
reports on both schemes stressed that this system benefited not only the
worker herself but also the firm. Industrial relations were more harmonious;
trained workers stayed at their jobs longer. The Aintree report added:

> 'From the state point of view the great question of the present day is the
> increase of the human race and infant welfare and any measures which
> tend to promote the greater well-being of the mother before and at the
> time of confinement and the health of the coming generation are to be
> encouraged.'[13]

Childcare

The evident and growing need for creches and other forms of childcare was
possibly the most difficult to reconcile with the official ideology of motherhood. Although hours could be shortened and home helps and other forms
of assistance provided, the separation of mother and child was inevitable.
The Ministry of Munitions examined schemes in operation in France,
Belgium and Italy where creches in or near the factories allowed munitions
workers to breastfeed their children, but eventually rejected them on the
grounds that they would place undue strain on mothers hurrying their own
meals in order to feed the baby! (One suspects that the disruption of the
work routine may have been an additional factor in the Ministry's mind.)
Another scheme considered and rejected was proposed by Dr Scurfield,
Medical Officer of Health for Sheffield: he advocated the provision of paid
and supervised minders. In a report to the Minister, the Welfare Advisory

Committee of the Ministry of Munitions claimed that their preferred system of creches near workers' homes was adequate, subject to the 'overriding consideration' that they should be strictly temporary:

> 'It is probably not . . . practicable in existing circumstances to confine the employment of women in factories to those who are unmarried or without children, but we consider that in so far as the establishment of Creches tends to facilitate the employment of married women, the extension of them should be confined within the narrowest limits.'

The Report went further and added that

> 'A large increase in the number of Creches must necessarily neutralise to a large extent the efforts which have been made over previous years to secure a better care of children by their own mothers, and in our view such a step would be retrograde and unjustifiable.'[14]

Public attitudes towards creches were more ambivalent and varied. In October 1917 *The Daily Chronicle* described running a creche as valuable war work:

> 'They were the prettiest, cleanest little children imaginable . . . They looked all that child life should be at its best. It is a picture you may see any day at the Whitefield Day Nursery, Whitefield Road, Tottenham Court Road. Here the little children of our splendid mothers who are making munitions or engaged in other productive work are fed and cared for. For 4d a day their mothers are able to leave them there, safe under the trained care of a sympathetic nurse and her assistants.'

The same paper had been equally fulsome in its praise of Sylvia Pankhurst's nursery, *The Mother's Arms*, and the work of the East London Suffrage Federation, but it gave little credit to the heroism of East End mothers. In 'Babies' Fairyland in Slumdom' (4 May 1915), the glowing account of the nursery clearly implied some criticism of the care normally received by the children.

> 'Tragedy comes in the evening. Just before seven, the babies are all undressed again, their old things brought out from the cupboard and they leave fairyland for the hard, humdrum existence of the ordinary London child. But they come back to fairyland again in the morning.'

The Labour Party adopted a generally hostile attitude to childcare, particularly to night-creches and those which took children on a weekly basis. The author of an article in *Labour Woman* in March 1917 was anxious to disassociate the Labour Party from anything which threatened family life. In the past, she wrote, anti-Socialist propaganda had claimed that 'the wicked Socialist wanted to take all the children away from their mothers and bring them up in barracks . . . It has often been said that the War has made Socialists of us all. If this were what Socialism meant, I, for one, would repudiate the title.' In general, though, the debate on childcare and creches remained fairly muted in the interests of the war effort. The Ministry of Munitions provided a seventy five per cent grant for creches on initial outlay and a subsidy of 7d per attendance from 1916, but by the end of the war it was actually subsidizing only forty one centres. The Board of Education was rather more supportive: it had provided grants to voluntary nursery schools and day nurseries since 1914 and was subsidizing 174 nurseries by 1918. Many of these were open-air nurseries run on Montessori lines which could be justified in terms of both health and education for the children. Since the Board was also responsible for the inspection of Ministry of Munitions creches, it was not difficult to blur the distinction between creches for working mothers and day-nurseries with primarily educational aims and thus to limit public concern over the separation of working mothers from their children.

The 1918/19 Annual Report from the Chief Medical Officer of the LGB showed the spirit in which nurseries were tolerated and provision for nursery schools made in the 1918 Education Act:

> 'Since the cessation of war conditions and the release of married women from industrial employment, some of these [creches] have been closed; but an increasing number of local authorities have become interested in the subject, as a means not simply of caring for the child, whilst the mother is at work, but for improving the health of the children who require special attention, and of instructing mothers, and girls in attendance at school, in the proper care of the young infant.'

This distinction, involving as it does the educational dimensions of the ideology charted above, was confirmed by the 1918 Education Act: nursery schools came under the jurisdiction of the Board of Education while day-nurseries, with no educational aspirations, were administered by the Ministry of Health. This distinction achieved wide public support. The Labour Party, for example, fully supported nursery schools but an article in *Labour Woman*, January 1920, described day-nurseries as 'from the labour point of view, a necessity of the moment, but not an ideal for the furture, for its main object is to provide for children whose mothers go out to work.'[15] With the end of the war, the educational approach to maternal and child welfare re-emerged as a central theme in the struggle to create a classless and specifically national image of motherhood.

Demobilisation

During the war women achieved an unprecedented status and independence. Many experienced regular paid employment for the first time. They
earned wages higher than had previously been known and proved their
ability to compete equally with men on the labour market. But they were
never allowed to forget that their primary role was that of wife and mother.
At the end of the war they were dismissed from the factories more or less *en
masse*.

Government controlled establishments set the pace. Even before the
Armistice, forty thousand women had been dismissed from government
work according to the *Woolwich Pioneer* of March 15, 1918. By April 1919, the
number of women employed in government establishments had been
reduced by 19.9% and in private industry by 13.7%. Some government
departments, including the Board of Trade and the Ministry of Munitions,
would happily have continued to use them as cheap labour on unskilled
work in light engineering, but the threat of social unrest resulting from high
post-war unemployment made the restoration of pre-war trades union
practices imperative. Any attempts to reabsorb women into employment
now had to channel them into areas where they would not be in competition
with men. The percentage of women in the industrial workforce (private,
municipal and government) rose from twenty six per cent in 1914 to thirty six
per cent in November 1918 and then fell rapidly back to twenty seven per
cent by July 1920. (In transport, the corresponding figures are two per cent
for 1914, twelve per cent for 1918 and four per cent for 1920.) Growth areas
for women's employment included retailing and catering and finance and
commerce where they worked mainly as clerks. In the latter category, they
already constituted twenty seven per cent of the total workforce in 1914,
rising to fifty seven per cent by 1918 and then down again to forty per cent by
1920.[16] Domestic service is not included in these figures but it provided the
main source of women's employment throughout the 1920s. Detested as it
was for its deplorable pay and conditions, it became, in effect, women's last
resort as one area after another was hit by the post-war economic crisis.
During the first six months of 1920, for example, this area alone accounted
for 67.2% of the total vacancies filled every month by labour exchanges.

Things might have been different if women had had the backing of
the labour movement. But a staunch trade unionist like Mary MacArthur,
Secretary of the National Federation of Women Workers, meekly accepted
the terms laid out by the Amalgamated Society of Engineers in the interests
of labour unity. Although the prospect of unemployment after the war had
been discussed at National Federation Conferences since 1916 and there had
been talk of finding alternative employment for the displaced women, it
failed to materialize. The National Federation devoted its main efforts to the

establishment of Trade Boards in the sweated industries which, although a worthy cause, avoided conflict with skilled male workers. The notion that a woman's place is in the home became a convenient alibi for failing to combat women's unemployment. Dorothy Jewson, Head of the Organization Department for the National Federation, wrote in *Reynolds News*, 'I wonder if it is really understood that though a woman's immediate value as a worker may be great, her potential value as a mother is greater . . . We are looking forward to the day when mothers will not be found in the industrial arena.' (11 May, 1919) Many women in the Labour Party thus found themselves sharing the official ideology of women's domestic role, partly through their strong commitment to the policy of the family-wage and partly through a genuine desire to improve the social and domestic conditions of the lives of working-class women. These class-conscious trade unionists cannot, however, be regarded as speaking for all, or even the majority of industrially employed women. One woman wrote to *Woman Worker* in January 1917:

> 'Do you think we women will be shouldered out of our jobs – some of us need them badly when the war is over, or do you think that some of us will fight to keep them in despite of the men. I would never keep a returned soldier out of his job, I hope, but the matter will be difficult. Can you give any advice or encouragement?'

Her dilemma does not appear to have been widespread among working women.

Despite the arduous nature of war work, women did not in general give up their jobs willingly. For many, it was not a choice between war work and domesticity, but between war work and poverty – either on the dole or in sweated industries. The improved health of women war workers and their families, indicated by increased claims for sickness benefit with the onset of post-war unemployment, underscored the importance of regular, well-paid employment, One investigation, reported at a Women's Labour League Conference in January 1917, had asked the question 'After the War do you want to return to your former work or stay in what you are doing now?' Out of three thousand replies, 2,500 favoured remaining in their wartime occupation.[17] At Woolwich Arsenal, in November 1918, women staged a spontaneous demonstration against dismissals which reached the Embankment and was only prevented from reaching Parliament itself by some hasty politicking by Mary MacArthur. Reports from labour exchanges in the North West reported that 'Many women who come to us express a real preference for factory work; that does not exist to any great extent. Then they consider what appeals to them next. Institutional or hotel work appeals to them rather than private domestic service.'[18] With ten million unemployed however, their wishes were unlikely to be fulfilled. Despite the extension of unemployment insurance in 1916 to cover just over a million munitions workers it was still clearly inadequate and the government hastily introduced the Out of Work Donation (OWD) or dole. This established for the first time the important principle of the right to maintenance while unemployed and reinforced the wartime precedent of separation allowances by including allowances for dependants. Women were entitled to the dole and to its successor, virtually universal national insurance, under the 1920 National Insurance Act, but since applicants were disqualified for refusing to accept jobs offered to them – often at extremely low rates – the effect was to return women to their pre-war jobs at pre-war rates of pay. And then, of course, there were always vacancies in domestic services.

Retraining schemes for women were limited in scope and, like the dole, directed towards returning women to their traditional feminine occupations: the lower grades of clerical work and, above all, domestic service. This was seen officially as good training for married life, but was hated and resisted by the women themselves despite heavy government promotion. In a similar vein, though with a more subtle emphasis, Adelaide Anderson, the Chief Factory Inspector, advocated the extension of training for midwifery, home helps, health-visiting, infant welfare work and nursery teachers as suitable openings for women made redundant at the end of the war. A Ministry of Labour leaflet meanwhile short-circuited all of these schemes by simply asking women to leave the labour market:

> 'A call comes again to the Women of Britain, a call happily not to make shells or to fill them so that a ruthless enemy shall be destroyed, but a call to help renew the homes of England, to sew and to mend, to cook and to clean and to rear the babies in health and happiness, who in their turn shall grow into men and women worthy of the Empire.'[19]

Faced with this – and with even the bulk of the trades unions and the Labour Party against them – those women who wanted to remain in industry had little chance of success. Their wartime release from domesticity had been partial and, indeed, 'for the duration only.'

Conclusion

There was a variety of complex elements comprising the ensemble of this national ideology of motherhood and of women's 'true role'; many subtle ideological manoeuvres, shifts and slides were needed to hold it together. Occasionally, these opened up a space for the development of some progressive and democratic potential as, for example, in the admission that it was sometimes necessary for women to work rather than subject their families to poverty or, as we have seen, in the tangential establishment of some limited welfare rights rather than privileges. These changes were presented as being purely temporary, though, the result of wartime expediency. After the war, women were ushered firmly back to the hearth and home.

But if for women in general few lasting gains had been made, several doors had been pushed ajar. In 1918 and 1928, the vote was given to women as a reward partly for their services as both mothers and war workers. Maternity and child-welfare services had begun to improve in a piecemeal way: feminists were to use these improvements as a basis for demanding the extension of rights for the mother and not just for her potential children. Separation allowances and the dole had established a precedent for dependants' allowances and for cash payments direct to the mother. This forced lengthy discussion of the question of mothers' pensions in government committees such as the War Cabinet Committee on Women in Industry (1919), as well as providing useful ammunition for the Family Endowment Society in its campaign for family allowances. It had also been proved that women's employment neither destroyed family life nor the woman's capacity for maternity. This was exploited by organisations like the Women's Industrial Council in it influential *Industry and Motherhood* enquiry, published in July 1918, which concluded that 'judging by any or all of the tests to which we have put our 934 cases, there is practically nothing to choose in quality of maternity between those who "go out to work" and those who stay at home.'[20] And, finally, the myth of the male breadwinner had been undermined to the extent that a large number of women had provided the main family income during the war, and many would continue as effective heads of family when men had been killed or disabled at the front.

None of these developments bore fruit immediately. Campaigns to reduce maternal mortality and morbidity only began in earnest in the 1930s. Family allowances were not conceded until 1945. And, in the meantime, the long period of the inter-war slump and unemployment had to be endured. But although the years immediately following the First World War represented a significant defeat for women, seeds of self-confidence and political awareness were sown and the lessons of the war years were not entirely lost.

Acknowledgments

I am particularly grateful to Marion Kozak for her valuable comments and suggestions, as well as for allowing me access to her own research, which has provided extremely useful and stimulating information.

Notes

1. A. Davin, 'Imperialism and motherhood', *History Workshop Journal*, no. 5, Spring 1978.
2. D. Chew, *Ada Nield Chew; the life and writings of a working woman*, London, Virago, 1982, p. 154.

3. A. Davin, op. cit., p. 56.
4. *Welfare Supervisor's Report, National Amatol Factory, Aintree*, Imperial War Museum, file MUN 26/6, 1918, p. 2.
5. *Maternity and Child Welfare*, October 1918.
6. R. Titmuss, 'War and social policy', *Essays on 'The Welfare State'*, London, Allen and Unwin, 1976, pp. 75–84.
7. Leaflet, Imperial War Museum, file WEL 1, 1918.
8. The question of state experts is dealt with more fully in Centre for Contemporary Cultural Studies State Group, *Crisis and Hegemony*, London, Hutchinson, forthcoming. Chapters by J. Clarke and C. Rowan deal particularly with state experts and working-class families.
9. B. Bentley Gilbert, *British Social Policy 1914–39*, London, Batsford, 1970, p. 286. See also C. Webster, 'Healthy or hungry thirties?', *History Workshop Journal*, no. 11, Spring 1982.
10. M. Kozak, *Women munition workers during the First World War, with special reference to engineering*, unpublished Ph.D. thesis, University of Hull, 1976, p. 404.
11. I. O. Andrews, *The Economic Effects of the War on Women and Children in Great Britain*, New York, 1918, p. 4.
12. *Yorkshire Factory Times*, 20 April 1916; *ASE Monthly Bulletin*, September 1916; Ministry of Munitions, *Final Report of the Health of Munitions Workers' Committee*, London, Cmd. 9065, 1918.
13. *Welfare Supervisor's Report, National Amatol Factory, Aintree*, Imperial War Museum file MUN 26/4, 1918,7pp. 6–14. See also H. Palmer-Jones, *A Report of Work Done for Expectant Mothers at the Sewing Depot, National Ordnance Factories, Leeds*, Imperial War Museum, file MUN 18.9/17, 1918.
14. Public Records Office, *MUN 5/93/546/140*, 1917.
15. *Labour Woman*, January 1920.
16. These figures from Kozak, op. cit., pp. 363–4.
17. Kozak, op. cit., p. 399.
18. Kozak, op. cit., p. 371.
19. Kozak, op. cit., p. 379.
20. *Women's Industrial News*, July 1918, p. 15.

Neil Grant

CITIZEN SOLDIERS: Army Education in World War II

What British society would be like when peace returned – 'the future being fought for' – became an important political question from an early stage of the Second World War. The propaganda of the period often projected an optimistic vision of future possibilities, but at the same time set limits on popular aspirations by referring back to notions of political citizenship, its rights and duties. The category of the *citizen* thus became central to the state's more explicitly educative role in mobilising support for the war – it informed contemporary legislation, and it also provided the point of reference for competing conceptions of what the social and political roles of the people should be in the post-war world. Some of the tensions within the state's educative strategies became particularly clear in the compulsory social education developed within the forces. One observer commented in 1945 that 'everybody in the Army was put into the same position as a child or adolescent, who must willy-nilly go to school, and by the accident of war circumstances an experiment became possible on a scale, and in terms, which no one would have dreamed of proposing in peace time.'[1] The 'experiment' was ABCA, the Army Bureau of Current Affairs. Its novelty was that, although a state initiative within the context of military discipline, it adopted popular and 'democratic' forms of learning. ABCA was seen by some commentators as having a radicalizing effect – R. A. Butler even suggested in his autobiography that it helped to lose the Conservative Party the 1945 election.[2] Whether or not it is wise to draw such direct political conclusions, the history of ABCA certainly reveals two cultural processes at work: how the liberal-democratic state attempts to shape popular national aspirations (through the work of intellectuals and education), and also how such educational initiatives are always negotiated by the people at whom they are directed.

Social Education in a Democracy

The idea of education for citizenship had already been floated in the 1930s, often in terms of the need to develop a defence against totalitarianism.[3] On the one hand, the subordination of German schools to Nazi ideology set alarm bells ringing. On the other, there was a fear that the failings of British schools might predispose children to authoritarian politics. In *Social Education and the Schools*, published in 1934, the New Education Fellowship outlined the tasks of social education in a democracy:

> '. . . one of the greatest dangers to the continuance and extension of democracy lies in the fact that the schools have not fully realised their responsibility for training the rising generation in the intelligent under- standing of the affairs of the contemporary world. As a consequence boys and girls, when they leave school, are not sufficiently aware of the complexity of modern problems . . . and therefore tend to fall an easy prey to the propagandist and manufacturer of party slogans.'

This concern with the political aspects of the 'problem of youth' as it was perceived in the '30s led to the formation of the Association for Education in Citizenship in 1934. Although it failed to convince the Spens Committee to incorporate formal teaching about citizenship in its report on Secondary Education in 1938, the AEC and other groups were conspicuously successful in promoting the idea that citizenship education could be a support to parliamentary democracy. A glance at the *Times Educational Supplement* and other educational publications in the pre-war years reveals the emergence and consolidation of a discourse in which education, democracy and citizenship were intimately connected.

The nature of that connection – what actually constituted 'good citizenship' – was a matter of dispute, not only with the movement's opponents but between its supporters. The Association's co-founder, the former Liberal MP Sir Ernest Simon, tried to persuade prominent political figures from across the spectrum that there was a common ground to be shared. Not all were convinced. The socialist G. D. H. Cole, a Council member of the Association, set out his reservations in a comment on the draft of one of its early publications:

> 'I feel that there runs through it an unspoken assumption that the existing basis of the political system, if not of the economic system as well, is adequate for bringing about such changes as may be desirable in the social order. Or, in other words, that the task is merely one of piecemeal adaptation and not one of fundamental reconstruction . . . I don't share that view.'[5]

Simon also had to face charges that Conservative, 'traditionalist' and relig- ious views could not easily be catered for in an association which drew most of its support from people of more radical and secular persuasions. Rep- resentatives from teachers' organizations also expressed the fear that any formal prescriptions about what should be taught could open the way to the use of schools for political 'indoctrination'.[6] Faced with such resistance, the politics of the AEC remained broadly Fabian. It failed to shift the government from its traditional notions of the curriculum and, despite the proliferation of publications about citizenship, the actual impact on teaching was limited. It was really only after the war that its advocacy bore fruit in the schools, in the 'social studies movement'.[7] During the war, however, new forms of adult education raised the debate about citizenship education to a more politically sensitive level.

Education for Citizenship in Wartime

Most members of the armed forces in the Second World War were not professional soldiers, but volunteers and conscripts – men and women drawn from a wide range of occupations and many different regional and social backgrounds. This created a potential problem, which George Wigg, later a Labour minister, perceived thus:

> 'What was certain, although the Army high-ups did not realise it, was that the recruits of 1939 . . . were completely disillusioned with the Establishment and all it stood for. They certainly lacked the innocence, or the enthusiasm, of the recruits of 1914. They were going into the war because it could not be avoided. They had no illusions that it meant fun and games, or that there was glory at the end of the road.'[8]

Military training alone was inadequate for such an army – the soldiers would have to be persuaded that theirs was a legitimate struggle, and that they were not only fighting *against* something but also *for* something. This task acquired a new urgency following the surrender of France and the return of the army to Britain. The general problem has been identified by another post-war Labour MP, Maurice Edelman: 'As in all wars, there are phases of violent action punctuated by long periods of boredom and apathy during which people had time to read and argue and discuss.'[9] Before the middle of 1940, educational schemes had been receiving only minimal attention: they depended heavily on civilian lecturers, they did not constitute a coherent programme, and, officially at least, they were not compulsory. Throughout the first two years of the war, there was considerable lobbying about what form of education would be appropriate for the services, which could both raise morale and enable the forces to have some involvement in the wider political discussions taking place in the country as a whole. Eventually, representations from educationalists and senior officers led to the formation of ABCA in 1941. It was to organize a compulsory programme which would be operated not by professional lecturers or the Army Education Corps, but by junior officers throughout the army who would lead weekly discussion groups on different themes.

ABCA was to be run by a civilian director, W. E. Williams, who before the war had been secretary of the British Institute for Adult Education and editor of the Workers Educational Association's magazine *Highway*. (He was also a director of Penguin books and, after the war, became secretary general of the newly formed Arts Council.) The Bureau's main task was to produce weekly information bulletins which were to serve as the basis for the officer's introduction to the discussion session. Publication started in September 1941: the bulletins alternated between *War*, which charted the military campaigns, and *Current Affairs*, which reviewed a comprehensive range of topics – Health, Social Insurance, Education, Housing, Employment, Women in the Post-War World, Public Opinion and many others – and also devoted issues to the other countries involved in the war. The bulletins were taken up by the other services, and in theatres of war like the Middle East they were reprinted (and sometimes even rewritten) locally. Local issues of both bulletins were also produced, at least in the Middle East.

Several influences seem to have come together in determining the Army Council's decision to set up ABCA.[10] While there was no doubt a genuine desire to improve morale and develop a better informed soldiery, ABCA could also provide a means of containing or, for that matter, identifying political grievances and those who held them. The appointment of Williams as director suggests an attempt to combine his experience of teaching about current affairs in adult education with the existing arguments about education for citizenship and the needs of a basically civilian army. In *Current Affairs in the Army*, an outline of the plan for ABCA published in 1941, the problem of morale was linked directly to the level of political ignorance:

'. . . lack of knowledge about national and international issues is a chronic condition among the citizens of this country, and it does not disappear because a man changes his dungarees or his pin-stripe trousers for a khaki battledress. But if an ill-informed or indifferent citizen is a menace to our national safety, so, too, is a soldier who neither knows nor cares why he is in arms.'

This is close to the earlier concerns about school children but here there was also an implicit invocation of the revolutionary tradition of the Cromwellian citizen-soldier.

This was expanded in a film produced for ABCA and issued in 1943.[11] The opening sequence recalled the critical spirit of the English Revolution:

'Three hundred years ago an Englishman, Oliver Cromwell, said these words, "the citizen soldier must know what he is fighting for, and love what he knows!" In that spirit Cromwell created a New Army, of the finest fighting men England had known to that day.'

The film reconstructs – rather self-consciously – the 'birth of ABCA'.

Williams explains why he coined the title: not only is it a nice short word, but it also suggests the intention of teaching the army a new kind of alphabet, the alphabet of world affairs. 'That sounds OK, Williams,' replies the Adjutant General of the Army without a hint of surprise. 'There's one thing we must be quite certain about. No propaganda, no long-winded lectures. The main thing is discussion. It's a big job, but I believe it can be done.' Officers were warned that they should avoid the tendency to lecture – their job was to act as a chairman – and that the *Current Affairs* bulletins were there '*not* to impose an official view, but to help the soldier to come to well-balanced views of his own.' Among the activities recommended was the production of wall newspapers: 'it gives a man a proper pride to see his name in print, and that starts something else that's very important, a sense of his own value as an individual.' The film ends by placing ABCA's educational work within a longer term political perspective:

> 'We recognize that the new world is in the building now. ABCA is helping to win the war by giving the soldier the weapon of truth and understanding. It is also laying the foundation of an enlightened society which will one day enjoy the peace.'

This educational strategy of ABCA's – and also the *British Way and Purposes* scheme prepared by the Army Education Corps – faced a basic contradiction. How could an army based on a strict top-down system of discipline tolerate activities in which officers could be challenged, their competences tried and incompetences exposed? Some sections did *not* tolerate it (despite the order to do so) or gave ABCA activities only minimal attention or encouragement. The obligatory weekly discussions were extended to the women in the Auxillary Territorial Service in 1943. One woman recalls the discomfort and boredom of being called to attention with other staff in the Pay Corps and lectured on 'current affairs' by an officer for half an hour – and even that encounter with ABCA was a rare one which certainly was not part of a weekly routine.[12] John Newsom found a similar response when researching his book *The Education of Girls* after the war:

> 'Discussing with a group of these young women the relative effects of their school education, pre-war jobs and service experience on their intellectuals interests, I was greeted with a gale of ironic laughter when I innocently suggested that Army Education might have been a help.'[13]

When ABCA operated as intended, it could sometimes intensify problems for the army, especially when junior officer had difficulty in coping with the greater experience and authority of soldiers with whom they disagreed. But generally the element of *compulsion* remained the dominant feature. Again this could cause problems, especially when a political topic was under discussion. The students in the classroom were also citizens sitting in judgment on what was being said. An officer trying to overcome suspicions about the political bias of the sessions might be faced with the solidarity of the 'Ranks' against officers and pupils against teachers. Angus Calder argues:

> 'Where ABCA was taken at all seriously the discussion was bound to range on to the controversial points which could not be cleared up with reference to the bulletins, and where the officer in charge was not always competent to intervene. If he did intervene, ABCA would be dismissed as more "bullshit". If he did not, an opinionated Marxist private could sweep all before him.'[14]

Although ABCA sessions were supposed to encourage thinking and prompt new questions, the ritualised weekly sessions could easily be seen as a device for controlling soldiers' desire to see things actually being changed. In his diary entry for 17 December 1942, J. L. Hodson remarked that:

> 'An intelligent private in the army writes that the feeling of frustration is accentuated by ABCA discussion; his argument is that after the men have discussed something with liveliness, they get a feeling that something must happen – and when nothing does happen, frustration increases. A novel point.'[15]

A former Army Education Officer who served in Cairo has reported similar sentiments among troops who wanted the decisions of their discussion groups communicated to politicians in England.[16]

In short, the ABCA scheme held out the possibility of a new form of participatory citizenship, but the army everywhere prevented its realisation. One occasion on which military requirements came into sharp conflict with educational and political aims was the publication of the Beveridge Report in 1942. Although generally viewed as a blueprint for post-war reconstruction, there were also widespread suspicions that its proposals would not be put into practice. These fears were exacerbated within the forces when an issue of *Current Affairs* written by Beveridge himself to explain his plan was withdrawn by the War Office after 100,000 copies had been issued. Their justification was that the report had not yet gone before parliament, but this seemed rather thin as the report was on public sale. On 1 February 1943, the *New Statesman* scathingly attacked 'Colonel Blimpery' in the War Office and noted, with a certain satisfaction, one unintended consequence of the action:

> '. . . we hear of units where the Beveridge Report, which along with other proposals has been regarded with indifference by disillusioned soldiers, has now suddenly become a matter of intense and vital

interest. If it frightens the War Office, then, it is argued, the Beveridge Report must really be worthwhile.'

The *Statesman* also published its own summary. Moreover, copies of the recalled ABCA pamphlet had disappeared in transit, and at least one found its way to Cairo, where a former staff sergeant who lectured for ABCA found it useful:

> 'Pamphlets were published in England, then forbidden for the troops abroad. I mean, an example of that was the Beveridge Report and they wouldn't allow that to be sent out to the troops in Egypt – in the whole of the Middle East as far as I know. I got a copy through a friend and I spend a very busy six months going round talking to groups on the Beveridge Plan, because they hadn't got this official ABCA pamphlet.'[17]

Such successes in getting around official intentions no doubt reinforced the suspicions of Conservative politicians that the work of ABCA would 'get out of hand' and encouraged hostile senior officers in their attempts to frustrate it – one general allegedly ordered the burning of thousands of copies of a *Current Affairs* bulletin which he thought openly seditious.[18] Equally, though, rank and file soldiers were often suspicious of ABCA on the grounds that if the army approved of or tolerated something, it *must* be harmless.[19]

The structured discussion of current affairs was also being developed outside the services, and not only by state agencies. *Picture Post* campaigned for an *Industrial Bureau of Current Affairs* to link factory discussion groups, and the format of the radio *Brains Trust* was copied both in the services and in local pubs. In an article for *Picture Post*, W. E. Williams extolled 'the greatest movement ever known in adult education.' 'Are we building a new British culture?' he asked, citing not just ABCA's work but also the 15,000 members of the National Fire Service who took part in organized discussion groups. A venture on that scale, he argued, must 'leave its mark on the post-war community.'[20]

But however widespread the enthusiasm for discussion – and Williams was certainly an optimist – the problem of generating real interest in the compulsory ABCA sessions remained. Mass Observation reports on early attempts record apathy, cynicism and resentment: 'the men don't like officers lecturing to them if they know nothing about their subject' and 'the men hated being told . . . that discipline is good for them . . . that the Englishman is top of the World . . . they disliked being talked to like children.'[21] Cartoons of the period, like David Langdon's in *Punch*, were also sceptical. Nicholas Montsarrat's later novel about the period, *The Cruel Sea*, is bleakly pessimistic:

"Now let this discussion on De-mobilization and Social Security be a lively one, with a spirited interplay of ideas, even if we have to be a half-minute late for tea."

David Langdon, *Punch*, 29 November 1944.

'. . . the serried eyes looked back at him unblinkingly, with very little discernible expression: a few of them were bored, a few hostile, most of them were sunk in a warm stupor; they were the eyes of men attending a compulsory lecture on British War Aims. As on so many previous occasions, thought Vincent, the heady magic of ABCA had not worked . . . He cleared his throat, sick of the whole thing, knowing only one way to play out time.

    "Any questions?"' [22]

This portrait certainly trivializes the political aspirations of ABCA in favour of a memory of war in terms of grand strategy and the masculine drama of military conflict. It also presents people in the services as an inert mass incapable of action without leadership, rather than as an active citizenry campaigning for the right to influence its own destiny. No doubt the passivity depicted by Montsarrat was a reality for many officers, but the comments about the educational competence or incompetence of officers reported by Mass Observation suggest that it may often have been a self-fulfilling prophecy, in which an unenthusiastic approach was met with an indifferent response.

    Given so many conflicting claims about the work of ABCA, how should the political impact of its discussion sessions be assessed? Did they really deliver the service vote for the Labour Party in 1945, or was it rather that army education focused a much wider political culture which had taken on a

"This week's subject for discussion is 'The World I Want After the War.' Would someone please prod Gunner Tomkins sharply in the ribs and ask him what sort of world he wants after the war."

David Langdon, *Punch*, 19 July 1944.

new intensity and scale during the course of the war? Certainly, although the forces appear to have voted for Labour, only a minority of those eligible to vote actually did so, and even if all the votes cast went to Labour, that would not account for the scale of its majority in the 1945 parliament. It was what ABCA permitted and made possible within the forces that was important; and the effect was probably achieved as much by the way the teaching was done as by its formal content. Where ABCA operated overseas, for example, the responsibility for running discussions often passed from officers to non-commissioned officers and other ranks. This opened up a more autonomous space for political debate and argument: it was important that such activity was defined as educational, because any other overt form of political involvement was illegal under King's Regulations. Officers too (and many of those commissioned during the war experienced the regular army as a thoroughly reactionary institution) risked the wrath of their superiors if they displayed more than a strictly professional interest in their educational work.[23] With these constraints operating, how was ABCA able to play a role in the radicalizing of the forces? One answer is that it was not so much the content of the bulletins, as the legitimacy it bestowed on the idea of discussion. This is the point Edward Thompson makes about his experience as an officer in Italy:

> 'I will not convince anyone now – least of all any young radicals – that those discussions were authentic and deeply significant. But everywhere across Italy, on wall newspapers, in bivvies around our tanks, in supply depots, the argument was going on. This curious half chauvinist, half anti-fascist, deeply anti-militarist and yet militarily competent army, debated the principles out of which the National Health Service came. They didn't debate these in terms of Beveridge's Giant This and Giant That, but in the direct terms of their own civilian experience.'[24]

It was this range of civilian experience and the level of ignorance about political problems of the time that gave politically committed soldiers the additional impetus to make political interventions. These went beyond the limits of army education, which were spelt out by one frustrated serving soldier in terms that echo G. D. H. Cole's criticism of earlier proposals for citizenship education:

> 'The lack of political education comes as a surprise to those who have read so much about Army education, ABCA and the Army Education Corps. However, all Army education is based on the notion that the Army is and has to remain a politically neutral body. This so-called political neutrality is the real stumbling block which makes the development of the Army as a progressive and clear-thinking political force so immensely difficult. All Army education, lectures and discussions are based on the alleged eternity and sacredness of our present social system.'[25]

Mock Parliaments

As ABCA was established and the discussion sessions became acceptable within the forces, the artificiality of the line between education and politics allowed increased scope for 'playing at politics' as an educational exercise. A particularly appropriate form for this – which had real political conse- quences – was the 'mock parliament'. Such parliaments had been promoted by citizenship educators in the pre-war years, and in a publication of the Association for Education in Citizenship. They were based more or less loosely on the rules of the House of Commons and operated as a kind of debating society. Some, like those at Twickenham and Hampstead, de- veloped a clear identity. During the war, Youth Parliaments were supported by local authorities, and a Women's Parliament in London passed resolu- tions and mock legislation.[26] During 1941 a small parliament was operating among soldiers in Gibraltar, [27] and there were certainly others in the Middle East by late 1943. They were set up mainly in areas at some distance from actual battlefields, where large numbers of people were based – especially RAF stations which were no longer on operational duties around the clock.

Much of the initiative for the forces' parliaments appears to have come from people not directly involved in ABCA or in Army Education, although circumstances varied. The length of these parliaments also depended on the enthusiasm and energies of those who were available to do the organizing work, and people were frequently transferred or 'posted', thereby disrupt- ing continuity. A few months appears to have been the maximum life, with meetings held fortnightly or monthly. The idea of the RAF Parliament at Kas Fareet, in Egypt, was first raised by an officer who in civilian life had been a Liberal Party candidate in the 1935 General Election. He had also regularly attended the 'Twickenham House of Commons' and had taken the precaut- ion of bringing its standing orders with him when he was posted overseas.[28] And at Kas Fareet it was the Liberals who formed the first 'government', the entire project having the tacit approval of the station commander. At Helwan, near Cairo, South Forces' Parliament met under the guidance of an Education Officer of the South African Defence Force. He happened to be an enthusiastic student of the British Constitution and of parliamentary proce- dure, later playing a central role as Speaker in the Cairo Forces' Parliament. The 'Heliopolis House of Commons', operating from an RAF base near Cairo, was organized by servicemen who supported the Labour or Com- munist Parties. As with other mock parliaments, however, there were regular planning meetings for other party groupings. At Heliopolis these were held every week during the life of the parliament.

These activities became politically embarrassing, for the Army author- ities especially, when news of them spread to a wider audience, and the parliaments were represented as something more than social or educational activities – as being, in effect, significant political developments in their own right. When the Cairo Parliament held elections, the results were reported all over the world. Commenting on these reports, German radio suggested that the troops were heading on a revolutionary path (although it sustained the allegation for only one broadcast.)[29] Subsequent events made the Cairo Parliament the best remembered of all the parliaments, as well as the centre of a protracted controversy in the Westminster Parliament.

The Cairo Forces' Parliament, of which there are, happily, many survivors, was significantly different from many of the others since it was held in a service club, Music for All, in the centre of Cairo. Others were held on Army or RAF bases, and could therefore be supervised directly by service authorities. Music for All was a well known social centre, with up to a thousand people a day passing through it,[30] and the Parliament was well publicized and open to any serviceman or servicewoman who had paid to enter the club. Civilian guests were also permitted to enter as observers and the press was welcomed. The Music for All Parliament, as it was known locally, grew out of a 'Thinking Aloud' discussion group which had operated in the club, in the best ABCA tradition, for some time. Following the example of other mock parliaments, it was decided to hold monthly sessions, alongside the weekly 'Thinking Aloud' meetings. One of the immediate reasons was, apparently, to revive flagging interest in the discussions.[31]

As the majority of active participants in the planning stage were declared Labour Party supporters, it was they who were given the task of preparing a Bill for debate. So, at its first meeting in December 1943, the parliament duly approved the 'Retail Trades (Nationalisation) Bill'. This Bill included some quite radical proposals, its second clause reading:

'The Bill shall provide that, as from an appointed day, the state shall assume sole responsibility for the marketing of all goods and commodities, after which appointed day it shall be illegal for any person, persons, or commercial concern to set up or seek to set up a shop, warehouse or any other organization for the purpose of buying and selling to the general public.'[32]

The legislation, and the parliament itself, was theoretically set in the immediate post-war period and had the brief of avoiding any criticism or comment on the war effort. The participants appear to have accepted and observed these conditions, although when it came to central questions of reconstruction the 'fiction' was rather difficult to sustain. The Army Education Corps gave its tacit approval for these sessions to continue, and officers attended both as participants and as members of the planning committee. But after the second session of the parliament in January 1944, when an 'Inheritance Restriction Bill' was passed, the procedures of the parliament were challenged by an officer member of the organizing committee. This officer, formerly a Conservative MP in the Westminster Parliament charged that the legislation being prepared was unrealistic and unrepresentative of service people attending the parliament, and that the planning committee was too biased towards left-wing measures. He called for changes to be made.

The next step can be traced through the words of one of the partici-pants, the secretary of the parliament, who also had previous experience as an MP – as an Honourable Member of a parliament organized by the Young Conservatives in Winson Green, Birmingham, before the war.

> '. . . it was decided then, all right, let's do it properly . . . let's organize an actual election, and so we advertised that we would have an election for the parliament and it would take place on a certain evening and there would be speakers from the main parties there and the audience would then vote as to what sort of government they wanted.'[33]

So 'mock' election addresses were prepared and, at the beginning of February 1944, the hustings and election were held. The play was acted through and, eighteen months before the real election, a Labour Govern-ment was returned with an absolute majority. Because Music for All was in the centre of the city, correspondents based in Cairo had no difficulty reporting the events of the evening and filed their stories. The news spread. On 13 April 1944, *Time* magazine recorded the election as a signal event – the educational activity had assumed a new importance. Headlined 'The Soldiers' Straw' the story observed:

> 'British and Dominion servicemen and women in Cairo elected a "Parliament" and thereby showed how their postwar minds are work-ing. The votes . . . were cast on British Parliamentary lines. Results, Labor 119; the new socialistic Common Wealth Party, 55; Liberals, 38; Churchill Conservatives, 17.'

For those involved, and *not* just the victors at the poll, the experience is recalled as one of great excitement – a freedom to give expression to political views, but released from the formal constraints of Army Education. More-over, their voices were being heard elsewhere.[34]

The following month the King's Speech was presented by Private Harry Solomons, the acting Prime Minister, who later became the MP for Hull during the 1960s. Anticipating many of the legislative proposals of the 1945 Labour Government, the speech was voted on and accepted by a gathering of several hundred. By this stage of the parliament's life local publicity had swelled attendances considerably. On the night of what proved to be the final meeting, 5 April 1944, over six hundred people packed the main hall of Music for All to hear the Chancellor of the Exchequer present a Bill nationalising the Bank of England. The 'Chancellor' – otherwise Aircrafts-man Leo Abse, now MP for Pontypool – was delayed by the arrival of the Commanding Officer of the Cairo Area accompanied by a senior Education Officer. It fell to this officer, who had previously led the opposition to the

Inheritance Restriction Bill, to read an order to the assembled parliament, stating that all future meetings must be held on Army premises under the name of 'Forces' Forum' and must abide by the rules of the Oxford Union. The parliament was, in effect, to cease operating. The Speaker, the South African officer mentioned earlier, prolonged the events of the evening by shrewdly ruling that the order, literally interpreted, did not apply to *that* evening's meeting but to future meetings. Offering his ruling to the parliament it was accepted by a vote of over 600, with one vote cast against. This solitary vote was apparently cast by the Commanding Officer who had crossed the fictional line to participate in the proceedings he had just banned – to the delight of all concerned. The meeting went ahead and the Bank of England was nationalised.

As a result of the closure, and what was regarded by the Army authorities as the 'demonstration' against it, several of the parliament's leading participants were moved away from Cairo. According to an Education Officer, in Cairo at the time, future parliaments were to be discouraged.[35] Abse was placed under open arrest until representations on his behalf resulted in his being posted back to Britain, several years before the end of his tour of duty had expired. The RAF authorities, apparently embarrassed by the Army authorities' response, took no further action against him. It should be said that the Cairo Parliament was closed at a time of widespread political upheaval among the forces based in the Middle East. The invasion of Europe was expected at any time and a mutiny of some sections of the Greek Navy and Army occurred during the latter stages of the Parliament's life. Although the mutiny of the Greek forces, based in Egypt, was unconnected to the parliaments in any formal sense, several of the parliament's participants were providing political support for them – an action which involved great personal risk.[36]

In retrospect it appears that the government in London and the War Office were anxious that there should be no appearance of disunity within the forces, and no opportunity for German propaganda to exploit criticism of the wartime government, even if it were only in a 'mock' form. It is this point which has caused surviving participants of the parliaments to argue that it was what they said and did which led to their suppression, rather than their participation in a parliament as such. 'Why,' one participant has argued, 'didn't the BBC broadcast a recording of the Cairo Parliament back to Germany, to show what democracy and debate were all about?' Had the parliament been solidly and uncritically in support of the main Party in the British Government things might have been rather different. In his account of the Cairo Parliament a former officer participant wrote:

'If the War Office was really sincere in its professed desire to develop adult education in the Army it would welcome every Forces' Parliament with enthusiasm. In fairness let it be said that it never raised any objection to a Parliament that "kept within reasonable bounds", that is has not been heard of outside the unit in which it operates, and has stuck to discussion that eschewed anything later than 1938 or earlier than 1960, and that kept clear of anything savouring of politics.'[37]

Whatever the intentions, the suppression of the Cairo Parliament achieved for it a fame, or notoriety, out of all proportion to the numbers who had actually attended. Questions were asked in Westminster, and in an Adjournment Debate on 4 October 1944, D. N. Pritt denounced the closure:

> 'It is a major scandal and I hope that anyone who has had anything to do with it will find all the soldiers' votes, and the votes of the families of all the soldiers, against him at the next election.'[38]

It was this interest among the civilian population in the forces' discussions about post-war Britain and the post-war world that made it difficult to suppress them. Indeed, the political debate in the army came to influence the conduct of domestic politics: the armed forces took on a symbolic role, as an expression of national identity and purpose. Politicians claimed to identify with the 'interests' of the forces – although a soldier writing in *Tribune* remained sceptical:

> 'Every public utterance regarding the Forces' attitude to post-war problems is either of the *"We owe it to our boys"* or *"The Forces will never tolerate . . ."* variety. The former is designed to utilise the public's well-meaning, though superficial, gratitude for pushing a certain measure. I have often wondered whether these self-appointed spokes-men – and the general public, for that matter – have ever tried to gauge the attitude of the Forces towards these questions . . .'[39]

While attempts *were* made in Westminster to extend greater civic rights to serving soldiers, these were frustrated.[40] It was this absence of a voice for the Armed Forces, combined with the knowledge that the Forces were discuss-ing what should happen in the post-war world, that gave an added edge to campaigns on their behalf. Perhaps the *Daily Mirror's* campaign prior to the 1945 General Election, demonstrates this most vividly. Under the slogan 'Vote for Them', relatives, and especially women relatives of serving soldiers, were urged to vote in the best interests of the services, to vote for and on behalf of those away from home. For the *Mirror* a vote for the services meant a vote for the Labour Party, an equation which was implicit by that stage of the war.

Although the wartime events were exceptional, and semi-autonomous activities like the parliaments remained atypical, they nonetheless drama-tised the inherent contradictions within forms of education which encourage critical thinking. These were intensified by the fact that the participants in the compulsory wartime schemes were adults who had the means to *reject* definitions of what was being offered as education. In other educational programmes we are rarely witness to the unfolding of those contradictions, and again in this respect the ABCA 'moment' was exceptional. Not only did the initiators of the programme walk a precarious political tightrope, but the subsequent programme was also conducted in public. The effects of ABCA can also *not* be simply reduced to the motives of those who initiated the schemes. Many other factors helped to shape the ABCA experience, not least the self-conscious efforts of those who sought to conduct another kind of politics within its parameters. It was to have both intended and unintended consequences which cannot be identified simply by mapping the different arguments present within any given context, or the uncritical acceptance of the idea either that ABCA caused the radicalization of soldiers or alternatively that it was part of a broader politics of containment by the state. What emerges most clearly is that conflicting conceptions of citizenship – whether in formal education or broader political discourses – are at the heart of strategies for defining or containing popular political consciousness.

Notes

1. Basil Yeaxlee, 'Army Education', in *Education: Today and Tomorrow*, London, Michael Joseph, 1945, p. 150.
2. R. A. Butler, *The Art of the Possible*, London, Hamish Hamilton, 1971, p. 129.
3. See Charmian Cannon, 'Social Studies in the secondary school', *Educational Review*, Birmingham University, vol. 17, no. 1, 1964. (Cannon confuses the Association for Education in Citizenship with the Council for Education in World Citizenship, a separate body established in 1939).
4. See Guy Whitmarsh, 'The politics of political education', *The Journal of Curriculum Studies*, vol. 6, no. 2, 1974.
5. Letter to Sir Ernest Simon, 20 November 1934, Simon Archive, Manchester Central Reference Library.
6. Similar responses have greeted more recent initiatives, such as the proposal by the Politics Association and the Hansard Society that political education should be expanded in schools: 'On the one hand, political education was seen as a subtle device for bolstering up a decaying capitalist system and, on the other, as a left-wing plot to destroy the fabric of British society.' (Tom Brennan, *Political Education and Democracy*, Cambridge University Press, 1981, p. 12.)
7. See, for example, Denis Lawton and Barry Dufour, *The New Social Studies*, London, Heinemann Educational Books, 1974.
8. George Wigg, *George Wigg*, London, Michael Joseph, 1972, p. 93.
9. Maurice Edelman, in *The Day Before Yesterday*, London, Granada, 1971, p. 13.
10. An important expansion of some of the points in this article, and especially the circumstances surrounding the setting up of ABCA, can be found in P. Summerfield, 'Education and politics in the British Armed Forces in World War 2', *International Review of Social History*, vol. XXVI, part 2, 1981.
11. *ABCA*, Ministry of Information with War Office Army Film Unit, 1943. Transcript held at the Imperial War Museum, AFU 33.
12. Interview with M. H., former ATS member, June 1980.

13. John Newsom, *The Education of Girls*, London, Faber, 1948, p. 133.
14. Angus Calder, *The People's War*, London, Panther, 1971, p. 290.
15. J. L. Hodson, *Home Front*, London, Gollancz, 1944, p. 263.
16. Interview with J. B., former Captain in Army Education Corps, February 1982.
17. Interview with S. B., former staff-sergeant in Middle East, March 1981.
18. W. Harrington and P. Young, *The 1945 Revolution*, London, Davis Poynter, 1978, p. 111.
19. One former Army Education Corps officer, writing shortly after the war, argued that ABCA was a deliberate attempt to channel political energies into harmless discussion: see Gilbert Hall, *The Cairo Forces Parliament*, NCCL pamphlet, no date but approx. 1945.
20. See *Picture Post* 23 October 1943, 6 March 1943 and 2 January 1943.
21. Report on the ABCA scheme for Mass Observation dated 16 November 1941, housed at the Mass Observation Archive, University of Sussex.
22. Nicholas Montsarrat, *The Cruel Sea*, Penguin edn. 1964, p. 427.
23. See, for example, Hall op. cit.
24. E. P. Thompson, 'A question of manners', in *Writing by Candlelight*, London, Merlin, 1980, p. 82.
25. Serving Soldier, 'The inarticulate revolution', *Tribune*, 10 March 1944.
26. See, for example, *Daily Worker*, 30 November 1944.
27. Interview with H. L., a former officer based on Gibraltar, February 1982.
28. Interview with B. G., former catering officer in RAF, August 1981.
29. German Home Service, 7 March 1944. Monitoring report held in Imperial War Museum.
30. *Music for All*, report and souvenir brochure, 1945.
31. Interviews with S. B and H. B., former servicemen in Cairo and participants in the parliament, March 1981 and February 1982.
32. Copy held by author.
33. Interview with S. B., March 1981.
34. There was considerable press coverage locally, especially in the *Egyptian Gazette*, an English language daily.
35. Interview with J. B., February 1982.
36. Interviews with L. A., S. B. and D. B., March 1981–February 1982.
37. Hall op. cit.
38. House of Commons Debates (Hansard), 4 October 1944, col. 1096.
39. Serving Soldier, op. cit.
40. See, for example, the debate on Army and Airforce (Annual Bill), House of Commons Debates (Hansard), 31 March 1944, cols. 1709–1768. This was substantially concerned with an attempt to allow people in the armed forces to take part in political activity while off duty. The move was heavily defeated.

Janice Winship

NATION BEFORE FAMILY:
Woman, The National Home Weekly, 1945–1953

'The war was over, peace was here but in 1946 the longed-for era of "plenty" had not come. The world of women was at its lowest ebb. It was a drab and dreary let-down after our high expectations. Rationing was still with us, more severe in some things than it had been during the war . . . There was little scope for gracious living of any sort, except vicariously from a hungry scanning of the colour food ads in the plush American magazines. . .'[1]

It is almost a commonplace among feminists today that the wider options opened up for women during the second world war quickly disappeared once peace returned. Whether they wanted it or not, women were ushered back to family, hearth and home and, following Betty Friedan's angry denunciations, women's magazines have been seen as making a significant contribution to that post-war closure.[2] Thus the incipient feminism of war-time discussions about working mothers performing men's jobs and a less complacent view of marriage and family life seemed to have been curtailed in favour of the post-war project of perpetrating an image of 'the happy housewife heroine' on readers. This view is not downright misleading; but it does not tell the whole story.[3]

In the first place, women's magazines did not really challenge traditional notions of femininity even during the war. If knotty social problems were discussed and unconventional roles for women were accepted, it was only because of the exceptional demands of war. Still marriage, domesticity and motherhood remained the unquestioned core of the magazines, no less than of the femininity more generally expected of women. And secondly, this exceptional state of affairs seems to have lasted well into the post-war period. The 'battles of war' were succeeded by the 'battles for peace'. To Mary Grieve, the editor of *Woman*, writing in January 1950, 'war' and 'peace' of the forties had merged into one 'momentous decade.'

'We have said farewell to a decade that has been momentous indeed. No ten years in history brought more tension and greater happenings to mankind. Although we struggled heroically for most of those years, we haven't yet succeeded in clearing up the mess they made; the fifties have started with a fairly large legacy of loose ends from the forties.'

The changes in what the magazines had to say about women came gradually. Only from about 1949, when the end of austerity was in sight, did appeals to the Dunkirk spirit give way to promises of a rosy future on the home front. This new era was perhaps best symbolised by the lavish coronation of Queen Elizabeth in the summer of 1953. She, the young, attractive, happy wife and mother was seen to be heralding a new era of gracious femininity and – at last – of plenty for women.

In retrospect, women's move back into the home may seem retrogressive. But it was not the neat turnabout that is sometimes portrayed. Certainly, the way it was represented at the time made it seem to be an *advance* for women on their war-time situation. Lottie, for example, was a woman who worked throughout the war, and continued to do so on a part-time basis throughout the fifties while her children were young. Yet, interviewed in the 1970s, she remembered that 'with the war, those of us who were married *couldn't wait* for our men to come home safely so we could have a normal life – we wanted homes of our own, and children. Being the housewife was the ultimate goal.'[4] During (and immediately after) the war, women were encouraged to look *outwards* beyond their primary concern with their families to do their bit for King and country – and the dollar drive. The extended crises of those years opened up possible new conceptions of woman's social place which seemed to move *beyond* the family. They did so, however, only insofar as they served the interests of the *nation*. Once the peace-time battles seemed to have been won – without conceding any changes which might have facilitated a wider role for women – women's responsibilities for the family were once again foregrounded.

Thus for A. J. Bradshaw, the General Secretary of the National Marriage Guidance Council, the year 1951 marked 'the end of war-time dislocations in family life and the beginning of what we must regard as normality.'[5] Women's concerns were thus once again turned *inwards* onto the family. There was, as Denise Riley has observed, a 'withering away of the post-war social democratic-reformist language into the particular familial speech of the fifties.'[6] It is, however, the changes in the women's magazines during what Riley refers to as the odd twilight years of austerity, that I am concerned with here. It is the period when, as Arthur Marwick puts it (in phrases reminiscent of the rhetoric of the time), 'the country lay in a crepuscular zone with the shadows of night as firm upon the landscape as the heartening hints of the rising sun.'[7] It is above all the arduousness of those years which may help to explain why women apparently gave up the feminist struggle and capitulated to what seemed the heartening hints of aspiring to be the happy housewife heroine.

I have chosen to focus on *Woman* as the best-selling women's magazine throughout the war period – a position it retained, astonishingly, until the mid-seventies. It had, however, begun modestly enough in 1937. Using idle machinery intended for an ailing *John Bull*, it failed initially to reach its guaranteed net sale. But as the first magazine to be printed by photogravure – that is, in colour – it was a glamorous novelty in the drab environment of the mid-thirties.[8] When Mary Grieve was rushed in to rescue it, her editorial skills allowed it to reap the benefits of that. By 1939 it was already selling three quarters of a million, but it was the war years that were crucial. As Mary Grieve recalled in her autobiography: 'There is no doubt that the war stretched the women's magazines and tested them as never before. And in this atmosphere of practicality and improvisation and strong comradely feeling the magazines throve.'[9] In 1946, with print restrictions still in operation, the *Woman* which readers were able to buy for threepence was still the flimsy, well-thumbed war-style issue of a mere twenty pages. The circulation stood at just over a million with each copy having a multiple readership. By 1951, when printing restrictions were at last lifted, the number of pages was doubled, their size increased, and the circulation rose to nearly two and a quarter million. In 1957 *Woman's* hundred-page issue cost 4½d and it was selling at a post-war record of nearly three and a half million – a figure never to be repeated nor matched by any other magazine.

Like most other women's magazines, *Woman* has always been conservative, having few pretensions about being an initiator of opinion or moral values. Even at the height of its 'intervention' into social problems the magazine approached any potentially controversial issue with a care bordering on timidity. Indeed it often dealt with them only in displaced ways. It therefore seems safe to assume that its radical edge, the incipient feminism to be found within it in the immediate post-war period, only touched the surface of the profound discontents *actually* felt by women. Further, given what appears to be a continuity of editorial policy and of contributors – Edith Blair, Evelyn Home, Helen Temple and Angela Talbot became household names, almost lifelong friends, to many women throughout the period of Mary Grieve's editorship until she retired in 1964 – the shift towards the domestic front in the period 1951–53 has to be explained in terms of events beyond the pages of the magazine.

A Land Fit for War Heroines?

Women's magazines immediately after the war have been described aptly as Utility Journals, whose watchword was 'Make Do and Mend'.[10] In striving (wo)manfully for standards of quality and practicality with only limited materials, they faced the same problems and preoccupations as they had during the war. According to Mary Grieve (*Woman*, 20 October 1945):

> 'Our people are underclothed, underfed and underhoused. Our country has got a fierce struggle ahead to hold its place in the world. In these spheres there is a national emergency. It can be dealt with only by the

same sort of emergency measures with which we, as a people, dealt with the emergency of war.

To rebuild our own homes and industries requires at least as much effort and discipline as to destroy the might of Germany and Japan.'

The war-time magazines had retained the typical features of beauty, fashion, problem page and fiction, but had approached them through the particular difficulties of the time. Letters to the problem page sought advice on whether to marry in haste when the man you loved faced possible death, on the difficulties of separation from boyfriends, husbands, parents and children, or on having a baby as an unmarried mother who had fallen for the soldier-who'd-gone-away. There were fashion tips on restyling last year's dress with scraps from a worn-out garment, on how to make your uniform look its best and even on how to make bras out of lace curtains ('good for uplifting morale if nothing else'). Beauty hints included hair styles suitable for a service cap or factory turban and skin care for land girls. There were ingenious recipes for fruit flans made from carrots, Siege Cake, Beet the Cold, Mock Marzipan made from haricot beans and Parsley Honey which contained no honey at all. Sometimes women were encouraged to practice their skills in less practical tasks, like embroidering *his* 'proud badge'.

These traditionally feminine concerns remained the core of *Woman* throughout the war. They asserted that women remained feminine even in unglamorous garments or when doing masculine jobs. In a report on a NAAFI canteen in her 'Women's War Service Bureau' series (*Woman*, 19 June

Woman, 17 July 1943.

1943), for example, Joan Lambert described how it was being run by a young woman with no comparable pre-war experience. Her husband, serving in Tunisia, hadn't wanted her to join the Service, 'but I don't think he'll mind the NAAFI.' Joan Lambert commented that: 'She has almost a maternal feeling for her canteen as she has watched it grow, literally from birth.' Her domestic skills and virtues in creating this 'home from home' were suitably rewarded: 'the military authorities showed their appreciation by sending a handsome brigadier to present the trophy to Rosemary, Phyllis, Ethel and Nannie.' In this report, there is a tension between a new image of women as efficient workers and an older domestic imagery. And it seems to have been the case more generally that, although women took on new jobs, they were still socially marked *as women*, as primarily wives and mothers.[11] The tension between new and old images tended to be resolved by representing women as infringing traditional feminine codes less than might appear at first sight – as in the NAAFI canteen.

The intention of Joan Lambert's regular 'Women's War Service Bureau' column was to boost women's morale in their role as war workers. It offered, as Joy Leman describes, 'unique exhortations, never repeated in peace time, . . . to participate in social and political decision making.'[12] For instance from January 1943:

> 'The last apprentice in many a factory is a woman, it may be you, and although you may be a novice where engineering is concerned, there are many other directions in which you can be bright (and practical) and so help the war effort. Your working conditions, the canteen and nursery services – all these are now admitted to be just as important as the most highly technical machine, and if you have any ideas on these, pass them on to the proper authorities.'

Nevertheless, as in the NAAFI article, the radical concern about conditions of work is mediated through notions of a traditional femininity – women are urged to use their *domestic* skills to improve the workplace.

In such ways, although the national demand for their labour made it possible for issues concerning women to be discussed in a way that would not have been possible before the war, this radical edge was partly recuper-ated. So long as the nation needed working wives and mothers, it was possible for the nation (and women) to contemplate responsibilities beyond the confines of the family. Once that need disappeared, the fragile and non-feminist basis of its legitimacy became apparent and women's interests were again limited to the family.

In the forties *Woman* dealt with the birth rate and family size, nurseries, homehelps for mothers and the problems shopping posed for (paid) work-ing housewives: ten years later, these discussions would have been inconceivable. At their heart was an image of Britain as democratic, a free (that is, not fascist) nation planning a better future for its children after its eventual victory in the war. In an editorial titled 'True Freedom' in June 1943, when the debate about the Beveridge Plan for welfare provision was at its height, Mary Grieve insisted that the Plan would not curtail individual responsibility. Democracy and the freedom it entailed, she maintained, meant:

> '. . . not having a system forced on you as in Hitlerite Germany with no free discussion, it is arguing and hammering out the best scheme for the common good; and then supporting and improving the agreed way of living. We are fighting for that way of life not only for ourselves but for all the people of the world.'

The magazine addressed its readers as responsible citizens acting in co-operation with the government. Two years later, in June 1945, Mary Grieve appealed to them to vote in the general election because of their special contribution as women citizens. 'Women, less steeped in party politics than men, can more easily listen to speakers of rival parties and vote for the candidate showing the clearest understanding of the common good . . . By using it [the vote] carefully we take our part in forming Britain's new life.'

One of the most contentious issues on which women's and the nation's interests conflicted was the question of the birth rate. Fears of its continuing fall generated national appeals to have at least four children. On this issue, *Woman* declared that it would 'gladly present' their readers' opinions as a contribution to the democratic debate: 'Their views on the families of the future are a vital contribution to the well-being and happiness of our land' (26 June 1943). The magazine received hundreds of letters from women lamenting the pressures being put on them. Their reasons, *Woman* insisted, were not 'selfish or trivial' and 'they must not be ignored or evaded.' Unsurprisingly, the overriding ones were economic – women just could not afford to feed, clothe and educate more children. 'Family allowances are asked for by the great majority,' reported the magazine, along with free secondary education. They were worried too about the availability and expense of accommodation, and though security in terms of jobs, provision during sickness and for larger families had all been recommended by Beveridge, they were concerned that as yet these remained 'vague promises.'

The most heartfelt reason, however, was the readers' 'loss of freedom.' Women remembered only too acutely the strains of their own mothers' lives. As Mrs F. C. (Stockport) wrote in the issue of 26 June 1943:

> 'I should dislike very much the life my mother had bringing up a large family with very inadequate help, she worked seven days a week, and I have seen her many times on Sundays after cooking a big dinner too

done up to eat her own. She had absolutely no freedom, no holidays, and there was one period of twelve years when she didn't leave home apart from shopping at the local small town. Do you wonder girls of today who come from large families are not going in for the same themselves?

There must be more nursery schools, trained mothers' helps, maternity hospitals and arrangements for mothers who have babies at home.'

The social reforms for mothers discussed within *Woman* may have been modest, but the magazine did recognise that motherhood was a tiring *job*, and that, if it was to be combined with paid work (as the government was still urging) without damaging the quality of child care or women's own health, then the government would have to provide nurseries, laundries and the like. Beyond the pages of *Woman* provisions ranging from anaesthetics at childbirth to family tickets on trains were being demanded. According to Denise Riley: 'For a short but intensive space, roughly, 1941 to 1947, "freeing mothers", work outside the home, and protonatalism were all held together in a tight though precarious balance.'[13]

Mary Grieve's statements at this time indicate that she considered the government's policies towards women misguided. They simply did not understand the burden of work women were already carrying. 'When a young mother has no home of her own, no domestic help, and her local day nursery is closing down, it is not surprising if she decides against increasing her family.' She therefore gave this advice to the government (21 July 1945):

'Let's stop theorising about babies not yet born, and concentrate on getting houses for the large number we have – reasonable help for their mothers. When we show what we can do for the families we've got we shall be well on the way to the bigger families we should all like.'

Joan Lambert made similar points in an article gloomily titled 'Is the day nursery doomed?' (3 March 1945). Against the Ministry of Health's pronouncement that it would be inappropriate to provide nursery care because 'the mother is the best person to look after the very young child,' she argued that the mother's responsibility should not mean working twenty-four hours a day for two years. 'A mother needs recreation; she needs to go out alone with her husband; she may want another baby during this time. Only a day nursery can adequately help her.' A year later, Joan Lambert was more optimistically urging women to lobby recently elected councillors who were about to decide their policy on the provision of care for the under-fives: 'Try to make certain that your own views are incorporated in that report' (9 February 1946).

What comes across most strongly in these discussions is the feeling

Is the day nursery doomed? Joan Lambert explains the points of view of the Government, the day nurseries and the mothers of the children

THE news that the wartime nursery is unlikely to carry forward into peace time is worrying many wives who hoped that the day nursery would find a permanent place in family life. What is actually happening. And can anything be done?

It is a three-sided problem. There is the Government's point of view; there is the nurseries' attitude, in particular that of the National Society of Children's Nurseries, pioneers since 1906; and there is the mothers' viewpoint.

I have interviewed all three, and this is what I find.

The Ministry of Health has cried Stop to any more wartime nurseries; they have closed down the short-term Child Care Reserve classes; they have decided that no more young probationers can start their 2-year training in wartime nurseries.

Why have they done this?

Official Statement

The Minister of Health gave the answer to the House of Commons recently:

Wartime nurseries have been provided at the cost of the Exchequer as an aid to war production. Their purpose has been to enable women with young children to help in the war effort, and where these facilities are no longer required their continuance for this purpose at the cost of the Exchequer cannot be justified. I hope, however, that it will prove possible for a number of the wartime nurseries where the site and the premises are suitable, to be taken over by local education authorities as nursery schools.

The N.S.C.N.'s reply to Mr. Willink's statement is that the wartime nurseries cost £2½ million a year—a mere drop in the ocean of millions *a day* which the war is costing—but in return pays handsome dividends in better national health. It is also argued that more women will have babies if there are day nurseries where the older children can be left in safety.

As for the local Education Authorities taking over the premises for nursery schools, this will affect only the children between two and five, and ignores completely the children below two. The nursery schools do not look after the children on Saturdays or during school holidays. Day nurseries would be open all the year round.

The closing down of the training is bound to result in a staff shortage later; and what alternative is offered to the girl of sixteen who wants to take up this work as her career? The wartime nurseries are the colleges for the working-girl who wants to earn as she's training. There are plenty of colleges for the wealthier girl.

The Ministry of Health have given me two reasons for their action.

(a) First, they believe that the mother is the best person to look after the very young child.

Quite a number of people agree with them on this point, but the N.S.C.N. has something to add. They say, of course the child is the mother's chief responsibility, but she should not be expected to work for twenty-four hours a day for two years. A mother needs recreation; she needs to go out alone with her husband; she may want another baby during this time. Only a day nursery can adequately help her.

And what about the mothers who *must* work after the war? There will be thousands who must do so because they need the money. Day nurseries will help them do so without worrying about the welfare of the children while they're away.

The Ministry's second reason for the ban is the risk of infection.

They have a battalion of medical opinion which believes that the risk of infection for the under-two's in nurseries is greater than any of the benefits.

But equally, the N.S.C.N. has an equally formidable battalion of doctors who state that the risk is no greater provided that adequate care is taken in equipping and staffing the nurseries.

Housing Shortage

So we laywomen can take our choice! Personally, I feel that the risk of infection when nursery-less mothers take their children out shopping, in buses or trains, or even to the cinema, is far greater than in any of the wartime nurseries I have visited in these war years where I have always been most impressed with the health and happiness of the children.

Then there is the postwar housing shortage as it affects the nurseries. Until

every mother has a healthy home of her own to bring up her children and nursery schools for the two to five's—and it will take years to bring this about—I feel that the day nurseries should be continued to help her in her task.

The adequate provision of nurseries would also help to prevent casualties on the roads, many of which are tiny children.

But don't let us be too downhearted. Even if the Treasury withdraws its grant, there is no reason why all nurseries should be doomed. Many housing estates plan to have nurseries attached. Some local authorities may continue to have municipal nurseries. Blitzed Coventry, for example, has already announced her intention of doing so.

Voice of the Mothers

Now, what are the mothers themselves thinking about this problem?

Here are extracts from five letters:

"I will always have to go to work as my baby has not got a father. I am his support now, so I will be thankful if our nurseries are kept on."

"It is impossible to bring up two children on a pension, and it is a most satisfactory feeling to know that while I am at work they are being looked after really well."

"My husband has been discharged from the Army and I had to go to work to help as he is not a fit man. What will happen if I cannot take my child to the nursery while I am at work?"

"I live with my five children in a cottage condemned before the war. I have two usable rooms—one living- and one bed-room—no garden, my front door opens on to main London Road. The street is their playground. What can I do if there is no nursery?"

A young wife in the Services writes: "I want children after the war but have had no training. I was looking forward to the parents' club to learn how to be a good mother."

These five women know what they want. It is only if they and all the others make their views known to their local authorities that the real need for nurseries can be proved.

Are the day nurseries doomed? They needn't be if you say, loud enough, that you want them in your postwar world.

Woman, 3 March 1945.

that married women were overworked. Many still had the dual burden of two jobs without compensating social or domestic facilities. And there were at least hints that many would give up paid work given half a chance. In her editorial 'Stand-by Summer' (9 June 1945), Mary Grieve toed the government line on women's work – but not without speaking up on women's behalf.

> 'Frankly, I feel that every woman who has domestic responsibilities is due for a break now, and I am sure every reader heartily agrees with me. But . . .
>
> Until the men come home and train for their peace time jobs, what is going to happen to industry? Those factories were never more needed than now. On the one hand we've got to supply the armies fighting the Japs; on the other we've got to begin producing goods to sell abroad (for Britain badly needs foreign money) – and in addition our own homes and wardrobes desperately need new additions.
>
> Now who on earth can carry this three-fold job through the critical time till the men are home? Yes, you've got it – women.'

Despite such appeals, married women did give up their jobs – from a peak of 7,253,000 (including part-timers) working in June 1943, the numbers had fallen to 5,806,000 by September 1946. At the same time, nurseries closed. If the country had got back on its feet economically, that might have been that. But the 1947 crisis intensified the mood of a 'battle for peace' and the debate about women's place was kept alive as the government tried to recruit married women's labour.

The Battle for Peace: the National Crisis, 1947/8

> 'Today we have a peace to win. Our future as a nation depends on whether we work for prosperity and save for it with as much courage and determination as we showed in the dark days of Dunkirk.'
>
> (Report to the Women of Britain no. 12, *Woman*, 5 June 1948)

Although the economy was in crisis and industrial production targets were not being met, the marriage rate had never been higher and the 'production' of babies was booming to deliver the nation with its post-war baby bulge. Against this background, it is not surprising that when the Ministry of Labour urged young married women to return to certain forms of work (especially in textiles), the problems of combining a paid job with domestic and maternal responsibilities provoked a sense of grievance against the new Welfare State. Necessities like nappies, prams and baby clothes were hard to come by, and women's complaints – and more clearly articulated feminist sentiments – were vehemently voiced in *Woman*. At the same time, the government tried to make more use of the magazine as a propaganda vehicle than it ever had during the war. Mary Grieve and her magazine were caught in a dilemma. On behalf of the government, they appealed to women to serve the nation. But at the same time they attacked the government for its shortsightedness on behalf of women. *Woman* spoke both for 'we the nation' and for 'we women'. The resolution between the two voices was always uneasy, and usually in the end favoured the nation at the hidden expense of women.

In January 1947 the magazine was still confidently assessing the employment prospects for girls in factories, shops, nursing, offices and domestic service. But by the following month, the optimistic tone had gone. The critical shortage of labour again led to pressure on married women. In 'Back to the Job?' (22 February 1947), Mary Grieve was probably giving voice to the feelings of many women:

> '"But surely you don't think they will call up women!" said my friend in tones of horror in the middle of our discussion on Britain's dire shortage of manpower . . . Looking at her shocked face I hardly knew what to say.'

The implication was that women would not want to return to paid work because of the extra burden it placed on them. 'If industry expects women to return to its ranks it must give them a better deal than it gave in war time,' she insisted. 'Married women left industry . . . because lack of day nurseries made it impossible for them to cope with a job and a family.'

At the same time as defending women's resistance to appeals by government and industry, Mary Grieve also supported the nation's struggle against the 'economic blizzard'. In 'First steps to victory' (15 March 1947), she explained the reduced size of *Woman*'s Crisis Numbers.

> '*Woman* like every other enterprise and every individual in the country, must accept and honourably fulfil the new conditions of living. Briefly these are that coal and manpower must be conserved while the country struggles to survive the economic blizzard.
>
>   Since you will be feeling the struggle in your homes and in your daily work *Woman* is proud to get into battle dress again with you . . . How long and severe will be the battle none of us can yet tell. But we have no doubt that our country can save itself as, in 1940, it saved the world.'

But in order for women 'to get into battle dress' once more, she insisted (22 March 1947), 'employers must co-operate' – for example, by offering more flexible part-time hours.

'It's no good offering a mother a job which starts, say, at 7.30 in the morning. Children don't start school till 9, and the gap is too long for any mother's peace of mind.'

Husbands too could help a lot. If they would 'jettison the idea that one man's comfort is one woman's whole-time job, it would be easier for many women to take part-time work.' Mary Grieve, backed up by Joan Lambert's column, tirelessly reiterated these arguments over the next few months. 'Women must be helped back,' she pointedly told government and industry. 'Do it now.' 'Mothers need help.'

> 'The housewife . . . has carried the heaviest end of war and post-war living. Unless widescale and efficient means are taken to relieve her of some of the burdens of homemaking, appeals to take on full time work – however genuine their urgency – will only infuriate and antagonise her . . . Appeals to women's patriotism are not enough.'
>
> (*Woman* 29 March 1947)

'Perhaps what we need,' she half-jokingly concluded one editorial (28 June 1947), 'is a Mothers' Union affiliated to the TUC!'

The despair that can be glimpsed behind Mary Grieve's pleas and exhortations was expressed less circumspectly by Ann Scott-James in *Picture Post*. 'How a housewife sees the crisis' appeared in April 1947, towards the end of the long winter during which people had been deprived of adequate heating and lighting as well as the Third Programme and the cinema, when rations had been more meagre than during the war and the Ministry of Food was promoting the unpalatable and unfortunately named fish *snoek*.[14] The housewife, said Ann Scott-James:

> '. . . wants more leisure and more colour as well as more food and clothes and less wearying work. But most of all she wants hope. That is why she is sadder now than during the war. Then there was always a target. Victory. Today, no one has tried to show her how or when the break may come. "I wouldn't mind the work," she says, "if I could see an end to it." That is the thought that is depressing all the Mrs Joneses and all the Miss Browns in the land.'

Regardless, His Majesty's Government continued its heavy-handed campaign to exploit women's patriotism and entice them into paid work. During 1947 and 1948 the series *Report to the Women of Britain* appeared among the ads in women's magazines. The tone of Report no. 5 is typical:

> 'Hats off to the 50,000 women who in one month joined the ranks of full time workers. They're real breadwinners these women, for they are making the goods that pay for the food we buy from abroad. But the factories and workshops could do with more of them especially in textiles and in some of the engineering trades. Part timers too are doing

fine work. Besides caring for their homes and families, over 500,000 women helped the export drive by part-time work in vital jobs.'

Despite the practical difficulties of this dual role, the campaign seems to have had some success. By January 1948, 70,000 women had returned to work.

The government was also running a number of other campaigns in the magazines. The National Savings Committee promoted the need to save for the country, as the other side of producing export goods to earn dollars and as an integral part of democracy and national security:

> '. . . you owe it to yourself, to those who died in the war, and to their children, not to use your money in any way that will jeopardise the future for which so high a price was paid. You will jeopardise the future if you save less and spend more before the battle for production is finally won.'

Sometimes the acerbic message that spending is for traitors was superficially sweetened by jolly jingles. 'The Woman Who Wouldn't', complete with cartoons, was the Report to the Women of Britain in *Woman*, 19 June 1948.

> 'The Woman Who Wouldn't said
> "I have a pretty good time on the sly,
> It's easy to cheat
> With light, petrol, heat
> As for *savings* or *work* – I don't try."'

Eventually, after several similar verses, it concludes:

> 'But thanks to the Women like You,
> To the millions who Would and who Do,
> Not selfishly spending,
> But saving and mending
> And working to see Britain through.'

If the battle for peace was to be won by eradicating the evils of spending, so too the national stock of babies, and workers, was to be improved by the elimination of other 'bad habits'. The Ministry of Health ran advertisements to warn against venereal disease. 'Can an unborn child be infected?' asked one entitled 'VD – and Baby' (*Woman* 5 June 1948). 'Yes, if a woman has Syphilis her baby may be born dead or diseased, but skilled treatment before or during pregnancy will almost always ensure a healthy baby.' The real safeguard, it advised somewhat ambiguously, is 'clean living.' Good eating habits too would help put the country on its feet. The Ministry of Food launched a series of recipes and advised on a balanced diet – 'What more pleasant way to health and beauty than a salad a day?' (*Woman* 17 July 1948.)

"I'm worried about the dollar gap"

Can we earn dollars in our sleep?

OF COURSE the Government is right to urge "more and more production" to earn the dollars we need. But what is a man to do if he begins the day already tired and feels like a piece of chewed string by the end of it? Not to mention his harassed wife, standing in queues and coping with rations!

You can't get blood out of a stone, they say. And you can't get more out of a man than the energy put into him.

Food and Sleep

Now energy, as we all know, is controlled by two things—food and sleep.

"Wonder where this lot's going?"

The experts disagree about whether we get enough food. On the *average*, we each get 2,681 calories (energy units) every day, which food authorities say is enough for good health and vigour—except for people doing very heavy work.

But nobody has ever met an "average" man. We all need different amounts. Anyway, there's no more food to be had until, as a nation, we can earn the dollars to pay for it.

Sleep is not Rationed

So what about sleep, which also controls our energy? Food is rationed, sleep isn't.

So perhaps we need more sleep to earn more dollars?

But the curious thing is that *long* sleep is not so important as *deep* sleep.

Tired after Long Sleep

Thousands of people sleep right through the night—and yet wake tired and un-refreshed in the morning. Their sleep is long enough; but the trouble is it isn't deep enough. Only deep sleep has the power to put back into your body and brain the energy and vitality you use up during the day.

Deep Sleep the Answer

Deep sleep — not long sleep

But once you begin to get the right kind of sleep, really deep sleep, you will be a different person. You will go through the day full of bounce and pent-up energy. You'll show the world!

One of the best ways to ensure deep sleep, is to drink Horlicks at bedtime. Horlicks soothes and relaxes. Horlicks helps the weary body to renew its store of energy. You'll wake up in the morning ready for anything. Export targets? Fish queues? You'll take care of them all!

* * *

DEEP SLEEP ... Do's and Don'ts

DON'T place your bed directly facing the window, especially if the window faces east. Sunlight striking your face on a summer morning may not always wake you, but it will make you sleep lighter.

DO keep your feet warm, your head cool. Deep sleep is encouraged if cool or even cold air circulates round the head.

DON'T go to bed immediately after some intense mental effort. You will have too much blood in your brain and you won't sleep deeply.

DO drink a cup of Horlicks last thing at night. Horlicks is more than a comforting drink— it is a promise of deep, restoring sleep for energy next day.

HORLICKS

Woman, 18 December 1948.

The mood even influenced commercial ads – 'Can we earn dollars in our sleep?' asked one. Yes, came the answer: with Horlicks.

Despite articulating women's dissonant voice, Mary Grieve in her *Woman* editorials also took on this rhetoric of 'we the nation'. It embraced government, industry, men and women in confronting the national crisis. 'In the six years of war thousands died that Britain should survive,' she wrote in April 1948. 'None of us will hold back now when the battle has moved into economic fields.' In this atmosphere, as she recalls in her autobiography, the government finally acknowledged 'the status which the magazine developed throughout the war time years.'

> '. . . the Home Secretary, the Minister of Health, the Minister of National Insurance and the Secretary of State for Scotland all arrived together one afternoon in the Kingsway offices of the Periodicals Proprietors Association to ask our assistance in explaining to the women of the country the five great acts which were coming into force in July of that year. These Acts were the National Insurance Act, the National Service Act, the National Assistance Act, the Industrial Injuries Act and the Children's Act. The four ministers spoke humanely about these new measures and answered questions readily and explicitly.'[15]

As a result, *Woman* ran features extolling the benefits of the National Health Service. One, on 12 June 1948, was illustrated by a photograph of a smiling family group with the caption 'They're a happy family – 8½d a week isn't much to pay to keep them healthy.' Norah Kingswood confronted the common moan that 'we will be paying large sums of money each week and getting precious little back' by stressing the more substantial advantages of free medical care. In the NHS and in National Insurance as in Utility clothes and furniture, it was the post-war virtues of co-operation, self-abnegation and quality without ostentation or excitement which were extolled.

A New Look: Questions about Womanhood

In *Woman*'s responses to government pleas to married women during the crisis of 1947/48, and in its arguments for social aids for women, we can now detect incipient feminist sentiments. Mary Grieve acknowledged the *work* that women do in the home, and men do not. She recognised women's need for space to themselves. She understood that men (and the government) do not see these things, and that woman's lot in full time work is harder because men do not have to perform a dual role. There was even some sense that women need to organise *as* women to get anything changed. In addition to these feminist perceptions, Mary Grieve also maintained an explicit allegiance to 'the nation' and hence, in a non-partisan way, to Labour's socialist policies. This was a potentially radical combination, but it did not really become widespread and the national interest usually won out. Insofar as the feminist demands were often a reaction to the awful conditions of *home* life, exacerbated by the pressure to do paid work as well, they tended to be satisfied (or at least negotiated) within the domestic sphere. Mobilisation around women's anger at these conditions did not become part of a broader political movement for reform – as Elizabeth Wilson has pointed out, one of the most effective organised groupings around these feelings was the primarily right-wing British Housewives League.[16] Perhaps in *Woman*'s limited demands we should see not so much a lost feminist moment as the emerging political horizons of the 'happy housewife heroine' consolidated during the complacent, Tory fifties.

Woman's wariness of feminism was sometimes expressed through a flippant approach. 'Your smoke gets in his eyes' (25 September 1948), for example, hints at a deep-seated (though displaced) criticism of double standards in judging men and women. In a 'new outbreak of an old sex war', women were being blamed for the shortage of cigarettes. Whereas 'tobacco is the solace of the working man,' it was apparently felt that 'women don't *need* cigarettes.' Rejecting the distinction, the writer concluded that 'the uncomfortable truth is that men don't like us to smoke.' Hence the double standard: 'A man is not less manly if he smokes 20 a day, provided he has the money and doesn't develop a revolting cough. A woman who does more than smoke an occasional cigarette is, for most men, less attractive as a woman.'

However, it was probably in the furore over the New Look in 1947 and 1948 that conflicting ideas about women's place and desires became most explicit. The fashion, as Ruth Adam has retrospectively described, became 'a moral and political issue, a focus on the question of what women's role was to be in post-war society.'[17] To many older style left-wing feminists it seemed outrageously extravagant. Mrs Mabel Ridealgh, a Labour MP who had been a Regional Controller for the Board of Trade's 'Make Do And Mend' campaign during the war, protested that 'padding and artificial figure aids . . . are extremely bad, because they make for over-sexiness.'[18] Mary Grieve's comment has a rather different slant. In 'It's got a fiery look now' (21 August 1948), she reported that the firechief of Middlesborough had denounced the New Look's long skirts as a hazard because women would not be able to feel scorching on their calves. Retorted Mary Grieve:

> 'I doubt if the accidents caused by feminine skirts are any more numer-
> ous than those created by masculine cigarette ends, dottles of smould-
> ering tobacco tapped from pipes or matches cast aside. (Women
> have reasonable smoking manners.) No, the root of the trouble is
> the New Look – something about its swinging bravado is incendiary.

I'll strike a bargain with Middlesboro'. I'll shorten my skirt when I hear that Middlesboro' firemen – including their chief – are wearing shorts – on and off duty.'

Despite the triviality of the incident, the response does seem to be in accord with the view of younger women like Miss Norah Alexander, who wrote to the *Daily Mail*: 'It's possible to wear skirts down to your ankles and still be one of the world's workers.'[19] That seems to have been the winning combination for the 'modern' woman – and so the eager adoption of the New Look can also be seen as marking another conservative resolution to the problems of being a woman.

On the domestic front, criticisms of men in *Woman* often took the form of rather fatalistic grumbles. 'Why, oh why do we girls long to be wives?' asked one reader's letter (4 September 1948). 'I spend from morn till night "doing" for my husband and two sons . . . I often think back to my single days when work stayed within the boundaries of 9.30 am and 5.30 pm, 5 days a week, and I was actually paid for it.' While *Woman* agreed that there seemed little in it but endless work and worry, it also unconvincingly invoked Bernard Shaw's theory of the 'Life Force, or the angels who protect the male sex from having to do its own chores' as explanation. Responding to another reader's tactic of treating her husband as a lodger (who therefore had to pay a salary as well as housekeeping), the magazine commented that: 'We can imagine husbands who would come out of it pretty badly' (7 January 1950). Even Evelyn Home's advice on marriage problems had not yet taken on the sugary optimism of the fifties – not least because of the problems posed by material disadvantages (caring for babies in cramped quarters, sharing with parents or in-laws) and the emotional dislocation of one or both partners returning from the excitement of war. A fictional account of such tensions was Jean Potts's story 'Stand Up Strike', in which a row about having relations to stay ends with the husband *hitting* his wife. Such a picture of domestic violence would not have been shown only a few years later.

Nor was it assumed, as it came to be in the fifties, that marriage automatically meant having a baby. What was accepted, despite the domestic problems, was that many married women would be combining marriage and motherhood with paid work. The Women's War Service Bureau continued after the war as a careers column. As late as 1952 a woman who wanted to know about bottle feeding because she wished to work after her baby was born was advised that she could breast feed *and* work. Only a few years later, medical opinion had become hostile to working mothers. In March 1957 one doctor declared authoritatively: 'Unless it is really unavoidable, no young mother should go out to work leaving in the care of others a child under three years.'

Woman, 18 February 1950.

In the post-war period, *Woman* encouraged its readers to be flexible within the home, as well as in combining work and domestic responsibilities. Whereas in the fifties Edith Blair advised them on the niceties of taste and 'contemporary' furniture, her advice in January 1947 on how to deal with the shortage of saucepans was of a different order:

> 'During the war it was found that women could do a wonderfully expert job on these tiny, intricate parts [i.e. bomb fuses]. And who says we in the home can't use this skill on our pots and pans?
>
> All that's needed is a stick of solder; a soldering iron; flux – and patience – it may not work out the first time . . .'

Role reversals which questioned feminine identity also occurred in several short stories at the time – career women, domesticated men, women who weren't 'born mothers'. But underlying most of these were notions that came to dominate *Woman*'s fiction in the fifties – the idea of marriage as a partnership, the individual resolution of the problems of motherhood, and a middle-class way of life that could afford alternative child care.

There was never a real challenge to the division of labour within marriage and home, in which it was women who bore the brunt of child care and domesticity. This view was characteristic of feminism more generally in this period. It perceived women and men as 'equal but different' and held to a notion of partnership in marriage. Even the Women's Freedom League's radical criticism that the Beveridge Report treated women as dependants within marriage did not challenge the status of the institution or the assumption that women are responsible for the home.[20] This feminism believed firmly in women's special qualities *as* women. As we have seen, one of Mary Grieve's consistent themes during the 1947 crisis was that women wanted part time work so that they could fulfil their special domestic and maternal obligations. It was never suggested that men should do an *equal* share of domestic tasks in order to free women for paid work. Mary Grieve's advocacy of women's special qualities as citizens extended to encouraging them to stand for local councils. 'To women falls so much work of the nation, from minding the babies to minding the looms, that it is time we ceased to think only of our family circle,' she argued (8 May 1948). 'We have special knowledge which makes us valuable helpers in the task of running not only our own flats and prefabs, but the whole of Britain.' Women's specialness, in other words, derives from their different place within marriage and the family. Single women scarcely appeared in *Woman*, except as the young and not yet married or as widows who have already been married. Even women's duty to the nation was characterised by Mary Grieve as a 'marital relationship'.

The Trimmings will come Later

By January 1948 it seemed that the worst of the economic crisis was over. In her editorial 'We're On Our Way', Mary Grieve wrote:

> '. . . we are doing for love and pride in our country what the cynics thought we would only do for personal gain. It is as though the young man had said to the girl "Darling, we love each other, let's get married . . . Let's get on with it and the fridge and all the trimmings will come later."
>
> The British people have made that proposal to each other, and accepted it – because it is one we understand and believe in. And our friends all over the world are watching with joy and admiration our new marriage – and not a few of them, the Dominions and America, for instance, are sending gifts to help us set up house again.'

Despite the forceful demands on behalf of women in the pages even of a conservative magazine like *Woman*, in the end women as citizens as well as wives laboured for love or patriotism. Women had to fit their interests around the nation's, just as they did around their husbands'. Few of the promised structural improvements – in the provision of child care especially

– were introduced to make the combination of domesticity and paid work easier. Nevertheless, part time work did become more readily available during the fifties: the increase in the number of married women in employment from 2,850,000 in 1950 to 3,770,000 in 1957 was largely accounted for by part time workers. This was a mixed blessing, though, as much a result of employers recognising its advantages as a response to women's desires. And, needless to say perhaps, it was seldom organised around school hours. The provisions of the welfare state, too, did produce benefits for women, however inadequate. Family allowances, unemployment pay and sickness benefits, the NHS and social security at least made caring for a family in bad times as well as good less of a financial strain. The rate at which people were rehoused gradually increased, easing domestic labour and some of the material pressures on family relations. Rationing was phased out by 1954, and supplies of food, domestic and personal goods increased. Some (only some) working-class women thus achieved the kinds of home their mothers could only have dreamt of. This was experienced as a *class* gain by many women, and that is how the magazines represented it, educating their readers in the new consumerism. It was also, of course, a spurious gain, trapping women as the 'happy housewife heroine' only able to perceive their oppression as a personal failure. It was politically effective too, contributing to the new consensus and the rhetoric of classlessness that characterised the fifties. All these changes contributed to the vision of post-war Britain that made it possible for the Conservative Prime Minister Harold Macmillan to utter his exultant promise in 1959, 'You've never had it so good.'

By then conspicuous consumption had become part of the image of Britain's success. 'We've got everything we want now,' one young housewife is reported to have said. 'I've a washer, and a TV set, and that's all I want in life.'[21] In the years of austerity I have been examining, the comparable domestic symbols were more modest and discreet. Britishness seemed to be summed up best, perhaps, in the practical but unglamorous Brown Betty teapot. In a 1981 Heal's exhibition of *Classics*, it was described as having a 'comfortable old fashioned shape.' In an editorial in June 1948 titled 'Little Brown Teapot', Mary Grieve described an earlier exhibition. Hundreds of brightly coloured pots, all marked *For export only*, were destined, according to the man on the stall, for 'the dollar countries where people dearly love a bit of gold.' On just one shelf, however, was 'a clutch of little brown teapots, some with a demure shoulder band of blue-grey.' It was in one of these, the man proudly asserted, that his wife liked to make their tea. 'Somehow,' he said, 'we don't take to fancy teapots.' Nor does the British nation, agreed Mary Grieve.

> 'As a nation we have always tended to love the simple, honest things –
> plain colours, good shapes, workable designs . . . I think that when

Woman, 5 May 1951.

once we have had a dose of rainbow hues, back we shall go to our old loves – simplicity, high quality, inconspicuousness which match so well the quiet domestic virtues we like to think of as especially characteristic of Britain.'

The symbolic status of the Brown Betty was confirmed by Godfrey Winn, a prolific contributor to women's magazines in the post-war period. In a sycophantic book, *The Queen's Countrywomen*, he detailed with glowing paternalism the lives of women ranging from 'Our Pat', the Conservative MP Patricia Hornsby-Smith, to 'The Red Coat', a young woman working at Butlins. In 'The Splendid Journeywomen', Winn takes tea with a family whose work is producing Spode china. The wife apologises for using not their precious Spode pot, but what Winn calls a 'dark tabby of a teapot.' 'Mind! I wanted to put my hands round it because it was so utterly, so solidly British,' he comments. 'Always on the hob, always there, at moments of celebration and equally as a cure for moods of depression.' Thus Britishness was about holding onto the traditional values represented by the teapot. Their core lay in the family and domestic life and was nurtured by women. '"Have a cup of tea, my dear," Mrs Brough said, reaching once more for her faithful, all-forgiving teapot.'[22]

Two events in the early fifties mark the shift from austerity to consumerism, but also the enduring hold of this Britishness: the Festival of Britain in 1951 and the Coronation in 1953. The Festival had all the trappings of modernity but, rather like the New Look, says Elizabeth Wilson, it was much more deeply conservative.[23] One of *Woman*'s contributions to the Festival highlights the way it was celebrated as both an individual and a collective British Achievement. The magazine offered a Festival Souvenir Map, 'traced on linen ready-to-embroider for only one shilling and ninepence (plus threepence packing and postage)' (*Woman* 19 May 1951).

> 'Show your pride in your country's achievements – and let others admire your craftsmanship – by embroidering this *Woman* sampler.
>
> This exquisite map of Great Britain is an artist's impression of the contribution the whole country is making to the Festival of Britain. Embroidered in gaily coloured cottons, it will make a treasured momento of 1951, the year when Britain's arts and industries were proudly displayed before the whole world . . . Cunning symbols represent the contribution of the cities and counties. A Beefeater welcomes visitors to the capital city; the brightly bedecked merry-go-round reminds us of all the fun of the fair we will have at Battersea Park. The national flags fly in Scotland and Northern Ireland . . . When you have embroidered the map make a flag to represent your own home town and its special contribution to the national Festival . . .'

Talking About Health
with **JOAN WILLIAMS, S.R.N., S.C.M.**

The Queen and the Duke of Edinburgh pick up their children
for the sort of photograph which every family loves to treasure

Family Life

NURSE WILLIAMS stresses the priceless
value of a happy home . . . symbolized by
the two children whose mother is the Queen

THIS week, as the pomp and pageantry unfold themselves, our hearts will be touched anew by the dignity and charm of the Queen who, in spite of her youth, combines her duties as leader of our country with those of a wife and the mother of two lovely young children. As women, we can understand a little of what these double responsibilities must mean.

Family life means much to the Queen but, because of her position, she is unable to devote herself wholly to it. She has only a limited amount of freedom and her husband is almost as heavily burdened.

But with his co-operation and her practical common sense, we can be sure that she has arranged for Charles and Anne an upbringing which both gives them a happy childhood and fits them for the positions they must hold one day.

We know, for example, that since their life is not their own, and the Royal parents must delegate much of the children's upbringing to others, those others will have been chosen with infinite care. They will be people whose characters, beliefs and principles are such that there will be no conflict between what the children learn from them and what they learn from their parents. There will be absolute consistency.

THE DIFFICULT CHILD

The importance of this cannot be over-estimated, for without unity between parents and teachers there is inevitably confusion in young children's minds. From this confusion may grow a feeling of insecurity which can do untold harm, striking as it does at the root of a child's happiness and well being.

It is the insecure child who is difficult to manage. Always he expresses his bewilderment and unhappiness in action. He can neither reason things out nor discuss them. He can only show the conflict in his mind by hitting out at a world that has hurt him. So he is rude, disobedient or dishonest. He lies, steals or bullies. He is the potential delinquent, the social misfit in embryo. Somehow, somewhere, his family have failed him.

It is in his family life that a child learns the values which will be his throughout life. If his background is sound and good, and the family relationship is one of loyalty and affection, the child will have his feet on solid ground.

He will be quite clear as to what is right and what is wrong, so that whatever comes to him will be met squarely and courageously, not with the misgiving and uncertainty which stem from inward insecurity.

FOUNDATION FOR LIFE

Obviously, the parents' own way of life is the greatest influence in their children's lives, particularly during the early and formative years and again during adolescence. The stronger their affection for each other, provided there is plenty for the children too, the more firmly will the children believe in the desirability of family life and the more likely they are to foster their own after they marry.

Conversely, they will have little faith in the value of family life if love and loyalty are missing, or if they are the victims of that other childhood tragedy, a broken home. The child whose parents are divided, either in actual fact or in their hearts, is sadly handicapped. No one but himself knows with what feelings of desolation, inferiority and injustice he is filled at times, and how deeply his life is influenced.

Every adult decides for himself what he considers right and wrong, what are his values and beliefs, what his code of living. But his choice will inevitably be influenced by his background and upbringing. If these have been sound, he is not likely to go far wrong. He may lose his head and his sense of values for a time perhaps but, sooner or later, he will find himself again and will try to live out in his own life all that he saw, admired and loved in his parents' lives and in the home they created for him.

The Royal children are fortunate indeed, for they are blessed with parents whose principles are of the highest and whose devotion to them and to each other is obvious to all the world. Here indeed is family life at its best. And the woman at its centre is a wise and understanding person as well as our loved Queen.

Willie Winkie and His Friends Play Kings and Queens

Auntie has ideas that are the greatest fun. This time it's a Coronation party and Willie Winkie is the host

Now they are well away! The special game is to be kings and queens and everyone is busy making a crown

What a magnificent pair of kings, bowing the knee before their queens as they sit in such stately beauty

The climax of an exciting afternoon—Larry shows the children Willie Winkie's own Coronation coach

The Festival was also, according to Elizabeth Wilson, obsessed with monarchy. So too, it appeared, was the nation as a whole – especially the half which was female. The year before the Festival, *Little Princesses*, the Royal Governess's story of Princess Elizabeth and Princess Margaret, had tugged at the nation's heart strings. For *Woman's Own*, which serialised it, it was a journalistic coup. It won the magazine 500,000 new readers – and if the editor James Drawbell is to be believed, it would have been even more if the production capacity had been available. Financially, it brought women's magazines into the big business league. The usual figure for such a story had been £5,000: *Woman's Own* bought it from the American *Ladies Home Journal* for £30,000. Mary Grieve, regretting that *Woman* had not won the serial rights, reckoned the story had everything: 'Crawfie's devotion to the two children, continuing into their young womanhood, and their affection for her; a way of Royal Family Life that few people knew much about . . . warm, authentic, a narrative tribute to a group of dedicated people, to an institution that has become something of a religion with the British people.'[24] Crawfie's story wove together the *nation* and *family* life, and so prefigured a post-war world for Britain built around the family.

This image was confirmed by the Queen's Coronation in 1953, the symbolic moment of transition from austerity to a future of plenty and comfort for the nation, with a special emphasis on married women and their families. The crowning of a woman, recorded the magazine (3 January 1953), had 'special significance and a depth of meaning' for women. The future seemed to lie in the hands of a wife and mother whose happy family was also metonymically the British nation. In the 'Talking About Health' slot for 30 May 1953, 'Nurse Williams stresses the priceless value of a happy home . . . symbolised by the two children whose mother is the Queen.' After all the discussion of women's wider contribution to the nation, this was finally the major burden of responsibility that women carried on the nation's behalf into the second half of the fifties. 'Here indeed is family life at its best,' concludes Nurse Williams. 'And the woman at its centre is a wise and understanding person . . .' She just happened also to be '. . . our loved Queen.'

Acknowledgment

Though they may disagree with some of its substance, this paper has, in one way or another, been nurtured in the Birmingham Feminist History Group on Women in the Fifties. My love and thanks especially to Lucy Bland, Angela Lloyd and Tessa Perkins.

Notes

1. James Drawbell, *Time On My Hands*, London, Macdonald, 1968, p. 45. Drawbell was editor of *Woman's Own* in the post-war period.
2. Betty Friedan, *The Feminine Mystique*, Harmondsworth, Penguin, 1965, Chapter 2. See also

Anthea Hinds, 'Cover Women', *Camerawork*, no. 20, December 1980; Jo Spence, 'What Do People Do All Day?' *Screen Education*, no. 29, 1978/9; and Elizabeth Wilson, *Only Halfway to Paradise*, London, Tavistock, 1980.

3. Denise Riley's very detailed and interesting work on the period suggests that my argument about women's magazines may apply more widely: I have therefore drawn on it extensively. See 'War in the Nursery', *Feminist Review*, no. 2, 1979, and 'The Free Mothers', *History Workshop*, no. 11, 1981.

4. In Suzanne Lowry, *The Guilt Cage*, London, Elm Tree/Hamish Hamilton, 1980, p. 127.

5. Quoted in Jane Booth, 'Watching the Family', *Women's Studies International Quarterly*, vol. 3, no. 1, 1980, p. 18.

6. Riley, 'War in the Nursery', p. 106. On the family in the fifties see also Birmingham Feminist History Group, 'Feminism as Femininity?', *Feminist Review* no. 3, 1979. On the contribution of women's magazines to 'familial speech' in the fifties, see my *Woman Becomes 'Individual': Femininity and Consumption in Women's Magazines 1954–69*, Stencilled Paper no. 65, Birmingham, Centre for Contemporary Cultural Studies, 1981.

7. Arthur Marwick, *British Society Since 1945*, London, Penguin, 1982, p. 22.

8. Cynthia White, *Women's Magazines 1693–1968*, London, Michael Joseph, 1970, p. 97.

9. Mary Grieve, *Millions Made My Story*, London, Gollancz, 1964, p. 134.

10. See White op. cit., p. 123 for several examples. For a general account of women's lives at the time, see Raynes Minns, *Bombers and Mash*, London, Virago, 1980.

11. My emphasis here differs from Joy Leman's in '"The Advice of a Real Friend" Codes of Intimacy and Oppression in Women's Magazines 1937–55', *Women's Studies International Quarterly*, vol. 3, no. 1, 1980. She argues that the magazines' 'fundamentally oppressive' attitude to women was indicated by their ability 'to adapt to this "new" image of women and still retain their basic character in terms of the ideology of femininity' (p. 65). The implication seems to be that women *did* take on a new image to which the magazines failed to respond adequately. This view is not borne out by, for example, Denise Riley's evidence.

12. Leman, *ibid.*, p. 73.

13. Riley, 'The Free Mothers', p. 96. By the late forties the birth rate had risen and by the fifties fears about its fall had dissipated.

14. See Susan Cooper, 'Snoek Piquante', in Michael Sissons and Philip French (eds), *The Age of Austerity*, Harmondsworth, Penguin, 1964.

15. Grieve, *op. cit.*, p. 126.

16. Wilson, *op. cit.*, p. 167.

17. Ruth Adam, *A Woman's Place*, London, Chatto and Windus, 1975, p. 159.

18. Quoted in Pearson Phillips, 'The New Look', in Sissons and French (eds), *op. cit.*, p. 149.

19. Quoted in *ibid.*, p. 151.

20. For a discussion of feminism in the forties and fifties, see Wilson, *op. cit.*, Chapters 9 and 10.

21. Quoted in John Montgomery, *The Fifties*, London, George Allen and Unwin, 1965, p. 208.

22. Godfrey Winn, *The Queen's Countrywomen*, London, Hutchinson, 1954, p. 19 and p. 23.

23. Wilson, *op. cit.*, p. 10.

24. Grieve, *op. cit.*, p. 85.

Louise London and Nira Yuval-Davis

WOMEN AS NATIONAL REPRODUCERS: The Nationality Act (1981)

On 1 January 1983 the British Nationality Act (1981) came into force.[1] Its arrival was somewhat overshadowed at the time by a revolt among right-wing Tory MPs against new immigration rules introduced by William Whitelaw: they thought them too liberal because they would amend existing immigration rules that a woman who is a British Citizen could not be joined in the UK by her spouse, unless she or at least one of her parents was born in the UK.[2] But more important than the Home Secretary's little local difficulties are the far-reaching changes introduced by this measure to what social groups belong to or are excluded from 'the British people' and 'the British nation'. In effect, the new law redefines what constitutes the national collectivity by narrowing down the legal category of British Citizenship and limiting the absolute right of abode to British Citizens.[3] It perpetuates more rigorously than ever the racial discrimination embodied in past legislation, and introduces a new element by asserting a constitutional legitimacy for this discrimination.

Previously, the acquisition and loss of citizenship of the United Kingdom and Colonies were governed by the British Nationality Act (1948). Passed in the twilight years of Empire, this contained a fairly wide definition of citizenship: it encompassed the whole of the British class structure within the national population, including the colonial division of labour which was crucial to Britain's rise as an imperial power. As the old colonies became independent Commonwealth states, citizenship was withdrawn from their nationals and later restrictions were imposed on their rights of entry into the UK. The Commonwealth Immigrants Acts of 1962 and 1968 introduced the concept of a right of abode in the UK established by virtue of ancestral connections, as a means of excluding many full UK citizens in the former and remaining colonies while preserving or creating rights of entry for white people in those countries. The 1968 Act was a direct and manifestly racist response by the Labour Government (and especially the then Home Secretary James Callaghan) to the panic about the immigration of East African Asians; it was also probably in breach of international law. These two pieces of legislation effectively created two tiers of citizenship, which were consolidated and extended in the Immigration Act (1971) which

'Brothers!' Vicky, *Evening Standard*, November 1963.

introduced the term 'patriality' for the absolute right of abode in the UK.

Patrial UK and Commonwealth citizens, whether or not residing in the UK, were free from immigration control while other full UK citizens (those classified as non-patrial) were not. The new Nationality Act secures this discrimination by finally removing the status of citizenship from people not defined as patrial under immigration law. In effect, having created a level of second-class citizens, the Government has now changed the labels so that this group no longer qualifies for citizenship at all. For the members of these groups two new second-class citizenships have been created (British Overseas Citizenship for those from former colonies and British Dependent Territories Citizenship for the rest): these carry with them no right of entry to any territory and are valueless. In addition, residents in the UK from former colonies will have only a limited period of time to exercise their right to register as citizens. If they fail to apply in time (*inter alia* because of the exorbitant fees charged for citizenship) they will lose it. In future, British Citizenship rather than patriality will guarantee freedom from immigration control. Being born in the UK will no longer automatically make children eligible for citizenship: it will have to be proved that the child has at least one parent who is a British citizen, or who is settled in the UK. For the first time, stateless children will be born in Britain.[4]

Between the 1948 Act and the 1981 Act, the definitions of nationality and citizenship have become increasingly restrictive. The new one is basically limited to already established resident citizens and the descendants of white British citizens. Previously eligible groups have been excluded, to break away from responsibilities deriving from Britain's colonial past, to mould the UK to be more like other EEC countries and to avoid the charge that the government is breaking international law or denying basic rights to some of its citizens.

Women, Nationality and Immigration

The new Nationality law and the system of immigration control do not differentiate between subjects according to racist criteria alone. Women are legally constituted differently from men, and generally more disadvantageously. If they are married, they are treated for immigration purposes not as independent individuals, but as appendages of their husbands. (Similarly, daughters aged between 18 and 21 are treated as dependent on their fathers, and widows on their adult sons.) Their dependency determines both how they live, economically, and also where they live – within or outside the UK. A woman can be deported along with her husband but not vice versa, for example, and she has less right than a man to be joined in Britain by her spouse.[5] In previous legislation, this presumed dependence had produced additional rights in some areas. But both the absolute right to citizenship for wives of citizens of the UK and Colonies under the 1948 British Nationality Act and to patriality under the 1971 Immigration Act have now been abolished by the new Nationality Act, while the extra disabilities continue. Under the new law, however, absolute rights to citizenship acquired by marriage have been weakened or removed especially when legal dependency no longer exists – as in the cases of divorced and widowed women.

But the most important difference between the old and new laws for women lies in the way they are constituted as *mothers*. Children continue to be perceived as an inseparable part of the mother (whether they are legitimate or not), but for the first time women can transmit citizenship to their children in their own right, even if the child is born abroad and regardless of whether the father is British. In other words, they are no longer merely 'means of reproduction': this represents a significant change in the constitution of women as reproducers of the British national collectivity.

Reproduction is a contentious and unresolved concept within feminist theory and debate,[6] but one classification common to several of the different approaches is to differentiate between the reproduction of labour power and a more general sense of reproduction in terms of the physical and ideological rearing of children. Elizabeth Wilson's influential book *Women and the Welfare State*,[7] for example, focuses on the interrelation between mothers and the state in the process of socialising children and moulding them into becoming members of society. In much of the literature dealing with human reproduction, membership in society is assumed automatically to include citizenship of the state – civil society and political society are treated as identical. The new British Nationality Act, with its exclusionary practices, shows perfectly that this is not necessarily so. Nor is this a unique example. To take just one other instance, children born to non-Jewish non-citizens in Israel, even if natives of the country, can also become stateless. In other words, not all women within a nation-state are the bearers of new members of the national collectivity, of the citizenry that constitutes the nation. Some women do not qualify as 'national reproducers'. In Britain, the new Nationality Act excludes several categories of women currently holding British passports or resident in Britain from passing on the full legal and political status of the citizen to their children: they are not part of the nation. On the other hand, though, those categories of women who do hold British citizenship are being granted additional rights to national reproduction. Up until now, British women have been only the biological tool for transmitting *patrilinear* British nationality – in most cases, especially when residing outside Britain, through the legal ties of marriage to British men. While

Arthur Horner, *New Statesman*, 12 March 1971.

withholding even these passive rights from some women, the new law grants those women within the redefined boundaries of nationality the independent power of national reproduction.

This differentiation has far-reaching political as well as legal implications. Through its welfare provision, the British state has been active in supporting women in their reproductive role in bearing and rearing children. A network of state apparatuses has come into existence – the National Health Service, social services and so forth – and through child benefits and family allowances the state has provided direct financial support to mothers beyond their dependence on men and whenever there was no man to maintain them. These apparatuses are concerned with the process of reproducing the labour force as well as the citizen body of the state, with creating a population physically and mentally fit to fill their social and economic roles. But there was always an explicit concern with national reproduction inherent in these policies. This was particularly clear in the fears around the declining birth rate during the 1940s, as in this justification of family allowances in the Beveridge Report: 'With its present rate of reproduction, the British race cannot continue; means of reversing the recent course of birth rate must be found.'[8] In the wake of the Nationality Act, it will be easier to discriminate against women excluded from the British collectivity in the provision of welfare services. Already checks are being made in NHS units to see that people are entitled to them. This discrimination, of course, will not be limited to potential or actual mothers, but will have far wider implications. In opposition to the formal ideology which justifies immigration control 'to enable the progress of racial harmony for those who are already in', the effect of the new law will be that racist discrimination will grow not only in relation to those who are not settled here, but to all ex-colonial British residents. It will not be all British citizens who will be required to provide proof of eligibility, but mainly those whose appearance and accent would make them suspicious in the eyes of a state bureaucracy itself subject to inconsistent and conflicting political and ideological forces.

Population Control

State control of national reproduction is not limited to the concern with the transmission of citizenship rights and the differential support of mothers as child rearers. The state also intervenes to control actual patterns of child bearing. This concern with population control was especially prominent when the British Empire was at its height. 'The maintenance of empire,' argued the prominent conservative journalist J. L. Garvin in 1905, 'would be best based upon the power of white population, proportionate in numbers, vigour and cohesion to the vast territories which the British democracies in the Mother country and the Colonies control.' Nor was he alone in these views: they reflect a powerful train of thought at the time. Then the threat was seen to consist not in indigenous colonial populations, but in other white imperial nations. The message was clear – population is power. 'Children belong not merely to the parents but to the community as a whole. They are a national asset.'[9] To protect and foster this asset, voluntary associations like the National League for Health, Maternity and Child Welfare, the Eugenic Education Society and the Women's League of Service for Motherhood were established. They had direct access to social policy decisions, were members of government commissions and were often called to give evidence to local authorities.

In the period since World War II, the focus of concern with national reproduction has switched from the empire to Britain itself. As the process of immigration and the internal colonisation of migrant workers began, fears about the constitution of 'the British people' took on a distinctly racist edge. Long before Mrs Thatcher expressed her fears about being 'swamped' by 'alien cultures', the Royal Commission on Population declared in its *Report* (1949):

> 'British traditions, manners and ideas in the world have to be borne in mind. Immigration is thus not a desirable means of keeping the population at a replacement level as it would in effect reduce the proportion of home-bred stock in the population.'

In comparing the population control policies of Britain with those of other states, however, it is clear that the ideology of national reproduction has periodically come into conflict with notions about the rights of individuals and families to decide how many children they should have. This gave rise to the provision of family planning clinics as a universal, free service and until now has dominated British policy on abortion legislation. Even during fears about the declining population during the 1940s, as Denise Riley has argued, the willingness to live with this tension in part reflected an awareness that Fascist countries had refused to allow birth control: the Commission on Population therefore emphasised how the provision of family planning differentiated British freedom and 'style'.[10] As Janice Winship describes in her article in this volume, women were encouraged to produce more children with better 'qualities' through ideological campaigns and improved welfare provision, not through a formal policy of denying access to birth control.

Until now, in Britain, the principle of universally provided state welfare has overshadowed policies of population control which differentiate between mothers of the white majority and of ethnic minorities. That could change over the next few years. Already it has been noted that in some cases, birth control advice in family planning clinics has often been transformed into an instrument of population control when directed at poor mothers in general and black mothers in particular – for example, the differential use of the notorious Depo-Pravera injections or the flooding of the clinics with birth-control leaflets in Asian languages, many more than in English. Several local councils – Bradford and Brent, for example – have expressed concern about the high proportion of welfare funds spent on 'minorities' children, and mothers whose children reside outside the UK (*inter alia* because of immigration policies) are not given child allowances for them. But despite the increasingly active role of the state, it would be wrong to assume that this is the only or even necessarily the primary factor in the reproduction of the national population. Traditional and religious ideologies and practices, as well as economic factors, remain central. These can act as countervailing forces to policies promoted by the state, or they can be incorporated as additional legitimating ideologies. Equally, questions of national reproduction are not the only consideration determining the state's intervention in women's reproductive role: these have to be balanced with the sometimes contradictory requirements around the reproduction of the labour force and the reproduction of the citizenship body of the state.

What is important is to examine in specific historical cases all the dimensions of national reproduction as composing a significant process through which sexism, racism and the state are linked together. The new Nationality Act is a prime example of the way these exclusionary practices interact and are given the power to define social categories by being embodied in legislation.

Notes

1. This article is based on two separate papers presented at History Workshop 1982.
2. Whitelaw's new rules were far from liberal. Women settled in the UK who are not citizens still have no right to have their husband settle with them, and the onus is now on a couple to prove that their marriage was not entered into primarily to obtain settlement.
3. Previously this right to abode was given to some categories of Commonwealth citizen.
4. Complex rules have been introduced to control the entry and stay of these children.
5. Any man settled here may be joined by his spouse whatever his citizenship – women only have this option if they are British citizens. Furthermore, a foreign husband must pass extra tests if he is to be allowed to enter or remain in the UK and will not be given settlement for at least twelve months.
6. See F. Edholm *et al*, 'Conceptualizing women', *Critique of Anthropology*, vol. 3, nos. 9/10; H. O'Brien, *The Politics of Reproduction*, RKP, 1981; and M. McIntosh, 'Gender and economics', in K. Young *et al* (eds.), *Of Marriage and the Market*, CSE Books, 1981.
7. E. Wilson, *Women and the Welfare State*, London, Tavistock, 1977.
8. Sir William Beveridge, *Social Insurance and Allied Services*, Cmd 6404 (HMSO, 1942), p. 154.
9. Quoted in A. Davin, 'Imperialism and motherhood', *History Workshop Journal*, no. 5, 1978.
10. D. Riley, 'The free mothers', *History Workshop Journal*, no. 11, 1981.